T0256895

Continuous Enterprise
Development in Java

Andrew Lee Rubinger and Aslak Knutsen

Beijing · Cambridge · Farnham · Köln · Sebastopol · Tokyo

Continuous Enterprise Development in Java

by Andrew Lee Rubinger and Aslak Knutsen

Printed in the United States of America.

Published by O'Reilly Media, Inc., 1005 Gravenstein Highway North, Sebastopol, CA 95472.

O'Reilly books may be purchased for educational, business, or sales promotional use. Online editions are also available for most titles (*http://my.safaribooksonline.com*). For more information, contact our corporate/institutional sales department: 800-998-9938 or *corporate@oreilly.com*.

Editors: Mike Loukides and Meghan Blanchette
Production Editor: Kara Ebrahim
Copyeditor: Kim Cofer
Proofreader: Becca Freed

Indexer: WordCo Indexing Services, Inc.
Cover Designer: Randy Comer
Interior Designer: David Futato
Illustrator: Rebecca Demarest

March 2014:   First Edition

Revision History for the First Edition:

2014-03-11:   First release

See *http://oreilly.com/catalog/errata.csp?isbn=9781449328290* for release details.

ISBN: 978-1-449-32829-0

[LSI]

Table of Contents

Foreword

Even ancient J2EE was never just about development.

From the advent of enterprise Java there has been a strictly defined holistic role concept. Component providers, assemblers, system administrators, and server providers have clear and distinct responsibilities, but these have been rarely upheld in the real world. Because of politics and organizational structures, often the developer assumes the responsibility of all these roles, with the possible exception of system administration and operations. The developer's main goal is development, and the well-intentioned role separation collapses quickly.

In the "real world," a dedicated operations department takes the results of the development cycle and attempts to install, run, and just keep it alive. Such an artificially separated model works, but is far away from being optimal. Sometimes it gets even worse, and signing off documents becomes more important than software quality.

If you are only interested in quick hacks, you will hate Java EE, application servers, and probably this book altogether. Packaging, deployment, monitoring, and management sounds like bloat and is bloat, if you are only focusing on development.

However the "DevOps" movement also considers operations and development as a single unit. Who needs beautiful code that cannot be properly installed in a predefined environment? DevOps is nothing groundbreaking; rather, it's a "back to the roots" movement.

This book is not just compatible with the "DevOps" ideals; it pragmatically shows how to build a Java EE application from scratch and also patches holes in the Java EE spec. Automation of project and archive creation, pragmatic integration of Maven builds into the process, and testing on all levels are deeply explained with concrete code. Rather than focusing on best-case scenarios, this book shows you how to test the inconvenient, including examples with SMTP servers or Message Driven Beans.

Although the tools, libraries, and frameworks introduced in this book were initiated by Red Hat employees, this book will be equally valuable for you if you are not using JBoss or WildFly at all. In fact, I used Arquillian, ShrinkWrap, and Forge to test applications on GlassFish and TomEE at the same time. Also, in my workshops (*http://airhacks.com*) I use Arquillian to test plug-ins, extensions, and sophisticated dependency injection without deploying mocks to a production archive.

It was fun to read this book on the flight to JavaOne 2013 in San Francisco; I learned a lot. I wish you happy reading—enjoy the lightweight Java EE development lifecycle!

—Adam Bien
http://adam-bien.com

Preface

Simplicity is the ultimate sophistication.

— Leonardo DaVinci

Software development for the modern Web continues to evolve at a furious pace. In recent years we've seen the trend of client-side state move to the server, only to correct itself back again. Despite JavaScript's obvious utility, two engineers are likely to yield three opinions regarding its worthiness. HTML5 ushers an armada of rich-media and concurrency support right into the browser. The proven, 40-year-old relational data model has fallen out of vogue to defiant NoSQL systems, and our version-control stores have undergone both implementation and paradigm overhauls.

Our tools constitute an ever-changing buffet of prescriptions, and sorting through the array of options presents a dizzying exercise.

In the meantime, engineers face the same central challenges raised by building any multiuser program; we like our code elegant and maintainable. We need it to run efficiently and securely. We must assert its correctness.

In the Java space, many answers have come from a set of specifications released under the heading of the *Java Enterprise Edition*. The overarching goal of this effort remains: hide away the syntactic complexity inherent in software development, and attempt to provide a clean standard model upon which to build. In other words, the Java EE Platform comprises an evolving toolkit, and a fallible one at that.

So a few years back we set out to fill some of the holes left unspecified by Java EE, and ended up holding the reins to a test framework that inspired our imaginations and proved more versatile than initially envisioned. In fleshing out ideas to best share the lessons we'd learned, it became clear that we didn't need to document any particular technology. Developers have been missing a cohesive map to navigate the murky waters of Java EE, its adjacent frameworks, and its services.

This text does not detail a singular specification. Those volumes may be found elsewhere, because we've found it makes little sense to begin our learning with the Solutions.

Instead, let's align our start with the Problems. We'll take a use-case–centric approach to the testable development of enterprise Java, and after a bit of exploratory theory and requisite background, each chapter will tackle a single high-level issue. The solutions we propose may span from the user interface to persistent storage, touching upon a number of standards or third-party projects along the way. All examples are executable, and as proof run in production on the companion website.

The newbie should expect to meet the players in an enterprise Java system, and bring a blank repository from scratch to a fully deployed, live public application on the cloud. Coders of all stripes may find appealing approaches to testing against seed data, pushing events to the client, interacting with a distributed data grid, validating the user interface, and more.

Quite simply, we'll aim to make the complicated much less so. With luck, this will empower greater productivity and enjoyment in your work.

At least, that's been our experience while employing the techniques that inspired this book.

Conventions Used in This Book

The following typographical conventions are used in this book:

Italic

> Indicates new terms, URLs, email addresses, filenames, and file extensions.

`Constant width`

> Used for program listings, as well as within paragraphs to refer to program elements such as variable or function names, databases, data types, environment variables, statements, and keywords.

`Constant width bold`

> Shows commands or other text that should be typed literally by the user.

`Constant width italic`

> Shows text that should be replaced with user-supplied values or by values determined by context.

> This element signifies a tip or suggestion.

This element signifies a general note.

 This element indicates a warning or caution.

Using Code Examples

Supplemental material (code examples, exercises, etc.) is available for download at *http://continuousdev.org*. We offer a guide to get started in Chapter 4.

This book is here to help you get your job done. All contents here are licensed under *Creative Commons Attribution-ShareAlike 2.0 Generic* (*http://creativecommons.org/licenses/by-sa/2.0/*), and we invite the community at large to contribute work including feature requests, typographical error corrections, and enhancements via our GitHub Issue Tracker (*http://bit.ly/1e7kQRD*). You may reuse any of the text or examples in compliance with the license, which requires attribution. See full license for details.

An attribution usually includes the title, author, publisher, and ISBN. For example: "*Continuous Enterprise Development in Java* by Andrew Lee Rubinger and Aslak Knutsen (O'Reilly). Copyright 2014 Andrew Lee Rubinger and Aslak Knutsen, 978-1-449-32829-0."

Safari® Books Online

 Safari Books Online is an on-demand digital library that delivers expert content in both book and video form from the world's leading authors in technology and business.

Technology professionals, software developers, web designers, and business and creative professionals use Safari Books Online as their primary resource for research, problem solving, learning, and certification training.

Safari Books Online offers a range of product mixes and pricing programs for organizations, government agencies, and individuals. Subscribers have access to thousands of books, training videos, and prepublication manuscripts in one fully searchable database from publishers like O'Reilly Media, Prentice Hall Professional, Addison-Wesley Professional, Microsoft Press, Sams, Que, Peachpit Press, Focal Press, Cisco Press, John Wiley & Sons, Syngress, Morgan Kaufmann, IBM Redbooks, Packt, Adobe Press, FT

Press, Apress, Manning, New Riders, McGraw-Hill, Jones & Bartlett, Course Technology, and dozens more. For more information about Safari Books Online, please visit us online.

How to Contact Us

Please address comments and questions concerning this book to the publisher:

O'Reilly Media, Inc.
1005 Gravenstein Highway North
Sebastopol, CA 95472
800-998-9938 (in the United States or Canada)
707-829-0515 (international or local)
707-829-0104 (fax)

We have a web page for this book, where we list errata, examples, and any additional information. You can access this page at *http://oreil.ly/continuous-enterprise*.

To comment or ask technical questions about this book, send email to *bookques tions@oreilly.com*.

For more information about our books, courses, conferences, and news, see our website at *http://www.oreilly.com*.

Find us on Facebook: *http://facebook.com/oreilly*

Follow us on Twitter: *http://twitter.com/oreillymedia*

Watch us on YouTube: *http://www.youtube.com/oreillymedia*

Acknowledgments

First and foremost we would like to give a huge thanks to the Arquillian community: wonderful, talented folks from around the world who have contributed their time and knowledge to help improve the project, from coding to writing to speaking to screaming on the Internet (yes, we pay attention to you).

A special thank you to all the Arquillian module leads: Karel Piwko, Bartosz Majsak, Lukáš Fryč, Dan Allen, Stefan Miklosovic, Jakub Narloch, Gerhard Poul, John Ament, Jan Papousek, Bernard Labno, Ståle Pedersen, Ken Finnigan, Tolis Emmanouilidis, Ales Justin, Martin Gencur, Vineet Reynolds, Davide D'Alto, Jean Deruelle, David Blevins, Mark Struberg, Thomas Diesler, Romain Manni-Bucau, Logan McGrath, and Alexis Hassler.

A big shout out to Sarah White and Cheyenne Weaver for giving us the visual identity and the storyline to play with. You make us look good!

And thanks to all the people who helped us throughout this book, correcting and commenting on the content.

Thanks to Meghan Blanchette for being so persistent on pushing us back to work. This probably (definitely) would never have reached revision if you hadn't!

And last but not least, a big thanks to our friend in code Adam Bien for the foreword.

This book is for the community from which our work was born, raised, and continues to evolve.

CHAPTER 1

Continuity

If everyone is moving forward together, then success takes care of itself.

— Henry Ford

The Zen of Prevention

At times it may feel that the universe mischievously conspires to destroy our work. And to some extent this is true: nature doesn't like order. This entropy manifests itself in many ways: we open a network socket, a router may fail. We write to a file, the disk could fill up. We fail to check for valid inputs, our program could blow up unexpectedly.

Causes of potential failure are both infinite and inevitable. As guardians of our own code quality, we're armed with two battle tactics: Be *reactive*, or be *proactive*.

Reactive Error Handling

Colloquially referred to as "firefighting," a reactive position calls us to action. In most cases, an undesirable situation has already presented itself, and now we're charged with fixing:

1. The initial cause of the error, if under our control

2. The unprotected areas of code that allowed the cause to wreak greater havoc

3. Any resultant artifacts that persist after the error is encountered

Anyone who's rifled through a database's binary logfile to restore data to a consistent state can attest to the stressful waste of time incurred in handling emergency situations after a breach in expected execution. Dealing with issues as they arise also imposes a sense of immediacy; the activities of a normal workday may be suspended to address more pressing concerns.

Clearly, the reactive model is not our best option if it can be avoided.

Proactive Quality Policies

"Only YOU can prevent ... fires" has been the plea of the United States Forest Service since 1947, underscoring the importance of limiting factors that contribute to disaster *before* they happen.

Related to the prevention of errors is the issue of *containment*. In the case of failure we'd like to know as soon as possible and handle the problem prior to its leaking into other areas of the system, where it might cause greater harm. Consider this simple bit of code:

```
public String welcome(String name) {
  return "Hello, " + name;
}
```

Assume a user were to accidentally pass `null` into the `welcome(String)` method. The `String` returned would be:

```
Hello, null
```

This is because the *Java Language Specification Version 7* (*http://bit.ly/1e7kLNX*) states in 15.18.1 (*http://bit.ly/1e7kJW5*) that concatenation with a single `String` operand will result in string conversion upon the other operand. The `null` pointer is therefore represented as the `String` "null" according to the rules dictated by 5.1.11 (*http://bit.ly/1e7kMBr*).

Likely this isn't the result we'd been expecting, but we've put ourselves in this position because we didn't *code defensively*. Enhancing the `welcome(String)` method to perform a *precondition check* would raise an `Exception` to the user and prohibit further normal execution flow:

```
public String welcome(String name) {
  if (name == null || name.isEmpty()) {
    throw new IllegalArgumentException("name must be specified");
  }
  return "Hello, " + name;
}
```

This *fail-fast* policy is equally as important at runtime as it is during development. Knowing how to limit our exposure to error remains a topic of vast research and refinement. Luckily, the study of the *software development process* provides us with a number of models upon which we may base our own practices.

Software Development Processes

Methodology. Doctrine. Paradigm. Whatever we call it, our process (or absence of one!) is the script we follow on a day-to-day basis that guides our approach to building software. Typically inspired by the central themes we believe contribute to quality and efficiency, a model for development workflow may be a powerful tool in keeping you and your team from heading down an unproductive path. Many well-documented approaches exist, and knowing their motivations can help inform your own decisions in choosing a sensible model for your project.

Serial Models

A *serial*, or *sequential*, process follows a linear path from project inception to completion. As each stage in the development lifecycle comes to a close, the next one in turn is started. Prior stages are typically not revisited, and this model is often visualized as a series of steps, as illustrated in Figure 1-1.

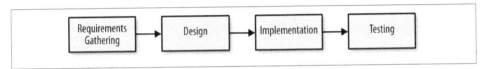

Figure 1-1. Waterfall Model

Development flows from one stage to the next, forming the basis for the nickname "Waterfall," often associated with serial models. Also called "Big Design Up Front," this process relies heavily upon a full understanding of all requirements from the project onset. The general theory supporting Waterfall Design is roughly "measure twice, cut once": by doing an exhaustive evaluation of all moving parts, the goal is to reduce wasted time by avoiding the need to go back and make corrections. In our opinion, this tack is best applied for projects with a long development cycle targeting a single release.

Though this might fit the retail software mold, the never-go-back mentality of a serial process makes it a particularly brittle approach to building adaptable code; the model is not designed to support changing requirements. For that, we might be better served by looking to a more random-access model where any development phase may be revisited (or many may be in-process at the same time!).

Iterative Models

In stark contrast to the linear workflow prescribed by the Waterfall Model, there exists a suite of well-known iterative designs built to encourage change and promote parallelism. By decomposing a large problem into more manageable components, we grant ourselves the option to solve each piece independently. Additionally, we might opt to take broad swipes on a first pass, further refining our solutions in repeated cycles; this is where "iterative" processes obtain their name.

Extreme Programming

Also known simply as "XP," *Extreme Programming* is a discipline that introduces a feedback loop into each phase of the development process. A practice that rose to popularity especially in the late '90s and early 2000s, XP lauds communication and other social aspects as centrally important themes. Figure 1-2 illustrates a typical workflow.

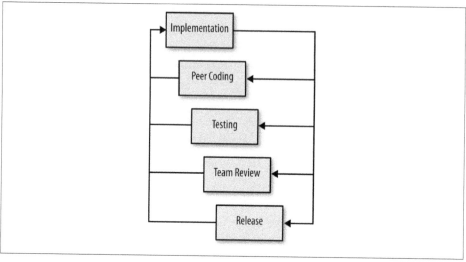

Figure 1-2. Iterative feedback loops in Extreme Programming

While the full reasoning behind XP is detailed by Kent Beck's *Extreme Programming Explained: Embrace Change, Second Edition* (Addison-Wesley, 2004), some of its primary tenets can be boiled down to:

- Short development cycles
- Daily, brief meetings
- Pair Programming, Team Ownership, and Accountability
- Doing only what needs to be done now, deferring nonessential work until later
- Garnering feedback from all stakeholders, not only programmers, early and often
- Test-Driven Development
  - The approach of first writing automated tests, then correcting/augmenting main code until it passes

In fact, XP, along with other models, has both inspired and acts as an implementation of a larger collection of iterative policies as outlined by the *Manifesto for Agile Software Development* (*http://agilemanifesto.org/*).

Testing Is Development

Move testing from the caboose to the engine.

— Tim Ottinger
Senior Consultant

No matter the development method your team prescribes, and no matter how rigidly you adhere to its principles, eventually you're going to need to assert that your code works. Of course you could handle this manually by deploying the application and letting a human user follow a scripted test plan, but wherever possible it's much more efficient and fail-proof to automate the test execution. So you're going to need to write some tests.

But it's our opinion that testing is not simply about making sure your code works as expected.

When you write tests, you're a *user* of your API. You'll see how intuitive it is to use, and you'll discover gaps in documentation. You might discover that it's too verbose or ugly, and most importantly: you can reevaluate your design before it's too late. You're putting yourself in the shoes of your target audience.

What's more, if you write tests alongside the development of your business logic, you might find your work to be more *enjoyable*. You'll know when a feature is completed; you'll have the satisfaction of seeing concrete feedback in real time. Proponents of *Test-Driven Development* even make the case for writing tests *before* implementation. In our experience, testing may be done alongside construction of the primary code such that the experience from one end of the tunnel can inform the other.

Automated testing can take many forms, and we'll categorize a few for use throughout this text.

Levels of Testing

Proponents of test-oriented software development processes may qualify tests in one or more flavors:

Acceptance
Asserts that code meets business requirements

Black-box
Asserts the contract of an API is working without respect to its internals

Compatibility
Asserts that code plays nicely with one or more outside components; for instance, a web application may need to display correctly on Internet Explorer, Chrome, Firefox, Safari, and mobile devices

Functional
> Asserts that code meets the technical requirements derived from business require-
> ments (i.e., that all *functions* are working as expected)

Load/stress/performance
> Asserts and measures how a system handles input under load, and how gracefully
> it degrades with increased traffic

Regression
> Asserts that previously identified errors have been corrected or that existing features
> continue to function

Smoke
> A subset of a full test suite, intended to run quickly and provide feedback that the
> system is generally intact from a simplistic level

White-box
> Asserts that an API is working as contracted, taking into consideration
> implementation-specific data structures and constructs

A well-tested application may have tests covering many of these areas, and we can further
organize these types according to scope.

Unit

The purpose of a unit test is to validate that a single functionality is operating as expected
in isolation. Unit tests are characterized as fast, simple, easy-to-run, and fine-grained.
They may dig into implementation details for use in white-box testing.

For instance, every Java object inherits the method `Object.hashCode()` and the value
equality test `Object.equals(Object)`. By API contract, calls to `hashCode` of equal-by-
value objects must return equal, that is:

```
/**
 * Test bullet 2 of the hashCode contract as defined by:
 * http://docs.oracle.com/javase/7/docs/api/java/lang/Object.html#hashCode()
 */
public void testHashCodeOfEqualObjects() {
  // Declare some vars that are equal-by-value
  MyObject a = new MyObject("a");
  MyObject b = new MyObject("a");

  // Now ensure hashCode is working for these objects as contracted
  assert a.equals(b) : "The objects should be equal by value";
  assert a.hashCode() == b.hashCode() : "Hash codes of equal objects not equal";
}
```

This test, implemented using the Java `assert` keyword, is a classic example of a unit
test: it checks for the smallest possible *invariant* (in this case that the `equals()` and

`hashCode()` implementations of `MyObject` are working with respect to one another). Many experts will advise that a unit test contains only one assertion; in our experience this is a fantastic guideline, but as the preceding example illustrates, use common sense. If more than one assertion is required to conclude that all participants in an invariant are in expected form, then use what's necessary.

In cases where a unit test may require inputs from unrelated components, the use of *mock objects* is a common solution. Mocks supply an alternate implementation used in testing that may help the developer to:

- Simulate an error condition
- Avoid starting up an expensive process or code path
- Avoid dependence upon a third-party system that might not be reliable (or even not available) for testing purposes
- Avoid dependence upon a mechanism that supplies nonidempotent (nonrepeatable) values
  - — For instance, a random-number generator or something that relies on the current time

Although mocks absolutely have their place in the testing arsenal, in the context of Enterprise development it's our opinion that their use should be limited. The Java Enterprise Edition is based on a *POJO* (Plain Old Java Object) component model, which enables us to directly instantiate servlets, Enterprise JavaBeans (EJBs), and Context and Dependency Injection (CDI) beans; this is great for validating business logic in simple calls. However, the true power of Java EE is in the *loose coupling* between components, and mocks do not account for the linkage between these pieces that's provided by the container. To fully test an application, you must test the whole runtime, not simply the code you've written on your own. For that, we need a more comprehensive solution to validation than is allowed by unit tests.

Integration

Imagine we'd like to build a pipe to carry water from a nearby reservoir to a treatment and purification facility. The unit tests we described previously would be responsible for ensuring that each section of the tube was free of leaks and generally of good quality. But the whole is more than the sum of its parts: the opportunity for water escaping between the cracks still exists.

And so it is with software: we must check that our components play nicely with one another. This is especially true for Java EE, where *dependency injection* is a commonplace tool. It's great that one bean not be explicitly bound to another, but eventually we rely upon a container to do the wiring for us. If our metadata or configuration is incorrect, our injection points may not be filled as we're expecting. This could result in a deployment-time exception or worse, making it imperative that we have test coverage for the interaction between components.

When we talk about *integration testing* in this book, it's within the context of a *container*. Historically, interaction with an application server has been notoriously difficult to test. For many, Java EE has become a dirty term as a result. It's the goal of this text to clearly delineate techniques for building enterprise applications in a testable manner. Though many may view this discussion as related to integration testing, instead we feel that it's more about *development*, and integration testing is a valued part of that equation.

In that sense, testing *is* development.

Foundation Test Frameworks

As you might imagine, *container services* really help us to cut down on the complexity in our application code. Dependency injection frees us from manual wiring, while features like *declarative security* and *transaction management* keep us from weaving technical concerns into our business logic. Unfortunately, nothing comes for free: the cost of enlisting a framework or an application server's help is that we've now added another integration point. And every integration point must be validated by an integration test.

Java has built-in support for the `java.lang.Assertion` error and the `assert` keyword, and these are fine tools when used in the right context. Because assertions using `assert` are only analyzed in the presence of the `-ea` switch at launch of the Java runtime, you need not worry about the performance implications of running extra checks in a production environment with this support disabled. For that reason, it makes sense to use `assert` for testing internal code. For instance:

```
private String welcome(String name) {
  assert name!=null && !name.isEmpty() : "name must be specified";
  return "Hello, " + name;
}
```

Because the visibility of this code is `private`, we do not need to worry about doing precondition checks on end-user input; the parameter `username` must be supplied by something *we* have written. Therefore, this need not be tested in production.

Of course, assertions may help us along the way, but they're not *tests*. Tests exercise a code path and validate one or more *post-conditions*. For instance, we might write the following client to validate that the public `welcome(String)` example from "Proactive Quality Policies" on page 2 is working as we'd expect:

```java
public class WelcomeJDKTest {

  /** WelcomeBean instance to be tested **/
  private WelcomeBean welcomer;

  private WelcomeJDKTest(WelcomeBean welcomer) {
    this.welcomer = welcomer;
  }

  public static void main(String... args) {

    /** Make a test client, then execute its tests **/
    WelcomeJDKTest tester = new WelcomeJDKTest(new WelcomeBean());
    tester.testWelcome();
    tester.testWelcomeRequiresInput();

  }

  private void testWelcome() {
    String name = "ALR";
    String expectedResult = "Hello, " + name;
    String receivedResult = welcomer.welcome(name);
    if(!expectedResult.equals(receivedResult)) {
      throw new AssertionError("Did not welcome " + name + " correctly");
    }
  }

  private void testWelcomeRequiresInput() {
    boolean gotExpectedException = false;
    try {
      welcomer.welcome(null);
    } catch (final IllegalArgumentException iae) {
      gotExpectedException = true;
    }
    if(!gotExpectedException) {
      throw new AssertionError("Should not accept null input");
    }
  }
}
```

Not too terrible as far as code coverage goes; we've ensured that the welcome method functions as we'd expect, and we even check that it bans null input at the right place, before that null pointer has a chance to make things more complicated later.

But our signal-to-noise ratio is way off when we write our own main(String[])-based test clients. Look at all the boilerplate involved just to get the execution running, as compared with the test code itself! Just as we use frameworks and component models to cut the redundant, rote bits in our business logic, we can take advantage of some popular libraries to help us slim our tests.

JUnit

The JUnit Test Framework (*http://www.junit.org/*) is one of the most widely known testing frameworks for Java. Initially ported from Kent Beck's work in testing the Smalltalk programming language (*http://en.wikipedia.org/wiki/Kent_Beck*), JUnit is the most-downloaded artifact in the Maven Central Repository (*http://search.maven.org/*) outside of libraries used to run Maven itself (as of August 2012).

Refactoring our `WelcomeJDKTest` to use JUnit might look a little like this:

```java
public class WelcomeJUnitTest {

    /** To be set by the {@link Before} lifecycle method **/
    private WelcomeBean welcomer;

    /** Called by JUnit before each {@link Test} method **/
    @Before
    public void makeWelcomer() {
        this.welcomer = new WelcomeBean();
    }

    @Test
    public void welcome() {
        final String name = "ALR";
        final String expectedResult = "Hello, " + name;
        final String receivedResult = welcomer.welcome(name);
        Assert.assertEquals("Did not welcome " + name + " correctly",
            expectedResult, receivedResult);
    }

    @Test
    public void welcomeRequiresInput() {
        boolean gotExpectedException = false;
        try {
            welcomer.welcome(null);
        } catch (final IllegalArgumentException iae) {
            gotExpectedException = true;
        }
        Assert.assertTrue("Should not accept null input", gotExpectedException);
    }
}
```

The first benefit we get is that we don't need a `main(String[])` method, and we don't need to manually call upon our test methods. Instead, JUnit will dutifully execute for us any lifecycle (i.e., `@Before`) or test (annotated with `@Test`) methods and report the results back to its initial runner. Secondly, we're given access to the JUnit library (for instance, a set of convenience methods in `org.junit.Assert`) to help us reduce the amount of code we'll need to write assertions.

JUnit also has widespread IDE support, making test execution during development much easier. For instance, consider the context menu available in Eclipse, as shown in Figure 1-3.

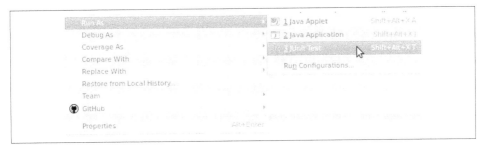

Figure 1-3. JUnit IDE runner integration

As opposed to our homebrewed `main(String[])` test client, JUnit supports reporting. In the IDE this may appear graphically, as shown in Figure 1-4.

Figure 1-4. JUnit IDE reporting integration

Often we'll make use of a *continuous integration server* to handle our builds and provide an auditable view of the codebase over time. During this more formal build process, output may be directed to an XML file for analysis by plug-ins. This can be very helpful in tracking progress of the failing and total number of tests. For instance, we can use the Jenkins Continuous Integration Server (*http://jenkins-ci.org/*) shown in Figure 1-5 to track the progress graphically.

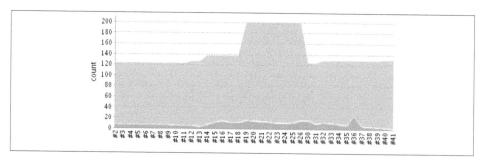

Figure 1-5. Continuous integration test reporting

Of course, JUnit is not the only kid on the block when it comes to test frameworks.

TestNG

If JUnit sets the standard for simplicity in Java testing, TestNG (*http://testng.org/doc/index.html*) touts greater flexibility to the developer by offering an arguably greater featureset. Although the differences between the two frameworks are beyond the scope of this text, there's quite a bit of overlap in concept. Refactoring our test for TestNG should look familiar:

```java
public class WelcomeTestNGTest {

    /** To be set by the {@link @BeforeTest} lifecycle method **/
    private WelcomeBean welcomer;

    /** Called by TestNG before each {@link Test} method **/
    @BeforeTest
    public void makeWelcomer() {
        this.welcomer = new WelcomeBean();
    }

    @Test
    public void welcome() {
        /// .. Omitting logic for brevity
        Assert.assertEquals(receivedResult, expectedResult, "Did not welcome " +
        name + " correctly");
    }

    @Test
    public void welcomeRequiresInput() {
        /// .. Omitting logic for brevity
        Assert.assertTrue(gotExpectedException, "Should not accept null input");
    }
}
```

Some of the parameter orders and API names for the annotations have changed, but the concept remains: write less, and let the framework wire up the call stack.

IDE integration, while not standard for Eclipse Juno, is simple enough to install (*http:// testng.org/doc/download.html*) and provides a GUI runner, as we see in Figure 1-6.

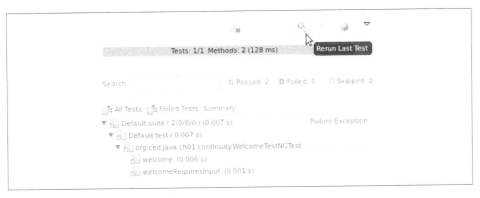

Figure 1-6. JUnit runner in Eclipse

Continuous Development

Followers of Extreme Programming and Agile methodologies are likely to be familiar with Continuous Integration (*http://bit.ly/1e7nG9j*), a practice that advocates frequent patching of the upstream development branch in order to catch errors as they're introduced. Such an approach involves:

- An authoritative source repository (which is *not* at odds with decentralized version control systems, as we'll soon see)
- A comprehensive test suite
- An automated build system
- Automated deployment

These general rules are applicable in most any modern language, are tool-agnostic, and are widely accepted throughout the development community.

So why the *Continuous Development* title of this book?

In addition to the successful ideology and theory espoused by the Agile community, we'll be looking at concrete tools and projects both within and extending the Java Enterprise platform to best address the real-world concerns of an Enterprise Java developer.

The authoritative Git repository containing the book and example application source for this text is hosted by our friends at GitHub (*http://bit.ly/1e7o0ox*). The accompanying book site is located at *http://continuousdev.org*, and the official Twitter channel is @ContinuousDev (*http://twitter.com/ContinuousDev*). The authors can be reached at *authors@continuousdev.org*.

All contents of the book's repository are licensed under Creative Commons Attribution-ShareAlike 2.0 Generic (*http://creativecommons.org/licenses/by-sa/2.0/*), and we invite the community at large to contribute work, including feature requests, typographical error corrections, and enhancements, via our GitHub Issue Tracker (*http://bit.ly/1e7kQRD*).

The print release of the book and its example source is set to be given the Git tag of 1.0.0 in the authoritative repository, and development will continue thereafter in the master branch to correct errata and add supplementary material, including new chapters and use cases. The community is welcome to suggest or request topics for additional coverage.

The example application accompanying the use cases raised in this book is called Geek-Seek, and it is publicly available at *http://geekseek.continuousdev.org*. The source is located in this repository under *code/application*, and instructions for building, testing, and running locally are detailed in Chapter 4 (*http://bit.ly/1e7wJqQ*). The build jobs for the application are kindly powered by CloudBees (*http://www.cloudbees.com*) at *http://bit.ly/1e7wRGN* and *http://bit.ly/1e7wQ5H*.

We welcome your contributions and hope you find the material covered here to be of interest and benefit to your work and career in testable enterprise development.

The first step is to meet some of the key players who will become thematic in this text.

CHAPTER 2

Enabling Technologies

I get by with a little help from my friends.

— Paul McCartney and John Lennon

There's a common misconception that the goal of a standard specification is to address *every* problem. This couldn't be further from the truth: creating a standard is meant to address the 80% case in a manner that's been proven through experience in the field. The Java Enterprise Edition (*http://bit.ly/1e7xn7H*) and its subsystems, governed by the Java Community Process (JCP) (*http://www.jcp.org/en/home/index*), is no exception.

By its very makeup, the JCP is designed to strive for consensus among all participants in an Expert Group on a given technology. Where corporate sponsors and individual contributors disagree or determine that a feature is not yet mature enough to be adequately standardized, latitude is given to specification implementors. This helps to foster creativity and provides differentiation between vendors. In fact, on a discussion regarding the Java EE7 Roadmap (*http://bit.ly/1e7xoIF*), Expert Group member David Blevins succinctly addressed the dynamic: "Vendors innovate, collectively we standardize."

Though it's not the goal of this book to provide exhaustive instruction on the complete featureset of Java EE, it is absolutely our intent to unify the development experience. Helping us along the way are a set of enabling technologies intended to smooth the rough edges of the EE platform and fill the gaps left open by its specifications.

The following open source projects are all made freely available for you to download, use, and modify (be sure to consult individual licensing terms).

Bootstrapping

For all the documentation surrounding Java EE and its use, the seemingly simple act of getting started gets quickly muddled:

- How am I going to build my sources into deployments?
- How should I organize my codebase?
- How can my team best collaborate in parallel on the codebase?
- What about libraries my code uses? How do I get those?

There are a number of valid answers to each of these questions, and the flexibility of choice can easily turn into a burden. Because we'll be exploring fully functioning examples that are intended to be reproduced in your own environment, by necessity we've had to make some decisions in the interest of keeping focus on the code as opposed to our development tools. The following projects, when combined, work very well together but are certainly not the only solutions to the preceding bullet points.

One approach to undertaking a new project is to first lay out the scaffolding on your local filesystem. This will create the structure for your source code, build descriptors, and other resources used by your project. Often this process is fairly rote, involving commands to make new directories and text files in some sensible layout. Although there's no formal rule dictating how your project tree is organized, some build systems employ a convention; others instead choose to allow you total control over your project's build by encouraging you to script or otherwise instruct each build task.

Our examples will be built using a *declarative build tool*, which has standard commands that do not change from project to project.

Apache Maven

Perhaps the most prominent figure in the Java automated build tool landscape, Apache Maven (*http://maven.apache.org/*) positions itself as a "software project management and comprehension tool." For simplicity's sake, we can view it as a build tool; it's capable of compiling, testing, and assembling.

One very nice feature of Maven is that it strives for "*convention over configuration.*" By following a set of recommended best practices, you're likely to trim down on the amount of metadata you'd otherwise need to explicitly define. Additionally, Maven actions (called *goals*) are bound to a documented lifecycle (*http://bit.ly/1e7xH6o*) that is common to all Maven-based projects. For instance, in order to compile, test, and package your project, the command $> mvn package applies. This standardization relieves us from having to declare or learn different build commands for each project.

At the core of the Maven engine is a sophisticated *dependency management* solution capable of resolving libraries by name from a Central Repository (*http://search.maven.org/*) (or additionally configured repository) onto a user's local system. This feature allows us to skip the manual process of adding dependencies into our version control system, and allows us to instead fetch them on demand as part of the build process. As an added bonus, the requisite dependencies for all projects consuming ours are well-documented and automatically fetched for us, as shown in Figure 2-1.

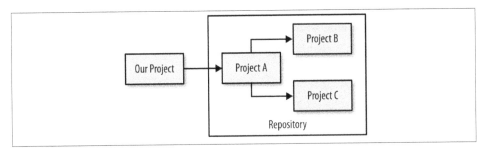

Figure 2-1. Project dependencies as fetched from an external repository

Maven is not without its detractors, however. It's been criticized for a few points. Among them are:

- Maven plug-in versions are not bound to Maven Core versions, making guaranteed reproducible builds between different environments difficult to guarantee.
- Project Object Model (POM, i.e., *pom.xml*) syntax, which is the metadata describing a project's makeup, is verbose.
- Transitive dependencies as a default trigger a lot of downloading on first build. Without care, a project may inherit more dependencies than are necessary or desired.
- Deviation from the defined Maven standard is often difficult to reconcile.

It *is* possible to use Maven-structured repositories from outside Maven. In fact, stand-alone dependency manager Apache Ivy (*http://ant.apache.org/ivy/*) (often used in concert with task-based tool Apache Ant (*http://ant.apache.org/*)), does just that. Groovy-based Gradle (*http://www.gradle.org/*) seeks to provide the flexibility of Ant with the dependency management of Maven.

That said, Maven continues to be a popular and widely used tool in Java development, and will satisfy our requirements to build our examples.

JBoss Forge

If you've spent any time developing Java EE–based projects (or any nontrivial application, for that matter!), you've likely invested a good amount of energy in creating the project layout, defining dependencies, and informing the build system of the relevant class paths to be used in compilation and execution. Although Maven enables us to reduce that load as compared with undertaking project setup manually, there's typically quite a bit of boilerplate involved in the *pom.xml* defining your requirements.

JBoss Forge (*http://forge.jboss.org/*) offers "incremental project enhancement for Java EE." Implemented as a command shell, Forge gives us the ability to alter project files and folders. Some concrete tasks we might use Forge to handle are:

- Adding *Java Persistence API* (JPA) entities and describing their model
- Configuring Maven dependencies
- Setting up project scaffolding
- Generating a view layer, reverse-engineered from a domain model
- Deploying to an application server

Because Forge is built atop a *modular, plug-in-based architecture* (*http://forge.jboss.org/plugins.html*), it's extensible to additional tasks that may be specific to your application.

Overall, the goal of Forge is to ease project setup at all stages of development, so we'll be employing it in this text to speed along the construction of our examples.

Version Control

From the moment we collaborate on a project with others or would like to inspect the evolution of our code over time, we need some form of *version control*. Until recently, the most common paradigm for synchronizing access to a shared codebase was the *client/server* model, wherein developers can keep a local working copy and check their changes into a centralized server, as shown in Figure 2-2.

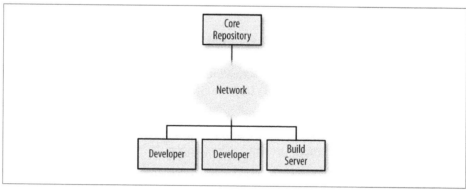

Figure 2-2. Clients interacting with a centralized version control system

Some systems utilize file-level locking to ensure that no conflicts arise during development; others allow concurrent access at the file granularity but cue the developer to resolve line-level conflicts upon committing changes upstream.

Likely the most widely deployed client/server version control system (VCS) from the 1990s through the 2000s has been Concurrent Versions Systems (*http://savan nah.nongnu.org/projects/cvs*), most often referred to by its acronym, *CVS*. Although CVS has enabled teams to freely work on all files in the tree through *unreserved checkouts*, its shortcomings (including nonatomic commits and absent tracking for file renames) prompted the development of Subversion (*http://subversion.apache.org/*) (SVN), heir apparent to CVS. Boasting a wider featureset and greater stability as contrasted with CVS, SVN has enjoyed its reign from the mid- to late-2000s.

These days, the centralized model has been superseded by *distributed version control systems* (DVCS), which are differentiated by their ability to store the full repository, including all history in any number of nodes.

This layout creates a "pull model," where developers on a common project are given the authority over their own repository, free to incorporate changes from others (or not!). At first, this can be a confusing topic to grasp for users vested in the centralized "push model," but it's our opinion that the benefits of this design easily justify the initial confusion inherent when considering many full-fledged repositories representing the same project.

Some immediate gains to consider:

- Repository operations such as committing and searching history are much faster.
- Network connectivity is not required to alter the respository's state.
- Every repository is a full backup of the codebase's history.

This is because each user is typically working on a local repository, and synchronization with a remote repository is only necessary when pushing changes to be visible by others.

In this text, we'll be using the open source DVCS *Git*.

Git

Originally developed to coordinate development of the Linux kernel, Git is a DVCS whose usage has taken off in recent years, arguably due to the user-friendliness of the socially aware hosting site GitHub (*http://www.github.com*). In fact, this book's text and examples are hosted on GitHub (*http://bit.ly/1e7o0ox*) for all to participate.

From a high level, we've chosen Git for our projects because it enables:

True feature (topic) development
    Branching is quick, easy, and cheap. You can work on feature X in isolation, with the ability to put your changes *on top of* development that may be occurring in the mainline branch.

Integration with third-party systems built to respond to Git events

> For instance, we'll be able to trigger builds and production deployments by pushing our local changes to a remote repository.

Rewriting of local history

> Often it's handy to commit liberally, giving yourself many "save" points along the way. However, before making these (sometimes breaking) changes visible to the rest of the world, it's good practice to "squash" the mini-changes into a cohesive, singular commit. This helps keep the version history sane and facilitates later auditing if a bug should arise.

Again, it is not our aim to fully delve into the mechanics of each tool we'll be employing. However, we will be issuing Git commands and explaining their use along the way. You can find a very good reference on the myriad Git subroutines in *Pro Git* (*http://git-scm.com/book*) by Scott Chacon (Apress, 2009), available for free in digital editions and in print via online retailers.

A Test Platform for Java EE

Java EE 5 introduced a *POJO* (Plain Old Java Object) programming model, which freed developers from having to adhere to any particular class hierarchy for its business objects. The introduction of Contexts and Dependency Injection (CDI) (*http://bit.ly/MAgJYs*) in Java EE 6 further pushed the notion of simple business objects by providing *typesafe injection.*

The benefit to objects that can be easily created using the new operator is the same as their drawback: when we manually instantiate objects for use in testing, we're not dealing with the same enterprise components we have in the target runtime. An EJB becomes such only in the context of an EJB container; a servlet is a servlet only when created by a servlet container. Any time we circumvent the target runtime environment to handle object creation and wiring on our own, we're using *mock objects.*

Although many will advocate on the usefulness of mocks, by definition they provide an approximation of how your application will behave in a production environment. Remember that you're responsible for validating that the full bevy of code running on your servers is working as expected, including the bits you *did not write.* Many not-so-subtle errors may arise while leveraging the full potential of the application server in production, and it's best to be testing in an environment as close to the real thing as possible.

True Java EE testing in this sense is an area left largely unspecified by the EE platform, and we'll be examining some tools to help bridge this divide.

Arquillian

Arquillian (*http://arquillian.org*) is an innovative and highly extensible testing platform for the JVM that enables developers to easily create automated integration, functional, and acceptance tests for Java middleware.

Picking up where unit tests leave off, Arquillian handles all the plumbing of container management, deployment, and framework initialization, so you can focus on the business of writing test logic. Instead of configuring a potentially complex test harness, Arquillian abstracts out the target runtime by:

- Managing the lifecycle of the container (or containers).
- Bundling the test case, dependent classes, and resources into a ShrinkWrap archive (or archives).
- Deploying the archive (or archives) to the container (or containers).
- Enriching the test case by providing dependency injection and other declarative services.
- Executing the tests inside (or against) the container.
- Capturing the results and returning them to the test runner for reporting.
- To avoid introducing unnecessary complexity into the developer's build environment, Arquillian integrates seamlessly with familiar testing frameworks (e.g., JUnit 4, TestNG 5), allowing tests to be launched using existing IDE, Ant, and Maven test plug-ins—without any add-ons.

The Arquillian project adheres to three core principles:

Tests should be portable to any supported container.
   Keeping container-specific APIs out of the tests enables developers to verify application portability by running tests in a variety of containers. It also means that lightweight containers can be used as a substitute for full containers during development.

Tests should be executable from both the IDE and the build tool.
   By leveraging the IDE, the developer can skip the build for a faster turnaround and has a familiar environment for debugging. These benefits shouldn't sacrifice the ability to run the tests in continuous integration using a build tool.

The platform should extend or integrate existing test frameworks.
   An extensible architecture encourages reuse of existing software and fosters a unified Java testing ecosystem. Regardless of how complex it becomes, executing an Arquillian test is as simple as selecting Run As → Test in the IDE or executing the "test" goal from the build tool, as shown in Figure 2-3.

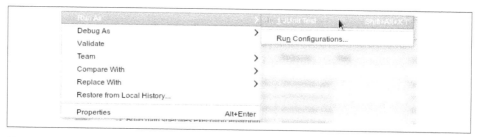

Figure 2-3. DCVS repositories and their relationships

ShrinkWrap

From the onset, ShrinkWrap was born from a need to more easily test Java Enterprise deployments. Traditionally defined as flat-file archives adhering to the ZIP standard, these have necessitated the introduction of some build step to package up all application resources. And a build step takes time:

```
$ mvn clean install
... terrifying output trace ...
[INFO] --------------------------------------------------------------------
[INFO] BUILD SUCCESS
[INFO] --------------------------------------------------------------------
[INFO] Total time: 1:13.492s
[INFO] --------------------------------------------------------------------
```

But as developers, we live in our coding environments. Switching out of that mind set to run a build is wasteful. So we asked: "What if we could declare, in Java, an object to represent that archive?" What resulted was a Java API analogue to the "jar" tool, a virtual filesystem with an intuitive syntax:

```
JavaArchive archive = ShrinkWrap.create(JavaArchive.class,"myarchive.jar")
    .addClasses(MyClass.class, MyOtherClass.class)
    .addResource("mystuff.properties");
```

This enables us to take advantage of the IDE's incremental compilation features, allowing us to skip the build, as shown in Figure 2-4.

Figure 2-4. Incremental compilation in the Eclipse IDE

This piece fulfills the design goal of Arquillian to run tests based on full-fledged deployments directly from the IDE.

Although ShrinkWrap is a standalone virtual filesystem, in our examples we'll be primarily exercising it as the deployment mechanism for Arquillian. Let's take a moment to review its usage.

The first step is getting your hands on the ShrinkWrap binaries. The Core is composed of three pieces, as outlined in Table 2-1.

Table 2-1. ShrinkWrap modules and separation of API, SPI, and implementation

Name	Maven coordinates
API	`org.jboss.shrinkwrap:shrinkwrap-api`
SPI	`org.jboss.shrinkwrap:shrinkwrap-spi`
Implementation	`org.jboss.shrinkwrap:shrinkwrap-impl-base`

Only the API should be available upon your compilation class path, while the SPI and the Implementation modules are both required for the runtime. This is to enforce good separation between classes intended for direct use and the project's internals.

In Maven, these can be brought in under the proper scopes easily by using the Shrink-Wrap Dependency Chain POM, available in Maven Central:

```
<project xmlns="http://maven.apache.org/POM/4.0.0"
  xmlns:xsi="http://www.w3.org/2001/XMLSchema-instance"
  xsi:schemaLocation="
  http://maven.apache.org/POM/4.0.0
  http://maven.apache.org/xsd/maven-4.0.0.xsd">
  <!-- snip -->

  <dependency>
    <groupId>org.jboss.shrinkwrap</groupId>
    <artifactId>shrinkwrap-depchain</artifactId>
    <version>${version.shrinkwrap}</version>
```

```
            <type>pom</type>
        </dependency>

        <!-- snip -->
    </project>
```

For projects not using the Maven repository system, the ShrinkWrap Distribution makes all modules available as a download, and you can set up the dependencies manually to suit your needs. Here are the prerequisites:

- JRE5+ runtime

- No additional dependencies

ShrinkWrap can run on any Java5 runtime or higher, but requires at least JDK6 for compilation.

The primary entry point to the ShrinkWrap library is the `org.jboss.shrink wrap.api.ShrinkWrap` class. From here you can call the `create` method to make a new `Archive`, a generic view of the virtual filesystem that allows the addition of content called `Assets` into a location called an `ArchivePath`. Table 2-2 more easily shows ShrinkWrap nomenclature next to more common terms.

Table 2-2. ShrinkWrap archive types

Archive type	Description
`org.jboss.shrinkwrap.api.GenericArchive`	Simplest type of concrete user-view of an `Archive`; supports generic operations
`org.jboss.shrinkwrap.api.spec.JavaArchive`	JAR type; allows addition of `Classes`, `Pack ages`, and `Manifest` operations
`org.jboss.shrinkwrap.api.spec.EnterpriseArchive`	Java EE EAR type; supports Manifest and related spec operations
`org.jboss.shrinkwrap.api.spec.WebArchive`	Java EE WAR type; supports operations common to web application deployments
`org.jboss.shrinkwrap.api.spec.ResourceAdaptorArchive`	Java EE RAR type; supports operations common to resource adapter deployments

To create an `Archive`, simply choose your desired archive type and optionally supply a name to the static `ShrinkWrap:create` method:

```
GenericArchive myArchive = ShrinkWrap.create(GenericArchive.class,
    "myArchive.jar");
```

That's it! You've got your first ShrinkWrap archive!

Of course, an object representing an empty archive is pretty useless. So let's have a look at adding in some content. As we noted before, content is modeled by the `Asset` class, so let's first take a look at some of the `Asset` implementations provided by ShrinkWrap (as listed in Table 2-3).

Table 2-3. ShrinkWrap asset types

Asset	Represents
org.jboss.shrinkwrap.api.asset.ArchiveAsset	Nested `Archive` content
org.jboss.shrinkwrap.api.asset.ByteArrayAsset	`byte[]` or `InputStream` content
org.jboss.shrinkwrap.api.asset.ClassAsset	Java `Class` content
org.jboss.shrinkwrap.api.asset.ClassLoaderAsset	A resource that can be loaded by an optionally specified `ClassLoader`
org.jboss.shrinkwrap.api.asset.FileAsset	`File` content
org.jboss.shrinkwrap.api.asset.StringAsset	`String` content
org.jboss.shrinkwrap.api.asset.UrlAsset	Content located at a given URL
org.jboss.shrinkwrap.api.asset.EmptyAsset	Empty (0-byte) content

Additionally, because `Asset` is an interface, you can provide your own implementation to supply any byte-based content that may be represented as an `InputStream`. For instance, the following snippet shows how to present an Activation Framework `Data Source` as an `Asset`:

```
final DataSource dataSource = null; // Assume you have this
Asset asset = new Asset() {
  @Override
  public InputStream openStream() {
    try {
      return dataSource.getInputStream();
    } catch (final IOException e) {
      throw new RuntimeException(e);
    }
  }
};
```

The `Archive:add` method allows us to pass in some `Asset` content and add it under an `ArchivePath`:

```
myArchive.add(myAsset,"path/to/content");
System.out.println(myArchive.toString(true));
```

Passing a `true` verbosity flag into the `toString` method of `Archive` creates a recursive `"ls -l"` -style output:

```
myArchive.jar:
/path/
/path/to/
/path/to/content
```

The `Archive` views we covered before are also really helpful, depending upon the type of content you're working with. For instance, a standard JAR file typically contains *.class* files and other resources, so the `JavaArchive` type lets you add these.

ShrinkWrap supports a simple mechanism allowing you to switch "views" of your archive, and it's provided by the `as` method of the `org.jboss.shrinkwrap.api.Assign able` interface; each view in turn extends `Assignable`. So to get your archive to use the `JavaArchive` view in order to easily add `Class` resources, you could simply write this:

```
myArchive.as(JavaArchive.class).addClasses(String.class, Integer.class);
System.out.println(myArchive.toString(true));

archive.jar:
/java/
/java/lang/
/java/lang/String.class
/java/lang/Integer.class
```

Using this mechanism is central to keeping ShrinkWrap's usage clean and intuitive, while providing for a versatility typically found in true multiple-inheritance languages.

Although ShrinkWrap has its roots in Java EE and close ties to the Arquillian Testing Platform, it's certainly not limited to these domains. In fact, ShrinkWrap on its own intentionally is scoped to go no further than to act as a virtual filesystem for archives. As such, it provides a simple mechanism for playing nicely with flat-file structures.

Borrowing from the previous example, perhaps we'd like to use ShrinkWrap to package up all of the *.class* files in the current package and output these as a standard JAR in ZIP format. The code for that would actually be pretty simple:

```
JavaArchive archive = ShrinkWrap.create(JavaArchive.class, "myPackage.jar")
    .addPackage(this.getClass().getPackage());
System.out.println(archive.toString(true));
archive.as(ZipExporter.class).exportTo(
    new File("/home/alr/Desktop/myPackage.jar"), true);

myPackage.jar:
/org/
/org/alr/
/org/alr/test/
/org/alr/test/TestClass.class
```

So let's see what's going on here. First we create a `JavaArchive` and add all the contents of the current `Class`'s `Package`. Then we dump the output to the console, just to see what's included. In the final line, we again use the `Assignable` facilities of the `JavaArch ive` view to get us into a new view: one capable of exporting to ZIP format. In this case we use the appropriately named `ZipExporter`, allowing us to export to a `File`, `Output Stream`, or even get the contents as an `InputStream` so we can deal with the bytes ourselves.

Table 2-4 lists the three types of exporters that ship with ShrinkWrap.

Table 2-4. ShrinkWrap exporter types

Exporter	Output format
org.jboss.shrinkwrap.api.exporter.TarExporter	TAR
org.jboss.shrinkwrap.api.exporter.TarGzExporter	TAR.GZ
org.jboss.shrinkwrap.api.exporter.ZipExporter	ZIP

Of course, we can also obtain a ShrinkWrap archive from a flat file in a similar fashion by using one of the standard importers shown in Table 2-5.

Table 2-5. ShrinkWrap importer types

Importer	Output format
org.jboss.shrinkwrap.api.importer.TarImporter	TAR
org.jboss.shrinkwrap.api.importer.TarGzImporter	TAR.GZ
org.jboss.shrinkwrap.api.importer.ZipImporter	ZIP

The code for running an import to roundtrip the previous example might look like this:

```
JavaArchive roundtrip = ShrinkWrap
  .create(ZipImporter.class, "myPackageRoundtrip.jar")
  .importFrom(new File("/home/alr/Desktop/myPackage.jar"))
  .as(JavaArchive.class);
```

Note how we can pass `ZipImporter` into the `ShrinkWrap.create` method, because it's `Assignable` as well! Beginning to notice a theme here?

This concludes our brief introduction into manipulating archive content with ShrinkWrap.

ShrinkWrap Resolvers

Although ShrinkWrap is ideally suited for creating new archives containing byte-based resources, often our applications are composed with prebuilt libraries bundled alongside our code, making for more complex deployments. These may bundle other archives together, as shown in the following example *Web application ARchive* (WAR):

```
$> jar -tvf myApplication.war
    0 Tue Apr 23 17:01:08 MST 2013 META-INF/
  128 Tue Apr 23 17:01:06 MST 2013 META-INF/MANIFEST.MF
    0 Tue Apr 23 17:01:08 MST 2013 WEB-INF/
    0 Tue Apr 23 17:01:08 MST 2013 WEB-INF/classes/
    0 Tue Apr 23 17:01:08 MST 2013 WEB-INF/lib/
 3654 Tue Apr 23 16:59:44 MST 2013 WEB-INF/lib/hibernate.jar
 3800 Tue Apr 23 17:01:00 MST 2013 WEB-INF/lib/commons-io.jar
 4015 Tue Apr 23 17:00:44 MST 2013 WEB-INF/lib/myEjbModule.jar
```

As you can see, under *WEB-INF/lib* are a couple of third-party libraries used as dependencies by our own code, and an *Enterprise JavaBeans* (EJB) module that we've written for our application. This packaging structure is consistent with the final deployments used by most WARs and *Enterprise application ARchives* (EARs).

Often we don't control the construction of these libraries, and we certainly shouldn't be in the business of reassembling them (and hence further differentiating our tests from our production runtime deployments). With the advent of Maven and other build systems, typically third-party libraries and our own dependent modules are obtained from a backing software *repository*. In this case we supply a series of coordinates that uniquely identifies an artifact in the repository, and resolve the target files from there.

That is precisely the aim of the ShrinkWrap Resolvers project; it is a Java API to obtain artifacts from a repository system. Grammars and support for Maven-based repository structures are currently implemented (this is separate from the use of Maven as a project management system or build tool; it's possible to use a Maven repository layout with other build systems).

ShrinkWrap Resolvers is comprised of the modules listed in Table 2-6.

Table 2-6. ShrinkWrap modules

Name	Maven coordinates
API	`org.jboss.shrinkwrap.resolver:shrinkwrap-resolver-api`
SPI	`org.jboss.shrinkwrap.resolver:shrinkwrap-resolver-spi`
Maven API	`org.jboss.shrinkwrap.resolver:shrinkwrap-resolver-api-maven`
Maven SPI	`org.jboss.shrinkwrap.resolver:shrinkwrap-resolver-spi-maven`
Maven Implementation	`org.jboss.shrinkwrap.resolver:shrinkwrap-resolver-impl-maven`
Maven Implementation with Archive Integration	`org.jboss.shrinkwrap.resolver:shrinkwrap-resolver-impl-maven-archive`

The separation between the Maven and non-Maven modules is there to enforce modular design and separate out generic resolution from Maven-specific grammars, should the project support other mechanisms in the future.

Adding ShrinkWrap Resolvers to your project

You can obtain ShrinkWrap Resolvers for use in your system in a single pass by declaring a dependency upon the depchain module in a Maven *pom.xml* file:

```
<dependencies>
    ...
    <dependency>
      <groupId>org.jboss.shrinkwrap.resolver</groupId>
      <artifactId>shrinkwrap-resolver-depchain</artifactId>
      <version>${version.shrinkwrap.resolvers}</version>
      <scope>test</scope>
```

```
        <type>pom</type>
    </dependency>
    ...
</dependencies>
```

This will bring the APIs into the test classpath and the SPIs and Implementation modules into the runtime classpaths (which will not be transitively inherited, as per Maven rules in runtime scope).

Alternatively, you can have finer-grained control over using ShrinkWrap Resolvers by bringing in each module manually:

```
<dependencies>
    ...
    <dependency>
      <groupId>org.jboss.shrinkwrap.resolver</groupId>
      <artifactId>shrinkwrap-resolver-api</artifactId>
      <version>${version.shrinkwrap.resolvers}</version>
      <scope>test</scope>
    </dependency>
    <dependency>
      <groupId>org.jboss.shrinkwrap.resolver</groupId>
      <artifactId>shrinkwrap-resolver-spi</artifactId>
      <version>${version.shrinkwrap.resolvers}</version>
      <scope>test</scope>
    </dependency>
    <dependency>
      <groupId>org.jboss.shrinkwrap.resolver</groupId>
      <artifactId>shrinkwrap-resolver-api-maven</artifactId>
      <version>${version.shrinkwrap.resolvers}</version>
      <scope>test</scope>
    </dependency>
    <dependency>
      <groupId>org.jboss.shrinkwrap.resolver</groupId>
      <artifactId>shrinkwrap-resolver-spi-maven</artifactId>
      <version>${version.shrinkwrap.resolvers}</version>
      <scope>test</scope>
    </dependency>
    <dependency>
      <groupId>org.jboss.shrinkwrap.resolver</groupId>
      <artifactId>shrinkwrap-resolver-impl-maven</artifactId>
      <version>${version.shrinkwrap.resolvers}</version>
      <scope>test</scope>
    </dependency>
    <dependency>
      <groupId>org.jboss.shrinkwrap.resolver</groupId>
      <artifactId>shrinkwrap-resolver-impl-maven-archive</artifactId>
      <version>${version.shrinkwrap.resolvers}</version>
      <scope>test</scope>
    </dependency>
    ...
</dependencies>
```

The general entry point for resolution is the convenience `org.jboss.shrinkwrap.re
solver.api.maven.Maven` class, which has static hooks to obtain a new `org.jboss.
shrinkwrap.resolver.api.maven.MavenResolverSystem`. Let's cover some of the
most popular use cases for ShrinkWrap Resolvers.

 If you happen to use Arquillian BOM in `<dependencyManagement>`,
it already contains a ShrinkWrap Resolvers version. You must import the ShrinkWrap Resolvers BOM preceding the Arquillian OM
in order to attain the 2.0.0-x version. Adding a ShrinkWrap BOM is
recommended in any case.

You can import the ShrinkWrap Resolvers BOM via the following
snippet:

```
<dependencyManagement>
  <dependencies>
    ...
    <!-- Override dependency resolver with latest version.
         This must go *BEFORE* the Arquillian BOM. -->
    <dependency>
      <groupId>org.jboss.shrinkwrap.resolver</groupId>
      <artifactId>shrinkwrap-resolver-bom</artifactId>
      <version>${version.shrinkwrap.resolvers}</version>
      <scope>import</scope>
      <type>pom</type>
    </dependency>
    ...
  </dependencies>
</dependencyManagement>
```

Resolution of artifacts specified by Maven coordinates

Maven coordinates, in their canonical form, are specified as follows: `groupId:artifac
tId:[packagingType:[classifier]]:version`. Often, those are referred as `G`
(groupId), `A` (artifactId), `P` (packagingType), `C` (classifier), and `V` (version). If you omit
`P` and `C`, you will get the default value, which uses `jar` as the packaging type and an
empty classifier. ShrinkWrap Resolvers additionally allows you to skip `V` in case it has
version information available from the POM; here are some use cases:

- The simplest use case is to resolve a file using coordinates. Here, the resolver locates
  an artifact defined by `G:A:V` and resolves it including all transitive dependencies.
  The result is formatted as an array of type `File`:

  ```
  File[] = Maven.resolver().resolve("G:A:V").withTransitivity().asFile();
  ```

- You might want to change the default Maven behavior and resolve only one artifact
  specified by `G:A:V`, avoiding Maven's transitive dependencies. For this use case,
  ShrinkWrap Resolvers provides a shorthand for changing resolution strategy, called

`withoutTransitivity()`. Additionally, you might want to return a single `File` instead of an array:

```
Maven.resolver().resolve("G:A:V").withoutTransitivity().asSingleFile();
```

- Very often, you need to resolve more than one artifact. The `resolve(String...)` method allows you to specify many artifacts at the same time. The result of the call will be an array of `File` composed of artifacts defined by `G1:A1:V1` and `G2:A2:V2`, including their transitive dependencies:

```
Maven.resolver().resolve("G1:A1:V1", "G2:A1:V1").withTransitivity().asFile();
```

- Resolving a dependency with a specific packaging type. The packaging type is specified by `P` in the `G:A:P:V` coordinates description:

```
Maven.resolver().resolve("G:A:war:V").withTransitivity().asFile();
```

Packaging can be of any type; the most common are listed here:

jar war ear ejb rar par pom test-jar maven-plugin

- Resolving a dependency with a specific classifier. With a classifier, such as `tests`, you need to include all `G:A:P:C:V` parts of the coordinates string:

```
Maven.resolver().resolve("G:A:test-jar:tests:V").withTransitivity().asFile();
```

- Returning resolved artifacts as a type other than `File`. ShrinkWrap Resolvers provides shorthands for returning an `InputStream` instead of `File`. Additionally, with `shrinkwrap-resolver-maven-impl-archive` on the runtime classpath, you can return results as ShrinkWrap archives, such as `JavaArchive`, `WebArchive`, or `EnterpriseArchive`:

```
Maven.resolver().resolve("G:A:V").withTransitivity().as(File.class);
Maven.resolver().resolve("G:A:V").withTransitivity().as(InputStream.class);
Maven.resolver().resolve("G:A:V").withTransitivity().as(JavaArchive.class);
Maven.resolver().resolve("G:A:war:V").withoutTransitivity().asSingle(
    WebArchive.class);
```

 It's the responsibility of the caller to close the returned `Input Stream`.

- Working with artifact metadata. Sometimes, you are more interested in metadata, such as dependencies of a given artifact instead of the artifact itself. ShrinkWrap Resolvers provides an API for such use cases:

```
MavenResolvedArtifact artifact = Maven.resolver().resolve("G:A:war:V")
    .withoutTransitivity().asSingle(MavenResolvedArtifact.class);
```

```
MavenCoordinate coordinates = artifact.getCoordinate();
MavenArtifactInfo[] dependencies = artifact.getDependencies();
String version = artifact.getResolvedVersion();
ScopeType scope = artifact.getScope();
```

You can still retrieve the resolved artifact from `MavenResolvedArtifact`:

```
File file = artifact.asFile();
```

- Excluding a dependency of the artifact you want to resolve. In case you need to resolve an artifact while avoiding some of its dependencies, you can follow the Maven concept known as `<exclusions>`. The following shows how to exclude `G:B` while resolving `G:A:V`:

```
Maven.resolver()
  .addDependencies(
    MavenDependencies.createDependency("G:A:V", ScopeType.COMPILE, false,
      MavenDependencies.createExclusion("G:B"))).resolve().
        withTransitivity().asFile();
```

- Using a strategy to control what will be resolved. In special cases, excluding a single dependency is not the behavior you want to achieve. For instance, you want to resolve all test-scoped dependencies of an artifact, you want to completely avoid some dependency while resolving multiple artifacts, or maybe you're interested in optional dependencies. For those cases, ShrinkWrap Resolvers allows you to specify a `MavenResolutionStrategy`. For instance, you can exclude `G:B` from `G:A:V` (e.g., the same as in previous examples) via the following snippet:

```
Maven.resolver().resolve("G:A:V").using(
  new RejectDependenciesStrategy(false, "G:B")).asFile();
```

 `withTransitivity()` and `withoutTransitivity()` are just convenience methods you can use to avoid writing down strategy names. The first one calls `TransitiveStrategy` and the second one calls `NotTransitiveStrategy`.

Strategies are composed of an array of `MavenResolutionFilter` instances and `TransitiveExclusionPolicy` instances. Defining the former allows you to transform a dependency graph of resolved artifacts, and defining the latter allows you to change default behavior when resolving transitive dependencies. By default, Maven does not resolve any dependencies in *provided* and *test* scope, and it also skips *optional* dependencies. ShrinkWrap Resolvers behaves the same way by default, but allows you to change that behavior. This comes in handy especially when you want to, for instance, resolve all provided dependencies of `G:A:V`. For your convenience, ShrinkWrap Resolvers ships with the strategies described in Table 2-7.

Table 2-7. Strategies available in ShrinkWrap Resolvers

Name	Description
`AcceptAllStrategy`	Accepts all dependencies of artifacts. Equals `TransitiveStrategy`.
`AcceptScopesStrategy`	Accepts only dependencies that have a defined scope type.
`CombinedStrategy`	Allows you to combine multiple strategies together. The behavior is defined as logical AND between combined strategies.
`NonTransitiveStrategy`	Rejects all dependencies that were not directly specified for resolution. This means that all transitive dependencies of artifacts for resolution are rejected.
`RejectDependenciesStrategy`	Rejects dependencies defined by `G:A` (version is not important for comparison, so it can be omitted altogether). By default, it is transitive: `RejectDependencies` `Strategy("G:A", "G:B")` means that all dependencies that originate at `G:A` or `G:B` are removed as well. If you want to change that behavior to reject defined dependencies but to keep their descendants, instantiate the following strategy: `Re` `jectDependenciesStrategy(false, "G:A", "G:B")`
`TransitiveStrategy`	Accepts all dependencies of artifacts. Equals `AcceptAllStrategy`.

- Control sources of resolution. ShrinkWrap Resolvers allows you to specify where you want to resolve artifacts from. By default, it uses the classpath (also known as Maven Reactor) and Maven Central repository; however, you can alter the behavior programmatically:

```
Maven.resolver().resolve("G:A:V").withClassPathResolution(false)
    .withTransitivity().asFile();
Maven.resolver().resolve("G:A:V").withMavenCentralRepo(false)
    .withTransitivity().asFile();
Maven.resolver().offline().resolve("G:A:V")
    .withTransitivity().asFile();
```

Although classpath resolution is handy for testing SNAPSHOT artifacts that are not yet installed in any Maven repository, making ShrinkWrap Resolvers offline lets you avoid accessing any repositories but local cache.

- Controlling classpath resolution and Maven Central comes in handy, but sometimes you might want to specify a completely different *settings.xml* file than THE default for your test execution. You can do this via the following API calls:

```
Maven.configureResolver().fromFile("/path/to/settings.xml")
    .resolve("G:A:V").withTransitivity().asFile();

Maven.configureResolver().fromClassloaderResource("path/to/settings.xml")
    .resolve("G:A:V").withTransitivity().asFile();
```

ShrinkWrap Resolvers will not consume *settings.xml* files specified on the command line (`-s settings.xml`) or in the IDE. It
reads *settings.xml* files at their standard locations, which are
~/.m2/settings.xml and *$M2_HOME/conf/settings.xml* unless
overridden in the API or via a system property.

Resolution of artifacts defined in POM files

While previous calls allow you to manually define what you want to resolve, in Maven
projects, you have very likely specified this information already in your *pom.xml* file.
ShrinkWrap Resolvers allows you to follow *DRY* (Don't Repeat Yourself) principles and
can load metadata included there.

ShrinkWrap Resolvers constructs a so called *effective POM model* (simplified, that is
your *pom.xml* file plus parent hierarchy and Super POM, the Maven default POM file).
In order to construct the model, it uses all local repositories, the classpath repository,
and all remote repositories. Once the model is loaded, you can automatically add the
metadata in there to artifacts you want to resolve. The following use cases are supported:

Resolving an artifact with the version defined in effective POM
> In case you want to resolve G:A:V, you can simply specify G:A instead. For artifacts
> with non-JAR packaging type or classifier, you must use alternative syntax with a
> question mark ?, such as G:A:P:? or G:A:P:C:?:

```
Maven.resolver().loadPomFromFile("/path/to/pom.xml")
    .resolve("G:A").withTransitivity().asFile();

Maven.resolver().loadPomFromClassLoaderResource("/path/to/pom.xml")
    .resolve("G:A:P:?").withTransitivity().asFile();
```

Resolving artifacts defined in effective POM
> ShrinkWrap resolvers allows you to import artifacts defined with a specific scope
> into the list of artifacts to be resolved. This way, you don't need to alter your tests
> if you change dependencies of your application. You can either use importDepen
> dencies(ScopeType...) or convenience methods that cover the most frequent usages
> (importRuntimeDependencies(), importTestDependencies(), and importRunti
> meAndTestDependencies()):

```
Maven.resolver().loadPomFromFile("/path/to/pom.xml")
    .importDependencies(ScopeType.TEST, ScopeType.PROVIDED)
    .resolve().withTransitivity().asFile();

Maven.resolver().loadPomFromFile("/path/to/pom.xml").
    importRuntimeDependencies().resolve().withTransitivity().asFile();
```

"Runtime" in convenience methods means all the Maven scopes that are used in the application runtime, which are `compile`, `runtime`, `import`, and `system`. If you need to select according to Maven scopes, go for `importDependencies(ScopeType...)` instead.

Specifying plug-ins to be activated

By default, ShrinkWrap Resolvers activates profiles based on property value, file presence, active by default profiles, operating system, and JDK. However, you can force profiles the same way you would via `-P` in Maven:

```
Maven.resolver().loadPomFromFile(
    "/path/to/pom.xml", "activate-profile-1", "!disable-profile-2")
    .importRuntimeAndTestDependencies().resolve().withTransitivity().asFile();
```

System properties

ShrinkWrap Resolvers allows you to override any programmatic configuration via System Properties, which are defined in Table 2-8.

Table 2-8. System Properties that alter the behavior of ShrinkWrap Resolvers

Name	Description
`org.apache.maven.user.settings`	Path to the user *settings.xml* file. If both settings are provided, they are merged; user one has the priority.
`org.apache.maven.global-settings`	Path to the global *settings.xml* file. If both settings are provided, they are merged; user one has the priority.
`org.apache.maven.security-settings`	Path to *settings-security.xml*, which contains an encrypted master password for password-protected Maven repositories.
`org.apache.maven.offline`	Flag there to work in offline mode.
`maven.repo.local`	Path to local repository with cached artifacts. Overrides value defined in any of the *settings.xml* files.

Experimental Features

The following features are in their early development stages. However, they should work for the most common use cases. Feel free to report a bug in the SHRINKRES project (*https://issues.jboss.org/ browse/SHRINKRES*) if you encounter problems.

ShrinkWrap Resolvers Maven plug-in

The ShrinkWrap Resolvers Maven plug-in allows you to propagate settings specified on the command line into test execution. Settings include paths to the *pom.xml* and *settings.xml* files, activated/disabled profiles, offline flag, and path to local repository. No support for IDE exists at this moment.

To activate the plug-in, you need to add the following snippet to the <build> section of your *pom.xml* file:

```
<plugin>
  <groupId>org.jboss.shrinkwrap.resolver</groupId>
  <artifactId>shrinkwrap-resolver-maven-plugin</artifactId>
  <version>${version.shrinkwrap.resolvers}</version>
  <executions>
    <execution>
      <goals>
        <goal>propagate-execution-context</goal>
      </goals>
    </execution>
  </executions>
</plugin>
```

Then, in your test you can do the following:

```
Maven.configureResolverViaPlugin().resolve("G:A").withTransitivity().asFile();
```

MavenImporter

The MavenImporter is the most advanced feature of ShrinkWrap Resolvers. Instead of the user being responsible for specifying how the testing archive should look, it reuses information defined in your *pom.xml* to construct the archive. So, no matter how your project looks, you can get a full archive because you would deploy it into the application server within a single line of code.

MavenImporter is able to compile sources, construct *manifest.mf* files, fetch the dependencies, and construct archives as Maven would do. It does not require any data to be prepared by Maven; however, it can profit from those if they exist. For instance, the following example takes advantage of metadata defined in the POM file to determine the build output:

```
ShrinkWrap.create(MavenImporter.class)
    .loadPomFromFile("/path/to/pom.xml").importBuildOutput().as(WebArchive.class);

ShrinkWrap.create(MavenImporter.class)
    .loadPomFromFile("/path/to/pom.xml", "activate-profile-1",
    "!disable-profile-2").importBuildOutput().as(WebArchive.class);

ShrinkWrap.create(MavenImporter.class).configureFromFile("/path/to/settings.xml")
    .loadPomFromFile("/path/to/pom.xml").importBuildOutput().as(JavaArchive.class);
```

`MavenImporter` currently supports only JAR and WAR packages. Also, it does not honor many of the Maven plug-ins—it currently supports only a limited subset.

Additionally, using different JDKs for running tests and compiling sources is not supported. However, it should work if you are compiling sources targeting JDK6 while being bootstrapped on JDK7.

By enabling resolution in a friendly, intuitive API, ShrinkWrap Resolvers arms ShrinkWrap archives with a powerful mechanism to create deployment units, which are applicable in real-world scenarios that require libraries and modules not owned by the current project.

Runtime

Being simply a component model, Java EE needs a concrete implementation to provide the runtime services to our applications.

WildFly

The latest community edition of the application server offered by JBoss has recently been renamed to *WildFly* (*http://wildfly.org/*), and this will be the default target runtime for our examples. Written from the ground up, WildFly (previously known as *JBoss Application Server 7*) was designed with the following goals at the core:

Speed
Startup, deployment, and request-processing demands leverage a concurrent-state machine and constant-time class loading.

Efficiency
Memory usage is kept to a minimum.

Modularity
Application libraries and server libraries are isolated from one another to avoid runtime conflicts.

Administration
Centralized settings via web interface, HTTP, Java, and command-line APIs.

Compliance
Java EE6 Full Profile Certification (*http://bit.ly/MAyPcP*).

Testable
Uses Arquillian and ShrinkWrap in its own internal test suite.

Because a quick feedback loop is important in testing during development, the speed afforded by WildFly makes it a compelling candidate for our target runtime:

```
19:16:06,662 INFO  [org.jboss.as] (Controller Boot Thread)
  JBAS015874: WildFly 8.0.0.Alpha2 "WildFly" started in 2702ms -
  Started 153 of 189 services (56 services are lazy, passive or on-demand)
```

The online user guide for WildFly is located at *http://bit.ly/MAyZAR*.

OpenShift

Although getting our applications running on our own machine is a great step in developing, the beauty of the Internet is that we can expose our content and services to the world at large. Until very recently, Java EE hosting typically involved a dedicated and expensive server colocated in a data center. With the rapid advent of virtualization and the cloud, we're now able to gain public access much more easily, and at a far reduced cost.

OpenShift (*http://www.openshift.com*) is Red Hat's free Platform as a Service (PaaS) for applications. Although it supports a variety of frameworks bundled as "cartridges," we'll be using OpenShift's built-in JBoss AS7 support. With just a little bit of initial setup, pushing changes from our local Git repository to the OpenShift remote will trigger a build and deployment of our application for all to see. We'll be relieved of the responsibility of obtaining a server, installing JBossAS, configuring the networking and firewalls, or manually deploying new versions.

On to the Code

Now that we've familiarized ourselves with the technologies we'll be using throughout the exercises, let's dig in and create a new Java EE application, making it public to the world.

CHAPTER 3

Scratch to Production

The way to get started is to quit talking and begin doing.

— Walt Disney

Enterprise Java has long suffered the (possibly correct) critique that it's difficult to bootstrap a new project. Couple the lack of definitive jumpstart documentation with vendor-specific techniques for application deployment, throw a mess of third-party dependencies into the mix, and we've got a prime recipe yielding barriers to entry for programmers new to web development in Java.

Of course, this all runs contrary to the mission of Java EE: to make our experience with enterprise features *easier*. So while the programming model has certainly evolved past the days of confusingly verbose and explicitly required metadata, the warts that lead to frustrating stack traces and unexpected deployment behaviors unfortunately persist.

Some of this is by design. The specifications that comprise the Java EE Platform intentionally leave room for vendors to implement features like server startup and deployment at their discretion. (Although there is some limited facility to, for instance, create an EJB container in a running JVM and bring EJB deployments on the classpath into service, a full-scale deployment is still typically achieved in a vendor-specific manner.)

In the interest of providing a uniformly workable solution to the reader, this text will routinely opt for vendor-specific approaches in favor of generic guidelines. By the end of this chapter, you should be comfortable creating a new Java EE web application and pushing it live to production using a few tools and services offered by the JBoss Community.

The Development Environment

Although all projects used here are ultimately standalone and require no plug-ins or special environments aside from a Java runtime, we're going to make our lives easier by taking advantage of the integration facilities provided by JBoss Developer Studio (JBDS).

The JBDS plug-ins atop the Eclipse Integrated Development Environment (IDE) will unify our development experience and allow us to stay inside one window. Installation is via an executable JAR available from the JBDS site (*http://bit.ly/MAzyup*) (see Figure 3-1).

To kick off the installation process, either double-click the icon (if your environment has the *.jar* extension correctly associated as a Java executable) or launch the installer from the command line via the Java runtime:

```
$> java -jar jbdevstudio-product-universal-7.0.0.GA-v20130720-0044-B364.jar
```

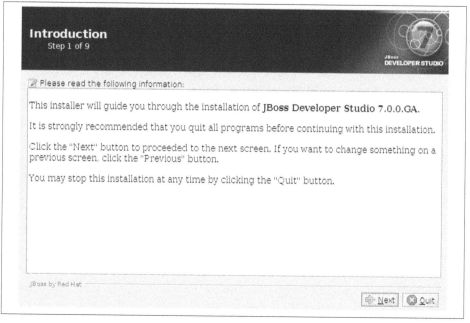

Figure 3-1. JBoss Developer Studio installation

Following the graphical wizard will install the JDBS IDE (and all requisite plug-ins we'll be using) onto your local machine.

A New Project

The previous chapter introduced us to JBoss Forge, a tool that aims to make project creation and enhancement more declarative and less manual. Because we're starting fresh now, it makes sense to use Forge to create our project layout. This will ultimately give us a functional skeleton from database to view layer that we can use either as a learning tool or a quick shortcut to writing some real code.

Forge's user interface is a shell, so it can be installed manually and used from the terminal like any other command-line application. However, JBDS removes the need for us to do this setup. As shown in Figure 3-2, selecting Window → Show View → Other will give us immediate access to the Forge Console.

Figure 3-2. Forge Console view selection

With our new *Forge Console* view, we're now free to start up the Forge runtime, which came embedded with the JBDS installation. Clicking the green play button, as shown in Figure 3-3, will give us access to the Forge shell:

```
    ____  _     ___ ___  ___ __ _ ___
   |  __|_   __   _   _ _      _ _
   | |_ / _ \| `__/ _` |/ _ \  \\
   |  _| (_) | | | (_| |  __/  //
   |_|  \___/|_|  \__, |\___|
                  |___/
```

```
JBoss Forge, version [ 1.3.3.Final ] - JBoss, by Red Hat, Inc.
[ http://forge.jboss.org ]
[no project] workspace $
```

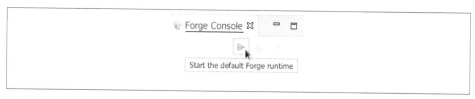

Figure 3-3. Click the play button to start Forge

JBDS integration with Forge is especially useful in this console because the IDE will automatically refresh any changes we make in Forge with our project view and open text editors.

As a decent shell, Forge supports tab-completion of commands and known parameters; if you get stuck, feel free to use the Tab key to see what's available.

To ease up on our configuration options, let's first start off by instructing Forge to accept defaults:

```
$> set ACCEPT_DEFAULTS true;
```

And now let's create the filesystem layout and *pom.xml* for our new Maven-based Java EE project. We'll be creating a simple application that will allow users to leave comments, so we'll name the application feedback:

```
$> new-project --named feedback --topLevelPackage org.cedj.ch03.feedback
   --projectFolder feedback;
```

Once we hit Enter, we'll see that Forge has dutifully created our new project's layout:

```
***SUCCESS*** Created project [feedback] in new working directory [./feedback]
Wrote ./feedback
Wrote ./feedback/pom.xml
Wrote ./feedback/src/main/java
Wrote ./feedback/src/test/java
Wrote ./feedback/src/main/resources
Wrote ./feedback/src/test/resources
Wrote ./feedback/src/main/java/org/cedj/feedback
Wrote ./presentations/feedback/src/main/resources/META-INF/forge.xml
```

Additionally, our project has appeared in the Project View, as shown in Figure 3-4.

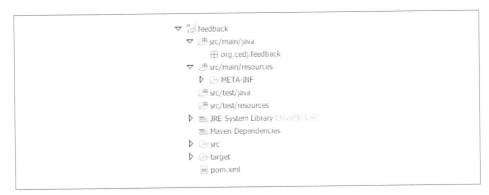

Figure 3-4. Our project created in Project View

Users of Maven Archetypes (*http://bit.ly/MABuTN*) may be familiar with this type of technique to create a new project, but because Forge is an *incremental* tool, it's capable of reading a project's state and adding behaviors after creation.

Let's add support for Java Persistence API (JPA) to our project, a task that typically would involve some searching for the correct dependencies for the spec APIs (as well as those for any vendor-specific extensions). Forge is helpful here as well, via its `persistence` plug-in:

```
$> persistence setup --provider HIBERNATE --container JBOSS_AS7;
```

In this case we've chosen Hibernate (*http://www.hibernate.org/*) as our persistence provider, and have targeted JBoss AS7 as our container. Forge will equip our POM with the proper dependencies and supply us with a default *persistence.xml* preconfigured to work with the AS7 runtime (for a list of supported options, look to tab completion):

```
***SUCCESS*** Installed [forge.spec.jpa] successfully.
***INFO*** Setting transaction-type="JTA"
***INFO*** Using example data source [java:jboss/datasources/ExampleDS]
***SUCCESS*** Persistence (JPA) is installed.
Wrote ./feedback/src/main/resources/META-INF/persistence.xml
Wrote ./feedback/pom.xml
```

A peek into the generated *persistence.xml* will show us a decent default configuration:

```
<?xml version="1.0" encoding="UTF-8" standalone="no"?>
<persistence xmlns="http://java.sun.com/xml/ns/persistence"
xmlns:xsi="http://www.w3.org/2001/XMLSchema-instance" version="2.0"
xsi:schemaLocation="http://java.sun.com/xml/ns/persistence
http://java.sun.com/xml/ns/persistence/persistence_2_0.xsd">
  <persistence-unit name="forge-default" transaction-type="JTA">
    <description>Forge Persistence Unit</description>
    <provider>org.hibernate.ejb.HibernatePersistence</provider>
    <jta-data-source>java:jboss/datasources/ExampleDS</jta-data-source>
    <exclude-unlisted-classes>false</exclude-unlisted-classes>
    <properties>
```

```
        <property name="hibernate.hbm2ddl.auto" value="create-drop"/>
        <property name="hibernate.show_sql" value="true"/>
        <property name="hibernate.format_sql" value="true"/>
        <property name="hibernate.transaction.flush_before_completion"
                   value="true"/>
    </properties>
  </persistence-unit>
</persistence>
```

Let's make one tweak; the property `hibernate.hbm2ddl.auto` is set to automatically drop the database tables so they can't be reused across deployments. Though this might be handy in development to ensure we're always coding from a clean slate, we'd actually like to use some real persistence later, so let's change that property to a value of `update`.

Java EE6 introduced the Bean Validation Specification (*http://jcp.org/en/jsr/detail? id=303*), which allows for validation constraints at the database, application, and view layers all with a single declaration. Let's enable BV for our project, similar to how we put in place support for persistence:

```
$> validation setup --provider HIBERNATE_VALIDATOR
```

Once again we're given the appropriate dependencies in our POM, as well as a valid *validation.xml* configuration file such that we don't have to apply any boilerplate XML on our own:

```
***SUCCESS*** Installed [forge.spec.validation] successfully.
Wrote ./feedback/src/main/resources/META-INF/validation.xml
Wrote ./feedback/pom.xml
```

The generated *validation.xml* should be fine for our uses without any modification:

```
<?xml version="1.0" encoding="UTF-8" standalone="no"?>
<validation-config xmlns="http://jboss.org/xml/ns/javax/validation/configuration"
xmlns:xsi="http://www.w3.org/2001/XMLSchema-instance">
  <default-provider>org.hibernate.validator.HibernateValidator</default-provider>
  <message-interpolator>org.hibernate.validator.messageinterpolation.
  ResourceBundleMessageInterpolator</message-interpolator>
  <traversable-resolver>org.hibernate.validator.engine.resolver.
  DefaultTraversableResolver</traversable-resolver>
  <constraint-validator-factory>org.hibernate.validator.engine.
  ConstraintValidatorFactoryImpl</constraint-validator-factory>
</validation-config>
```

Now we're all set to add some entities to our project. For the uninitiated, this will be our interface to accessing persistent (i.e., database-backed) data as an object. For now we'll just create one simple bean to represent a database table, and we'll call it `FeedbackEntry`:

```
$> entity --named FeedbackEntry;
```

Forge will create a new Java class for us, adding the proper `@Entity` annotation, an ID field to represent our primary key, a version field for optimistic locking, and stubbed-out methods for the value-based `equals(Object)` and `hashCode()`:

```java
package org.cedj.feedback.model;

import javax.persistence.Entity;
import java.io.Serializable;
import javax.persistence.Id;
import javax.persistence.GeneratedValue;
import javax.persistence.GenerationType;
import javax.persistence.Column;
import javax.persistence.Version;
import java.lang.Override;

@Entity
public class FeedbackEntry implements Serializable
{

    @Id
    private @GeneratedValue(strategy = GenerationType.AUTO)
    @Column(name = "id", updatable = false, nullable = false)
    Long id = null;
    @Version
    private @Column(name = "version")
    int version = 0;

    public Long getId()
    {
        return this.id;
    }

    public void setId(final Long id)
    {
        this.id = id;
    }

    public int getVersion()
    {
        return this.version;
    }

    public void setVersion(final int version)
    {
        this.version = version;
    }

    public String toString()
    {
        String result = "";
        if (id != null)
            result += id;
        return result;
    }

    @Override
```

```java
    public boolean equals(Object that)
    {
        if (this == that)
        {
            return true;
        }
        if (that == null)
        {
            return false;
        }
        if (getClass() != that.getClass())
        {
            return false;
        }
        if (id != null)
        {
            return id.equals(((FeedbackEntry) that).id);
        }
        return super.equals(that);
    }

    @Override
    public int hashCode()
    {
        if (id != null)
        {
            return id.hashCode();
        }
        return super.hashCode();
    }
}
```

Our FeedbackEntry entity should be capable of recording feedback for some user with a Twitter ID, so let's add fields to represent that data (as well as some validation constraints dictating that these cannot be null):

```
field string --named twitterHandle;
constraint NotNull --onProperty twitterHandle;
field string --named feedback;
constraint NotNull --onProperty feedback;
```

It's worth noting now that our Forge prompt reads that the current location is *inside* our entity, because that's where we're currently working. Forge's ls command is handy for seeing the current state of our entity as we build:

```
[feedback] FeedbackEntry.java $ ls

[fields]
private::Long::id;
private::String::feedback;
private::String::twitterHandle;
private::int::version;
```

```
[methods]
public::equals(Object that)::boolean
public::getFeedback()::String
public::getId()::Long
public::getTwitterHandle()::String
public::getVersion()::int
public::hashCode()::int
public::setFeedback(final String feedback)::void
public::setId(final Long id)::void
public::setTwitterHandle(final String twitterHandle)::void
public::setVersion(final int version)::void
public::toString()::String
```

With our sole entity in place, it's time to let Forge generate a UI layer for us as a starting point for the view in our web application. The `scaffold` command makes short work of this:

```
$> scaffold setup
***SUCCESS*** Installed [forge.maven.WebResourceFacet] successfully.
***SUCCESS*** Installed [forge.spec.ejb] successfully.
***SUCCESS*** Installed [forge.spec.cdi] successfully.
***SUCCESS*** Installed [forge.spec.servlet] successfully.
***SUCCESS*** Installed [forge.spec.jsf.api] successfully.
***SUCCESS*** Installed [faces] successfully.
Wrote ./feedback/src/main/webapp
Wrote ./feedback/pom.xml
Wrote ./feedback/src/main/webapp/WEB-INF/beans.xml
Wrote ./feedback/src/main/webapp/WEB-INF/faces-config.xml
Wrote ./feedback/src/main/webapp/favicon.ico
Wrote ./feedback/src/main/webapp/resources/scaffold/paginator.xhtml
Wrote ./feedback/src/main/webapp/resources/scaffold/pageTemplate.xhtml
Wrote ./feedback/src/main/webapp/index.html
Wrote ./feedback/src/main/webapp/index.xhtml
Wrote ./feedback/src/main/webapp/error.xhtml
Wrote ./feedback/src/main/webapp/resources/add.png
Wrote ./feedback/src/main/webapp/resources/bootstrap.css
Wrote ./feedback/src/main/webapp/resources/false.png
Wrote ./feedback/src/main/webapp/resources/favicon.ico
Wrote ./feedback/src/main/webapp/resources/forge-logo.png
Wrote ./feedback/src/main/webapp/resources/forge-style.css
Wrote ./feedback/src/main/webapp/resources/remove.png
Wrote ./feedback/src/main/webapp/resources/search.png
Wrote ./feedback/src/main/webapp/resources/true.png
Wrote ./feedback/src/main/webapp/WEB-INF/web.xml
```

As shown by the somewhat lengthy output, we're now equipped with a *src/main/ webapp* folder laid out with a nice starting point from which we can build our own UI. With just one more command, we can generate a CRUD (Create, Read, Update, Delete) interface to our entities:

```
$> scaffold from-entity org.cedj.feedback.model.*;
***INFO*** Using currently installed scaffold [faces]
***SUCCESS*** Generated UI for [org.cedj.feedback.model.FeedbackEntry]
Wrote ./feedback/src/main/java/org/cedj/feedback/view/FeedbackEntryBean.java
Wrote ./feedback/src/main/webapp/feedbackEntry/create.xhtml
Wrote ./feedback/src/main/webapp/feedbackEntry/view.xhtml
Wrote ./feedback/src/main/webapp/feedbackEntry/search.xhtml
Wrote ./feedback/src/main/webapp/resources/scaffold/pageTemplate.xhtml
Wrote ./feedback/src/main/java/org/cedj/feedback/view/ViewUtils.java
Wrote ./feedback/src/main/webapp/WEB-INF/classes/META-INF/forge.taglib.xml
Wrote ./feedback/src/main/java/org/cedj/feedback/model/FeedbackEntry.java
```

And that's enough for now; we've created the skeleton for a fully functional application. Of course, the thematic element of this book is *testable development*, so it's best we throw in the facility to run some integration tests on our little application.

Writing Our First Integration Test with Arquillian

We've mentioned before that Forge is based on a plug-in architecture; all commands we've used thus far are actually plug-ins called by the Forge runtime when we request them in the console. Up to this point, we've used support that comes standard with the Forge distribution. Now we'd like to add some tests, and we'll use the Arquillian Test Platform as both the programming model and the JUnit test runner. The first order of business is to install the Arquillian plug-in into our Forge runtime, and we do this by way of the forge install-plugin command:

```
$> forge install-plugin arquillian
Connecting to remote repository [https://raw.github.com/forge/plugin-repository/
master/repository.yaml]... connected!
***INFO*** Preparing to install plugin: arquillian
***INFO*** Checking out plugin source files to
          [/tmp/forgetemp1365281623326595751/repo] via 'git'
***INFO*** Switching to branch/tag [refs/heads/1.0.2.Final]
***INFO*** Invoking build with underlying build system.
...
***INFO*** Installing plugin artifact.
***SUCCESS*** Installed from [https://github.com/forge/plugin-arquillian.git]
              successfully.
```

This instructs Forge to connect to its plug-in repository, grab the latest version of the requested plug-in, build it from source, and install the binaries into the current runtime. Because Forge is built on a modular class-loading architecture, we're able to load in plug-ins without the need to restart the process or concern ourselves with conflicting dependencies.

With the Arquillian plug-in installed, we now have access to the arquillian command. Let's instruct Forge to equip our POM with the dependencies needed to run Arquillian tests on the JBoss AS7 container:

```
$> arquillian setup --containerType REMOTE
    --containerName JBOSS_AS_REMOTE_7.X --testframework
```

You'll be prompted for the versions of Arquillian, JUnit, and JBoss AS7 that you'd like to use, and the available options will expand over time as new versions are released. These instructions have been tested with:

```
[org.jboss.arquillian:arquillian-bom:pom::1.1.1.Final]
[junit:junit:::4.11]
[org.jboss.as:jboss-as-arquillian-container-remote:::7.1.1.Final]
```

With the POM config changes out of the way, let's ask Forge to now create for us a jumping-off point from which we'll write our test:

```
$> arquillian create-test
    --class org.cedj.ch03.feedback.model.FeedbackEntry.java
Picked up type <JavaResource>: org.cedj.feedback.model.FeedbackEntryTest
Wrote ./feedback/src/test/java/org/cedj/feedback/model/FeedbackEntryTest.java
```

The newly created FeedbackEntryTest is technically an Arquillian test, but it really doesn't do too much for us. After all, we can automate quite a bit, but in the end it's up to us to write our own business and test logic. So let's replace the contents of this class with:

```java
package org.cedj.feedback.model;

import java.io.File;
import javax.persistence.EntityManager;
import javax.persistence.PersistenceContext;
import org.jboss.arquillian.container.test.api.Deployment;
import org.jboss.arquillian.junit.Arquillian;
import org.jboss.shrinkwrap.api.ShrinkWrap;
import org.jboss.shrinkwrap.api.spec.WebArchive;
import org.junit.Assert;
import org.junit.Test;
import org.junit.runner.RunWith;

@RunWith(Arquillian.class)
public class FeedbackEntryTest {
    @PersistenceContext
    private EntityManager em;

    @Deployment
    public static WebArchive createDeployment() {
        return ShrinkWrap.createFromZipFile(WebArchive.class, new File(
                "target/feedback.war"));
    }

    @Test
    public void canFindFeedbackByUser() {
        final FeedbackEntry feedback = em.createQuery(
                "from " + FeedbackEntry.class.getSimpleName()
                    + " where twitterHandle='@ALRubinger'",
```

```
                    FeedbackEntry.class).getSingleResult();
            Assert.assertNotNull(feedback);
        }

        @Test
        public void testIsDeployed() {
            Assert.assertNotNull(em);
        }
    }
```

Before going forward, let's break down the anatomy of this test.

First, we'll note that there are no references in the import statements to any particular
application server or target container. This is because Arquillian is designed to decouple
the programming model of the test from the target runtime; any container that can
handle the capabilities demanded by the test will work. This keeps the portability goals
of Java EE intact, moving the mechanics of startup and deployment to configuration
elements. In this case, the Arquillian runner will note that the JBoss AS7 container
adaptor is available on the classpath because it was defined in the POM when we ran
the setup command for the Arquillian Forge plug-in.

The next point of interest is the class-level annotation:

```
@RunWith(Arquillian.class)
```

@RunWith is a standard JUnit construct that directs control to a specified test runner.
This is Arquillian's entry point; from here Arquillian can receive lifecycle events from
JUnit and perform its own handling. The benefit to this design decision is that Arquillian
requires no special plug-ins or configuration on the part of the user. Anything that is
capable of launching a JUnit test—be it a Maven build, an Ant task, a manual command,
or an IDE—can take advantage of Arquillian without any additional handling. For instance, you can use JBDS and Eclipse to launch a full-scale integration test with Arquillian by right-clicking on the class and selecting Run As → JUnit Test.

Next up is the class declaration:

```
public class FeedbackEntryTest {...}
```

The important bit here is what's *not* required. Because of the Arquillian JUnit Test Runner, you're free to use whatever class hierarchy you'd like, and there's no need to extend
a base support class. This keeps Arquillian tests in line with the POJO programming
model originally introduced in Java EE5.

Another feature of Arquillian is its capability to provide services like injection to the
test. Here we're going to interact with persistent storage via the JPA EntityManager:

```
@PersistenceContext
private EntityManager em;
```

The EntityManager is typically used by server-side business components like EJBs or CDI beans, but because this test is going to run *inside* the container as part of a deployment, we'll be able to interact with it directly.

Because Arquillian aims to follow the standards set forth by Java EE, instead of requiring the user to do a lookup or manual creation of the EntityManager, we'll be able to receive an instance by requesting injection via use of the @PersistenceContext annotation.

The final important fixture of the Arquillian test anatomy is the @Deployment method:

```
@Deployment
  public static WebArchive createDeployment() {
      return ShrinkWrap.createFromZipFile(WebArchive.class, new File(
              "target/feedback.war"));
  }
```

Because Java EE application servers work off deployments like *Web Archives* (WARs), *Java Archives* (JARs), or *Enterprise Archives* (EARs), we need to instruct Arquillian with the artifact to be deployed. This method must be static and return any ShrinkWrap Archive type; for this first exercise we'll simply grab the output of the current project's build *feedback.war*, but as we'll soon see in later examples, we don't need to rely on flat files at all! This will free us to skip the build entirely in between code changes and test runs, instead letting us rely on ShrinkWrap's packaging of *.class* files created from the IDE's incremental complication features.

The rest of the file is all test logic! Remember, the focus of the Arquillian programming model is to allow you to write less boilerplate and setup, and focus on the bits of code that only you as the developer can write. It's not your job to deal with bootstrapping an application server or calling upon vendor-specific deployment hooks; Arquillian will handle all of that for you behind the scenes.

Running the Application Locally

Time to see our generated application in action. First we should run the build to package our flat-file deployable *feedback.war* for manual deployment into JBoss AS7. We can trigger Maven from the Forge Console:

```
$> build --notest --profile arq-jboss_as_remote_7.x;
```

After a series of informative build output messages from Maven, we should see BUILD SUCCESS, indicating that the WAR has been properly built from sources.

The missing bit is that we need a server into which we can deploy our web app! JBoss AS7 has a simple installation process (simply download and unzip onto the filesystem), but again Forge can help automate this for us, so we don't need to locate the JBossAS binaries. For this we'll turn to the Forge JBoss AS7 plug-in, which is installed similarly to the Arquillian plug-in we put in place in the previous section:

```
$> forge install-plugin jboss-as-7
```

Once installation is complete, we can use the newly acquired as7 command to set up our server:

```
$> as7 setup
```

You'll be prompted for your $JAVA_HOME location and JBoss AS7 version; be sure to align the versions with the Arquillian Container Adaptor Version we chose before. Again, in this example we recommend 7.1.1.Final. Forge will additionally ask for the location to a JBoss AS7 installation on the filesystem, but simply hitting Enter will download the server for us into the target directory of our project.

Now it's time to fire up the server. We'll first cd into the root of our project in the Forge shell, then execute the following command:

```
$> as7 start --jboss-home target/jboss-as-dist/jboss-as-7.1.1.Final/
```

If you've opted for a different version of JBoss AS7, you may have to make substitutions to point to JBOSS_HOME correctly. Assuming all goes as planned, you should see the JBoss AS7 startup sequence in the Forge shell, followed by:

```
***INFO*** JBoss AS 7.1.1.Final has successfully started.
```

With the server up, let's deploy our application:

```
$> as7 deploy
```

Again, after a series of JBoss AS7 deployment messages, you should see:

```
The deployment operation (FORCE_DEPLOY) was successful.
```

We're up and running! Point your browser of choice to the root of the application at http://localhost:8080/feedback, and you should see the home screen of the UI that Forge has generated for us, as shown in Figure 3-5.

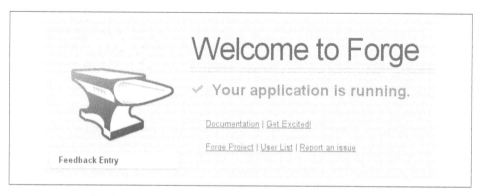

Figure 3-5. Feedback application home page

Clicking the Feedback Entry button in Figure 3-5 will grant us access to the CRUD editor for this entity. From here we can create a new row in the database table, as shown in Figure 3-6.

Figure 3-6. New feedback entry

Although CRUD applications are little more than a UI frontend to an entity, the benefit here is in having a fully functioning application to use as a base from which to start. For newcomers to Java EE, this is especially useful as a learning tool.

With our new entry now persisted into the database, let's undeploy the application in preparation to perform our first integration test run with Arquillian:

```
$> as7 undeploy
...
The deployment operation (UNDEPLOY_IGNORE_MISSING) was successful.
```

Running the Arquillian Integration Test

At this point, we still have a running JBoss AS7 server and have undeployed the feed back application. Because we'd chosen the JBOSS_AS_REMOTE_7.X option as part of the Forge Arquillian plug-in setup command, our POM is equipped with a profile that enables a dependency on the JBoss AS7 Arquillian container:

```
<profile>
  <id>arq-jboss_as_remote_7.x</id>
  <dependencies>
    <dependency>
      <groupId>org.jboss.as</groupId>
      <artifactId>jboss-as-arquillian-container-remote</artifactId>
      <version>7.1.1.Final</version>
    </dependency>
  </dependencies>
</profile>
```

Let's inform JBDS that we should consider the metadata in this profile; this will impact our compilation and JUnit runtime classpaths. Right-clicking the *pom.xml* file and using the Maven context menu will give us the option to select a Maven profile, as shown in Figure 3-7.

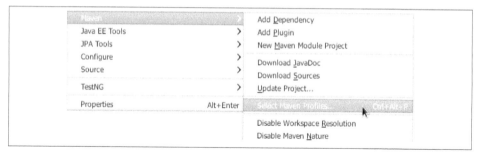

Figure 3-7. Selecting a Maven profile

Now the Arquillian test launcher will know to pick up the proper adaptor to a remote JVM instance of JBoss AS7 when running tests; it will connect to the currently running instance, deploy the defined @Deployment, execute the tests, and undeploy to clean up. If we'd like to allow Arquillian to automatically control the server start/stop lifecycle alongside each test suite, we could alternatively use the JBOSS_AS_MANAGED_7.X setup option, which defines org.jboss.as:jboss-as-arquillian-container-managed as a dependency in a POM profile.

With JBDS now configured with the proper classpath for test execution, all that's left to do is launch the test. A simple right-click on the test class in the Project Explorer yields the option Run As → JUnit Test. The IDE's JUnit launcher will create a new process, fire up JUnit, and yield control to Arquillian. We'll receive results just as we'd expect from any other JUnit test; The standard JUnit Test Report for Eclipse is shown in Figure 3-8.

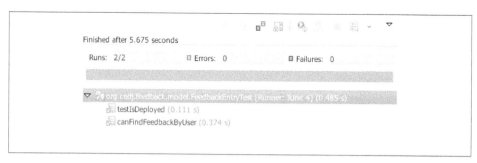

Figure 3-8. Passing the tests

With assurance that our application has some minimal level of tested functionality, let's take a risk and move this off the isolation of our local machine and into the public realm, accessible to the world.

Deploying to OpenShift via JBoss Developer Studio

JBDS provides us a convenient user interface to the OpenShift cloud service, which will run our applications on the publicly available Web. Complete information is available at the OpenShift (*https://www.openshift.com/*) site; for our purposes we'll be running the Java EE web app we created earlier in a JBoss AS7 *cartridge*, OpenShift's moniker for a canned set of cloud services.

Before continuing, we are required to create an account; we can do this by clicking the Sign Up button from the home page and completing the requisite form, as shown in Figure 3-9.

Figure 3-9. OpenShift signup

Existing users can simply log in to see active applications, as shown in Figure 3-10.

Figure 3-10. OpenShift login

With that accomplished, we can use JBDS to connect our current feedback project to a new application on OpenShift and bring it all the way to deployment. The actions we need are available in the "OpenShift Explorer," a *view* in JBDS (see Figure 3-11).

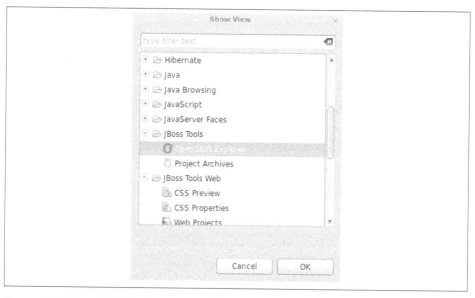

Figure 3-11. OpenShift Explorer view selection

In the Explorer, we can sign in to OpenShift from JBDS using the Connect to OpenShift button, as shown on the far right in Figure 3-12.

Figure 3-12. OpenShift Explorer

This will open the prompt shown in Figure 3-13 for us to enter our authentication information; simply provide the same credentials you used to log in to the OpenShift site.

Figure 3-13. Sign in to OpenShift

Right-clicking our account will allow us to create a "New OpenShift Application…" As shown in Figure 3-14, here we'll supply a name ("feedback" seems appropriate) and choose the target cartridge or "type" as "JBoss Application Server 7 (jbossas-7)."

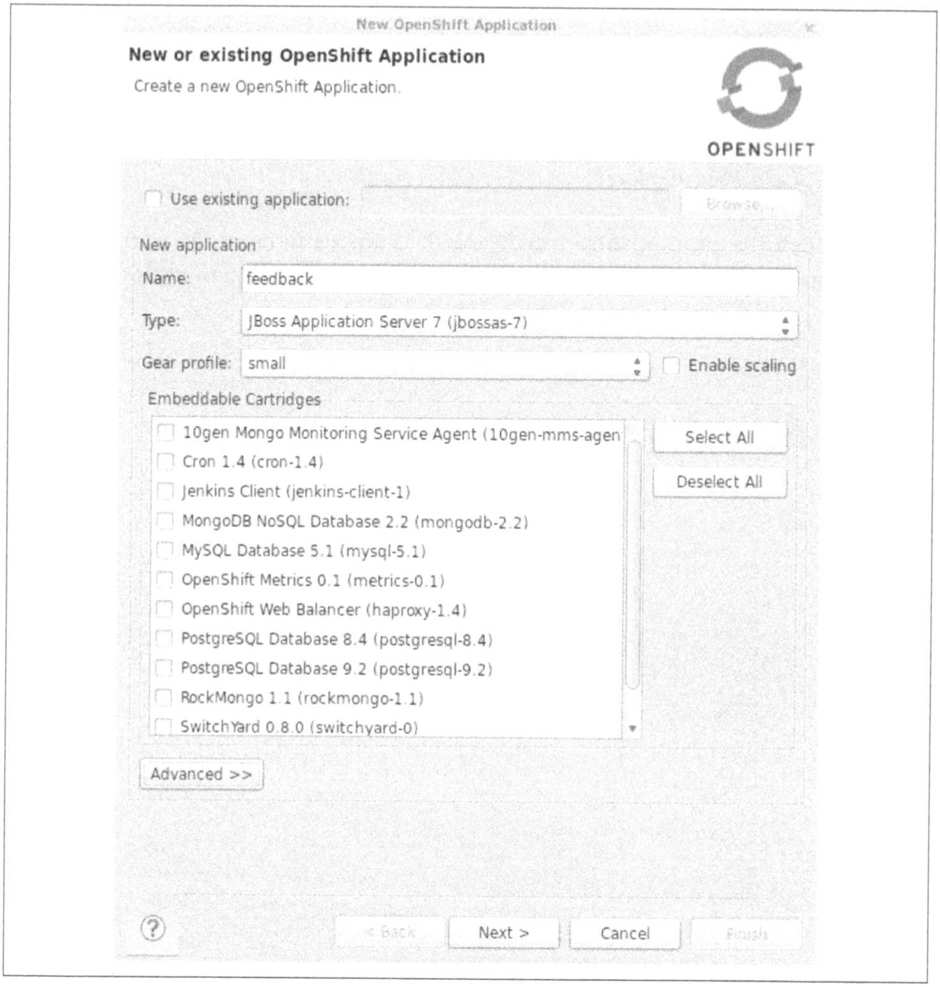

Figure 3-14. New OpenShift application

Next we'll be asked to set up a new project to back the application on OpenShift. Because we just created the project, we can choose "Use existing project" and select the *feedback* project from our JBDS workspace (see Figure 3-15).

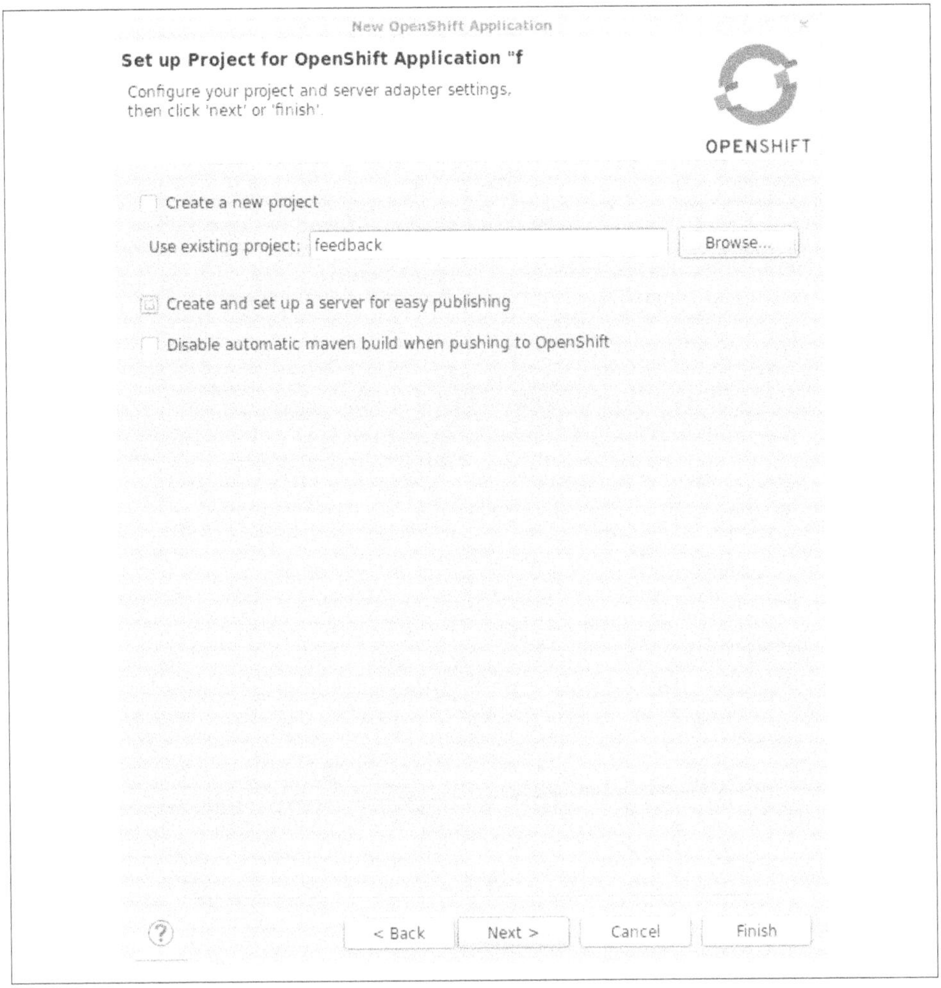

Figure 3-15. Project for OpenShift application

Because the OpenShift deployment mechanism is powered by Git, JBDS will now prompt us to accept some defaults for the Git metadata it'll write into our local project directory. You can tailor these as you see fit, though we use the defaults in this example. Figure 3-16 shows the dialog to import an existing OpenShift application.

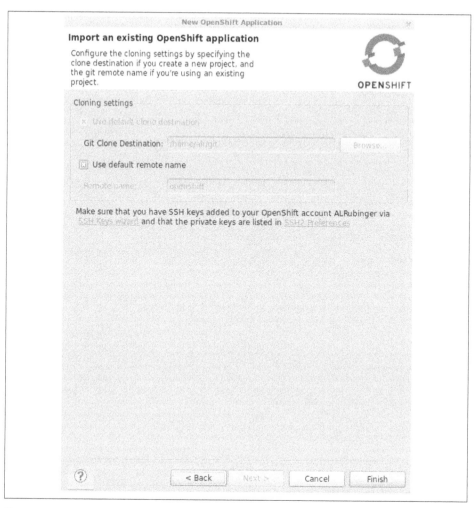

Figure 3-16. Import existing OpenShift application

Finishing this setup will trigger the deployment of our built artifacts from our project, and JBDS will report this for us (see Figure 3-17).

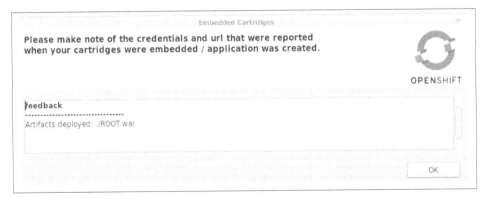

Figure 3-17. Embedded cartridges

We'll also want to confirm the Git metadata to be written into our project directory a final time. As JBDS notes, this cannot be undone (though you can manually delete the *.git* directory from your project should you choose to disconnect your local workspace from any OpenShift or Git references). Figure 3-18 displays the dialog allowing us to confirm the addition of Git metadata.

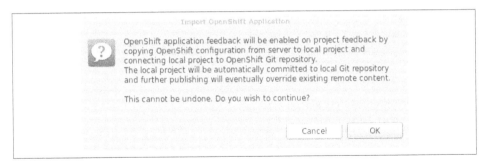

Figure 3-18. Adding Git repo information to the project

Because OpenShift is using Git under the covers, and by extension SSH authentication, there may be some system-specific confirmation needed to continue. For instance, we may need to confirm that it's OK to connect, as shown in Figure 3-19.

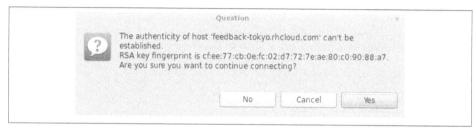

Figure 3-19. Establishing SSH keys

And if you have a passphrase enabled on your SSH key, you will be asked to provide this as well, as shown in Figure 3-20.

Figure 3-20. Unlocking SSH keys

With these steps completed, our console view should show us output similar to the following:

```
Deploying JBoss
Starting jbossas cartridge
Found 127.13.6.1:8080 listening port
Found 127.13.6.1:9999 listening port
/var/lib/openshift/52390eb55973cafc7000008a/jbossas/standalone/deployments
/var/lib/openshift/52390eb55973cafc7000008a/jbossas
CLIENT_MESSAGE: Artifact: ./ROOT.war is still deploying
/var/lib/openshift/52390eb55973cafc7000008a/jbossas
CLIENT_RESULT: Artifacts deployed: ./ROOT.war
```

Although this is not indicative of the steps we'd traditionally take to develop a more realistic application, we've found that Forge, JBoss AS7 (WildFly support forthcoming), and OpenShift make a powerful team in quickly prototyping or learning the components involved in bringing a blank slate to a fully deployed, live, Java EE application.

CHAPTER 4

Requirements and the Example Application

> *Whatever pursuit you undertake, the requirements should start*
> *with a love of what it is that you are pursuing.*
>
> — Bill Toomey

Although the previous chapter provides decent proof that it's possible to jumpstart development on a greenfield Java EE project without too much hassle, we all recognize that this may be a far cry from how applications are built in the real world. The benefits of quickly going from a blank canvas to a deployed, functioning application are largely educational or handy in rapid prototyping, but in the majority of cases we're likely looking to:

- Have greater control over the architectural design of our program
- Augment an existing application with new features
- Integrate one or more systems
- Increase modularity during development

In short, the preceding chapter introduced us to some potentially new technologies and is capable of getting us up and running, but the end result is a toy that would need a lot more work before it became a viable product.

This book will aim to address some of the common issues encountered during enterprise development. Our primary goal is education, and that will inform some of the design choices we make in building our application; for instance, we may expose more technologies than necessary to fulfill our objectives. But just as a guide on design patterns doesn't advocate usage of every technique at the same time, neither should these examples. It's your responsibility as developer to choose appropriate tools for the job, and we'll aspire to help you make informed decisions.

Introducing GeekSeek

Our example application will be a software conference tracker, roughly modeled after the excellent Lanyrd (*http://lanyrd.com/*) service. Its purpose will be to expose information to aid conference-goers in planning their experience around technical sessions and related activities. The goal is to provide a single example with all layers working in concert to showcase how various technologies interact, and each use case detailed in the book will dig into various slices of the application. We've lovingly named this example *GeekSeek*.

Reading this book should not be a passive endeavor; we've designed the example application to be an executable proof of the approaches we'll use to satisfy our broad use cases. Readers will likely get the greatest benefit by pulling down the GeekSeek source and building, testing, and running the application locally.

The live "production" GeekSeek site is hosted at *http://geekseek.continuousdev.org*; let's first have a look at the requirements comprising this application.

Featureset

We'll start by outlining in broad strokes the features provided by GeekSeek. This will provide a high-level view of the actions users may take, and from these we can start to drill down into more technical requirements.

Account-centric actions

- Users may sign up by associating the site with their Twitter account
- Users may track others whom they follow on Twitter
- Users may see others who may be interested in their activity (their Twitter followers)
- Users may get updates on the activity of their followee's followees (transitively, the people followed by the people you follow)

Directory view

- Users may display upcoming and prior Conferences in the system

Conferences and sessions

- Users may add Conference and Session data, additionally associating them with a Venue and Room
- Users may define who is speaking at or attending a Session
- Users may add arbitrary Attachments (media) information to a Conference, Session, Venue, or Room

- Users may track Conferences and Sessions to receive alerts for updates and changes

Search
- Users may search for a Conference, Session, or User by some criteria

Conceptual Data Model

Because we're still in the process of defining what our application does and the types of data it'll be dealing with, this is not the place to delve into database design just yet. This is the stage where we describe our *conceptual data model*; first we need to understand:

- What kind of data is to be represented?
- Who are the major players (entities), and what are their fields?

Here we speak at a very coarse level of granularity, and we seek to define from a business perspective the *nouns* of our application. In our case, we have:

User

Name	String
Twitter ID	String, unique among all users
Bio	String

Conference

Name	String
Tagline	String
Start	Date/Time
End	Date/Time

Session

Title	String
Outline	String
Start	Date/Time
End	Date/Time

Attachment

Content	Binary
Type	Media Type (i.e., JPEG, PDF, etc.)

Venue

Name   String

Location Place

Room

Name   String

Location Place

Once we've got a solid understanding of the kinds of data we'll be addressing, we can go a bit further and see how these nouns might play out in the context of our proposed featureset.

Logical Data Model

We've taken the first step in describing our data types by acknowledging the information we'll need to capture. Now we need to take into account some additional concerns:

- What are the relationships inherent between entities?
- How much data are we expecting in each entity?
- What features will be demanded of our entities?

It's questions like these that will help us to arrive at a *logical data model*, a representation of our data that isn't yet tied to any specific storage mechanism but still addresses the preceding questions. Decisions at this step are instrumental in our later choices, which will have heavy impact in areas like efficiency and performance.

This is because database systems have varying strengths when we couple data representation with the requests we may make. Actions like searching and sorting can take milliseconds or days, depending only upon the backing data structures and implementation used! Therefore, it's very important for us to define the relationships required between our data, and recognize cases where we could have potentially large result sets; it's here that we'll need to design efficiently.

Relationships

Relationships are the bonds that tie our entities together, and come in three flavors of *cardinality*:

Cardinality	Name	Example
1:1	One-to-one	I have one nose; my nose belongs to only me.
1:N	One-to-many	I have many fingers; my fingers belong to only me.
N:N	Many-to-many	I have many friends; my friends also have many other friends besides me.

So in the case of the entities for our application as defined by our desired featureset, we can draw the following relationships:

#	Entity 1	Entity 2	Cardinality	Description
1	Conference	Session	1:N	A conference may have many sessions.
2	Session	Room	N:N	A session may take place in, many rooms (spanned together).
3	Venue	Room	1:N	A venue may have many rooms; a room exists only in one venue.
4	Conference	Venue	1:N	A conference may take place in many venues.
5	Conference	Attachment	1:N	A conference may have many attachments.
6	Session	Attachment	1:N	A session may have many attachments.
7	Venue	Attachment	1:N	A venue may have many attachments.
8	Room	Attachment	1:N	A room may have many attachments.
9	User	User	N:N	A user may follow many other users on Twitter, and may also have many followers.

In graphical terms, this may look a little like Figure 4-1.

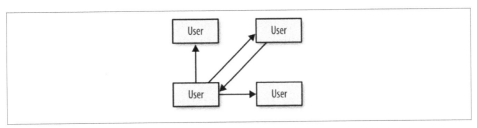

Figure 4-1. Cardinality in a relational database management system (RBDMS)

Intended use

When considering the efficiency of operations like database lookups, we should attempt to strike a balance between premature optimization and planning for performance. For instance, it really wouldn't matter how complex the relationships between these entities are if we were only expecting a small, finite number of records; these would likely be cached at some level and held in memory, avoiding the need for lengthy tasks like full table scans. At the other end of the spectrum, it'd be an oversight to recognize that we're expecting lots of data in a *normalized* form, and anticipate that querying against this model has time complexity that's linear ($O(n)$), geometric ($O(n^2)$), or worse.

Unfortunately, a quick peek at our data types and featureset shows that given enough time and interest in the application, we could reasonably expect entries for each of our main data types to grow, unbounded.

Of particular note is the many-to-many relationship among users. Because a user may have both many followers and may follow many people, we have two unidirectional relationships; a follower of mine is not necessarily someone I follow. This is in contrast to a mutual "friend" model employed by, say, the Facebook (*http://www.face book.com*) social networking site. In effect, this relationship has a graph structure.

Although we might store and model this structure in any number of ways, it's worth noting that requesting transient relationships can be a problem with geometric time complexity. That is, we'd need one query to find all of a user's followers. Then, *for each* of the results in that set, we'd need another query to find *their* followers. With each level we drill in to find followers, the problem becomes more prohibitively complex and unsolvable when organized in standard tables and rows.

Because the relationship is naturally a graph, it will likely make sense to store our relationship data in this fashion. That way, instead of querying standard records, we can walk the graph (simply obtaining a value from a pointer is an operation with constant time complexity, and thus will perform many factors better when we compound the process in a loop).

Another interesting area revolves around the system's attachments. An attachment can be associated with a conference, session, venue, or room, and ultimately consists of some arbitrary series of bytes. This amounts to a natural "key/value" store, where we can add a bunch of content, associate some metadata with it, and draw a relationship to its "owner." Again, we might tackle this in a standard table representation, but perhaps the problem domain suggests a native solution more in tune with the key/value model.

Now that we've developed a better understanding of our data, what requests we'll make of it, and how much we might have, we can move on to designing some user-based and technical use cases to drive the construction of our application.

Obtaining, Building, Testing, and Running GeekSeek

We mentioned earlier that we'd be using the distributed version control system Git to store the source for this book and its examples, and our *authoritative repository* is kindly hosted at GitHub (*http://bit.ly/1e7o0ox*). Unlike centralized version control systems, Git stores the full repository history in each clone; when you "fork" or "copy" our repo, you'll get the entire history with every commit made since the book's inception. The *authoritative repository* refers to the one we elect to act as the *upstream*; changes that are approved to make it into new releases go here.

Obtaining the source

The first step toward obtaining the source is to sign up for a GitHub account. Though it's absolutely possible to clone the authoritative repo locally, without an account either here or at some other writable host you won't have an avenue to push changes of your own or contribute ideas. Because signing up for an account is free for our uses and has become commonplace especially in open source development, it's the avenue we'll advise.

As shown in Figure 4-2, signup is fairly simple, and the process starts at *https://github.com*.

Figure 4-2. GitHub signup

Once logged in, you'll *fork* the authoritative repo into your own publicly viewable repository. You do this by visiting the book's repo and clicking the Fork button, as shown in Figure 4-3.

Figure 4-3. Forking a GitHub repository

With the fork in your account, now you'll be able to *clone* this repository locally. And because you have your own fork on GitHub, you'll be able to *push* the *commits* you make locally to your own fork, where you have write access. This provides two important benefits. First, it serves as a backup in case of disk failure, loss of machine, or a synchronization point if you develop on many machines. Second, it allows others to see the changes you've made and optionally bring them in for their own use.

Before bringing in your fork of the repository locally, you'll need to have a Git client installed. This is a command-line tool available on many platforms, but there are also GUI wrappers included in many IDEs, like Eclipse or IntelliJ IDEA. We'll offer instructions based on the command line.

Installation is platform-specific, but in flavors of Linux, this is easily enough achieved via your package manager of choice:

```
$> sudo apt-get install -y git
```

`apt-get` is the default for Debian-based distributions including Ubuntu and Linux Mint; for others (including RHEL and Fedora), `yum` may be more appropriate:

```
$> sudo yum install -y git
```

You can obtain the Git Client for Windows as an executable installer at *http://git-scm.com/download/win*. Similarly, the client for Mac is available at *http://git-scm.com/download/mac*.

You can verify your installation at the command prompt by executing:

```
$> git --version
git version 1.8.1.2
```

With your Git client installed locally, now you're free to pull down the book's repository from your public fork on GitHub to your local machine. You do this by first finding the URI to your repository on your GitHub repo's home page, as shown in Figure 4-4.

Figure 4-4. GitHub URI to clone

Then simply move to a directory in which you'd like to place your local clone, and issue the `git clone` command, passing in the URI to your GitHub repository. For instance:

```
$> git clone git@github.com:ALRubinger/continuous-enterprise-development.git
Cloning into 'continuous-enterprise-development'...
remote: Counting objects: 2661, done.
remote: Compressing objects: 100% (1170/1170), done.
remote: Total 2661 (delta 534), reused 2574 (delta 459)
Receiving objects: 100% (2661/2661), 1.19 MiB | 1.24 MiB/s, done.
Resolving deltas: 100% (534/534), done.
```

This will create a new directory called *continuous-enterprise-development*, under which you'll be able to see the book's source in the root and all supporting code under the *code* directory. The *GeekSeek* application root is housed under *code/application*:

```
$> ls -l
total 492
-rw-r--r-- 1 alr alr   468 Jul  6 17:18 book.asciidoc
-rw-r--r-- 1 alr alr  3227 Jun 26 03:20 Chapter00-Prelude.asciidoc
-rw-r--r-- 1 alr alr 23634 Jun 28 18:03 Chapter01-Continuity.asciidoc
-rw-r--r-- 1 alr alr 40527 Jun 28 18:03 Chapter02-EnablingTechnologies.asciidoc
-rw-r--r-- 1 alr alr 29803 Jun 28 18:03 Chapter03-ScratchToProduction.asciidoc
-rw-r--r-- 1 alr alr 20772 Jul  7 17:29
 Chapter04-RequirementsAndExampleApplication.asciidoc
-rw-r--r-- 1 alr alr 32765 Jun 28 18:03
```

```
Chapter05-JavaPersistenceAndRelationalData.asciidoc
   ...etc
drwxr-xr-x 8 alr alr  4096 Jul  6 20:24 code
drwxr-xr-x 6 alr alr  4096 Jun 26 03:20 images
-rw-r--r-- 1 alr alr  2733 Jul  7 16:19 README.asciidoc
```

This will pull the current upstream version of the application into your local disk. If, for instance, you'd like to work against one of the authoritative repository's tags, you can:

- Create a `remote` reference to the authoritative repo: `git remote add upstream` `https://github.com/arquillian/continuous-enterprise-development.git`
- `fetch` all the tags from the remote repo: `git fetch -t upstream`
- checkout the tag as a local branch: `git checkout -b remotes/upstream/1.0.0` (checks out tag `1.0.0`)
- Work on your new branch, based off the tag you've specified: `git branch`

Building and testing GeekSeek

We'll be using the Maven software management tool to handle our build, test, and packaging needs. The Java 7 JDK is a prerequisite we'll assume is installed on your system, referenced by the environment variable `JAVA_HOME`, and the executables in *$JAVA_HOME/bin* available on the system PATH; you can simply download and extract Maven on your drive to *MAVEN_HOME* from *http://maven.apache.org/download.cgi*. Ensure that *MAVEN_HOME/bin* is on your PATH, and you'll be good to go:

```
$> mvn -version
Apache Maven 3.0.5 (r01de14724cdef164cd33c7c8c2fe155faf9602da;
2013-02-19 08:51:28-0500)
Maven home: /home/alr/opt/apache/maven/apache-maven-3.0.5
Java version: 1.7.0_25, vendor: Oracle Corporation
Java home: /home/alr/opt/oracle/java/jdk1.7.0_25/jre
Default locale: en_US, platform encoding: UTF-8
OS name: "linux", version: "3.8.0-19-generic", arch: "amd64", family: "unix"
```

You build and test GeekSeek by invoking the `package` phase of Maven on the *pom.xml* file located in *code/application*:

```
application $> mvn package
   ...lots of output
[INFO] BUILD SUCCESS
```

The first run is likely to take some time because Maven will resolve all dependencies of the project (including the application servers in which it will run), and download them onto your local disk. Subsequent runs will not require this initial "downloading the Internet" step and will execute much faster.

The test phase will instruct Maven to fire up the application servers and run all tests to ensure that everything is working as expected. If you'd like to save some time and simply fetch the dependencies, build the sources, and package the application, execute mvn package -DskipTests=true. Here's a full list of the Maven lifecycles (*http://bit.ly/1e7xH6o*).

Packaging the full application will result in a WAR (Web Archive) file located at *application/target/geekseek-(version).war*. It's this file that can be deployed into an application server to run GeekSeek locally; by default, we'll be using *WildFly* from the JBoss Community.

Running GeekSeek

Although we've configured the build to obtain and use WildFly for use in testing Geek-Seek automatically, you may prefer to have an installation on your local disk to use manually. This is useful for testing with remote containers (as covered in Chapter 11) as well as poking around the running application locally.

WildFly is available for free download (*http://www.wildfly.org/downloads*), and should be extracted to a location we'll call *JBOSS_HOME*. By executing *JBOSS_HOME/bin/standalone.sh*, the server will start:

```
wildfly-8.0.0.Alpha2 $> JBOSS_HOME=`pwd`
wildfly-8.0.0.Alpha2 $> cd bin/
bin $> ./standalone.sh
=============================================================================

  JBoss Bootstrap Environment

  JBOSS_HOME: /home/alr/business/oreilly/git/continuous-enterprise-development/
  code/application/target/wildfly-8.0.0.Alpha2

  JAVA: /home/alr/opt/oracle/java/jdk7/bin/java

  JAVA_OPTS:  -server -XX:+UseCompressedOops -Xms64m -Xmx512m -XX:MaxPermSize=
  256m -Djava.net.preferIPv4Stack=true -Djboss.modules.system.pkgs=org.jboss.
  byteman -Djava.awt.headless=true

=============================================================================

18:08:42,477 INFO  [org.jboss.modules] (main) JBoss Modules version 1.2.2.Final
18:08:43,290 INFO  [org.jboss.msc] (main) JBoss MSC version 1.2.0.Beta1
  ...trimm output
JBAS015874: WildFly 8.0.0.Alpha2 "WildFly" started in 8624ms - Started 153 of 189
services (56 services are lazy, passive or on-demand)
```

Copying the *application/target/geekseek-(version).war* file into *JBOSS_HOME/standalone/deployments* will trigger deployment of the GeekSeek application:

```
$> cp code/application/application/target/geekseek-1.0.0-alpha-1-SNAPSHOT.war
code/application/target/wildfly-8.0.0.Alpha2/standalone/deployments/
geekseek.war -v
'code/application/application/target/geekseek-1.0.0-alpha-1-SNAPSHOT.war' ->
```

```
'code/application/target/wildfly-8.0.0.Alpha2/standalone/deployments/
geekseek.war'
```

This will trigger something similar to the following on the server console:

```
18:11:46,839 INFO  [org.jboss.as.server] (DeploymentScanner-threads - 2)
JBAS018559: Deployed "geekseek.war" (runtime-name : "geekseek.war")
```

Once deployed, you'll be able to launch your web browser of choice, point it to `http://localhost:8080/geekseek`, and explore the screens powering the featureset we've covered here.

Use Cases and Chapter Guide

Each chapter from here on out will address a set of related technical and user-centric use cases. They'll be organized as follows:

Chapter 5: Java Persistence and Relational Data

Our featureset demands a variety of operations that depend upon persistent data; information that must be saved longer than a user's session or even the application's startup/shutdown lifecycle. It's likely we won't be able to hold all of our data in memory either, so we'll need to tackle issues like serialization and concurrent, multiuser access.

As our logical data analysis has exposed, we have plenty of data types that might work well arranged in a table/row/column structure as provided by the *relational* model, and that's exactly what we'll cover in Chapter 5.

We'll also give a brief overview of mapping from a relational database to an object model that's more familiar and friendly using the *Java Persistence API* and transactional support via *Enterprise JavaBeans*, and we'll be sure to test that our domain layer is properly tested against known data sets using the handy *Arquillian Persistence Extension*.

Chapter 6: NoSQL: Data Grids and Graph Databases

Although it enjoys popularity as the most widely deployed database management system flavor, the relational model is not the only representation we have at our disposal. In recent years a paradigm shift has been prevalent in the persistence space.

NoSQL is a blanket term that has varied definitions, but generally refers to any number of database systems that do not employ the relational model. Popular implementations include a document store (i.e., MongoDB (*http://www.mongodb.org/*)), a key/value store (i.e., Infinispan (*http://www.jboss.org/infinispan/*)), or a graph database (i.e., Neo4j (*http://www.neo4j.org/*)).

We noted earlier that our user relationship model is a natural graph and that our attachments might be well-served from a key/value store, so Chapter 6 will take a look at implementing persistent storage through these mechanisms.

Chapter 7: Business Logic and the Services Layer

With our persistence layers covered, we need to expose some way of allowing users to interact with the data and carry out the business logic demanded by our requirements. Java EE recommends encapsulating business logic in components such as *Enterprise JavaBeans* (EJBs) or *Contexts and Dependency Injection* (CDI) beans; we'll be using primarily EJBs.

EJBs and CDI beans are very handy for either direct calling or using a *remote procedure call* (RPC) style, but they don't do much to inform us as users about the possible state transitions and available operations as we navigate the application.

Our use case will explore the testable development of an SMTP service and interacting with an external, asynchronous, nontransactional resource.

Chapter 8: REST and Addressable Services

REST (*Representational State Transfer*) is an architecture of patterns that reveal services as resources in a fashion consistent with the guiding concepts behind the Web itself. Chapter 8 will introduce the exposition of enterprise services using REST guidelines, and will be implemented with Java EE's JAX-RS framework. Additionally, we'll test our endpoints using *Arquillian Warp* and the REST-assured project (*http://code.google.com/ p/rest-assured/*).

Chapter 9: Security

Our featureset requirements clearly couple user registration with an existing Twitter account, so we'll need plenty of implementation and testing to ensure that the integrity of our users is not compromised.

Chapter 9 will involve OAuth authentication using security and identity management from the PicketLink project (*http://www.picketlink.org*). We'll again look to REST-assured to help us with our client testing strategy.

Chapter 10: UI

The user interface represents the visible elements with which end users will interact to submit form data and view our domain objects in a unified aggregate view. We test the UI through *Arquillian Drone, Arquillian Warp*, and hooks into the Selenium project (*http://www.seleniumhq.org/*).

In this fashion we automate and emulate real user input by writing tests to push data into the browser and reading the response after it's been rendered.

Chapter 11: Assembly and Deployment

Once we've abided by proper modular design principles, it's time to bring everything together and do some full-scale integration testing upon the final deployable archive. Chapter 11 will combine our application and set up some test configurations to flex all layers of GeekSeek working in tandem.

With our bird's-eye view of the GeekSeek example application complete, it's time to dig into some code.

CHAPTER 5

Java Persistence and Relational Data

Energy and persistence conquer all things.
— Benjamin Franklin

If we really boil down the primary objective of most applications to bare metal, we'll find that nearly everything we do involves an interaction with *data*. We supply it when we make a new online order. We pull it out when we research on a wiki. We update it when we change our credit card's billing address.

The information contained in a system at any point in time comprises the *state* of the application, and state comes in a variety of *scopes*, including:

Request
    Limited access within one request/response cycle

Session
    Limited access within one user session

Conversation/Sequence/Transaction
    Limited access to a sequence of events (treated as one unit) within one user session

Application
    Shared throughout the application

Environment
    Shared throughout the host environment

Depending upon your view or framework of choice, there may be other ways to slice visibility, but this list outlines some of the most commonly used paradigms.

As is thematic throughout the study of computer science, the rule of thumb is to limit ourselves to the smallest scope required. Fine-grained access to data helps to ensure that we don't leak out state where it can cause security issues or difficult-to-debug behaviors.

Can you imagine what it'd be like if one user's access to his online bank account were to be replicated to all active sessions?

In addition to the notion of scopes, which limit data's visibility, we also have the concept of *persistence*. Persistence is a property that dictates whether or not state will survive outside of its confining scope. For instance, we may allow a user to log in and change her online profile, but if we don't synchronize these updates with some sort of persistent storage, they'll be lost as soon as her user session (which defines the scope of this data) is closed.

Perhaps the simplest way to handle persistent storage is to directly serialize information to the filesystem. At first glance, this looks like a nice approach; we open up a file, write whatever we want in there, and close it up. Later we go in and read as needed. Easy!

…until we start to think through how this is going to play out in practice. Our applications are multiuser; they support any number of operations going on in parallel. How are we to ensure that we don't have two writes happening on the same file at once? We could put a read/write lock in place to ensure that only one write happens at a time, but then we could potentially queue up lots of write requests while work is being done. And what about auditing our changes, or ensuring that the integrity of our data model is preserved in case of an error? Very quickly we'll discover that the task of persisting our data is a first-class problem in and of itself, and one that probably doesn't belong on our desks as application developers.

It'd be much better to delegate the task of persistent storage to another component equipped to handle this efficiently and securely. Luckily, we'll have our pick of any number of database management systems (DBMSs) that do just that. Figure 5-1 illustrates apps using centralized persistent storage.

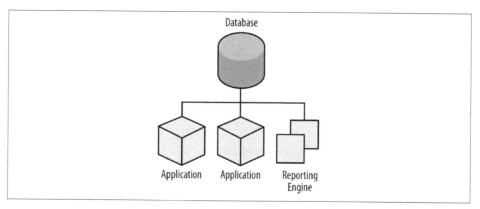

Figure 5-1. A series of applications backed by an RDMBS

The role of a DBMS is very generally to store and provide access to data. They come in a variety of flavors, which are differentiated in terms of how they internally organize information:

Relational (RDBMS)
Like data is grouped into tables where columns represent data types and rows represent records. Most often employs a protocol language called *Structured Query Language* (SQL) for interaction. Examples: MySQL (*http://www.mysql.com/*), PostgreSQL (*http://www.postgresql.org/*).

Graph
Stores objects with relationships in a graph structure; ideal for traversing nodes. Example: Neo4j (*http://www.neo4j.org/*).

Key/value
Nested Map or document-oriented structure, has become very popular in recent years. Examples: Infinispan (*http://www.jboss.org/infinispan/*), MongoDB (*http://www.mongodb.org/*).

Column-oriented
Stores data in columns, as opposed to an RDBMS, where the records are kept in rows. Best suited for very large tables. Examples: Apache HBase (*http://hbase.apache.org/*), Apache Cassandra (*http://cassandra.apache.org/*).

This chapter will focus on today's most commonly used relational model (NoSQL will be covered next, in Chapter 6).

The Relational Database Model

To best understand the relational model, let's highlight how it differs from the object model with which we're already familiar. For this example we'll seek to describe a family.

Each member of the family can be represented by a `Person` object:

```
public class Person {

    // Instance members
    private Long id;
    private String name;
    private Boolean male;
    private Person father;
    private Person mother;
    private List<Person> children;

    // Accessors / Mutators
    public Long getId() {
        return id;
    }
    public void setId(final Long id) {
```

```
            this.id = id;
        }
        /* Other properties omitted for brevity... */
    }
```

Simple enough: this value object that explicitly declares the relationship between a parent and child is sufficient for us to further infer siblings, grandparents, cousins, aunts, uncles, and so on. If we populate a few of these objects and wire them together, we'll end up with a *graph* representing our family, as shown in Figure 5-2.

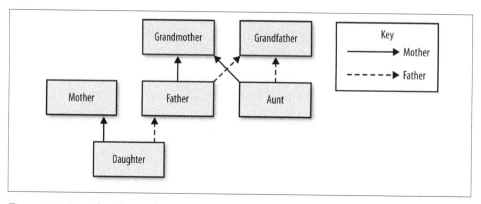

Figure 5-2. Family relationships represented as a graph

Now, let's take a look at how that same information might be represented in a relational database in Table 5-1. Much like a spreadsheet, classes from our object model are instead organized into tables.

Table 5-1. Data types representing a "person"

Data type	Field name
UNSIGNED INTEGER (*PK*)	id
VARCHAR(255)	name
BIT(1)	male
UNSIGNED INTEGER	father
UNSIGNED INTEGER	mother

Already we see some differences here. The id, name, and male fields are as we might expect; simple data types where a Java Long is now represented as a database UNSIGNED INTEGER, a Java String maps to a VARCHAR(255) (variable-length character String with maximum length of 255), and a Java Boolean becomes a BIT type. But instead of a direct reference to the mother or father, instead we see that the data type there is UNSIGNED INTEGER. Why?

This is the defining characteristic of *relationality* in RDBMS. These fields are in fact pointers to the *primary key*, or the identifying id field of another record. As such, they are called *foreign keys*. So our data may look something like Table 5-2.

Table 5-2. Relationships among family members

id	name	male	father	mother
1	Paternal Grandpa	1		
2	Paternal Grandma	0		
3	Dad	1	1	2
4	Mom	0		
5	Brother	1	3	4
6	Sister	0	3	4

Note especially that there is no direct data reference to the children of a person in the relational model. That's because this is the "many" side of a "one-to-many" relationship: one person may have many children, and many children may have one father and one mother. Therefore, to find the children of a given person, we'd ask the database something like:

"Please give me all the records where the mother field is my ID if I'm not a male, and where the father field is my ID if I am a male."

Of course, the English language might be a bit more confusing than we'd like, so luckily we'd execute a query in SQL to handle this for us.

The Java Persistence API

It's nice that a DBMS takes care of the details of persistence for us, but introducing this separate data layer presents a few issues:

- Though SQL is an ANSI standard, its use is not truly portable between RDBMS vendors. In truth, each database product has its own dialect and extensions.
- The details of interacting with a database are vendor-dependent, though there are connection-only abstractions (drivers) in Java (for instance, Java Database Connectivity, or JDBC).
- The relational model used by the database doesn't map on its own to the object model we use in Java; this is called the *object/relational impedance mismatch*.

To address each of these problems, Java EE6 provides a specification called the *Java Persistence API* (JPA), defined by JSR 317 (*http://bit.ly/1e84urW*). JPA is composed of both an API (*http://bit.ly/1e84sjL*) for defining and interacting with entity objects, and an SQL-like query language called *Java Persistence Query Language* (JPQL) for portable interaction with a variety of database implementations. Because JPA is itself a spec, a variety of open source–compliant implementations are available, including Hibernate (*http://hibernate.org/*), EclipseLink (*http://www.eclipse.org/eclipselink/*), and OpenJPA (*http://openjpa.apache.org/*).

So now our tiered data architecture may look something like Figure 5-3.

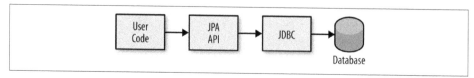

Figure 5-3. Persistence layers of abstraction from user code to the database

 Though a full overview of this technology stack is beyond the scope of this book, we'll be sure to point you to enough resources and explain the basics of interacting with data via JPA that you'll be able to understand our application and test examples. For readers interested in gaining better insight into JPA (and its parent, EJB), we recommend *Enterprise Java Beans 3.1, 6th Edition* by Andrew Lee Rubinger and Bill Burke (O'Reilly, 2010).

POJO Entities

Again, as Java developers we're used to interacting with objects and the classes that define them. Therefore, JPA allows us to design our object model as we wish, and by sprinkling on some additional metadata (typically in the form of annotations, though XML may also be applied), we can tell our JPA provider enough for it to take care of the *object/relational mapping* for us. For instance, applying the `javax.persistence.Enti ty` annotation atop a value object like our `Person` class is enough to denote a JPA entity. The data type mapping is largely inferred from our source Java types (though this can be overridden), and we define relationship fields using the `@javax.persistence.One ToOne`, `@javax.persistence.OneToMany`, and `@javax.persistence.ManyToMany` annotations. We'll see examples of this later in our application.

The important thing to keep in mind is the concept of *managed entities*. Because JPA exposes a POJO programming model, consider the actions that this code might do upon an entity class `Person`:

```
Person person = new Person();
person.setName("Dick Hoyt");
```

OK, so very clearly we've created a new `Person` instance and set his name. The beauty of the POJO programming model is also its drawback; this is just a regular object. Without some additional magic, there's no link to the persistence layer. This coupling is done transparently for us, and the machine providing the voodoo is the JPA `Entity Manager`.

`javax.persistence.EntityManager` (*http://bit.ly/MAXk9G*) is our hook to a defined *persistence unit*, our abstraction above the database. By associating POJO entities with the `EntityManager`, they become monitored for changes such that any state differences that take place in the object will be reflected in persistent storage. An object under such supervision is called *managed*. Perhaps this is best illustrated by some examples:

```
Person person = entityManager.find(Person.class, 1L); // Look up "Person" with
                                                       // Primary Key of 1
System.out.println("Got " + person); // This "person" instance is managed
person.setName("New Name"); // By changing the name of the person,
                            // the database will be updated when
                            // the EntityManager is flushed (likely when the
                            // current transaction commits)
```

Here we perform a lookup of the entity by its primary key, modify its properties just as we would any other object, then let the `EntityManager` worry about synchronizing the state changes with the underlying database. Alternatively, we could manually attach and detach the POJO from being *managed*:

```
Person person = new Person();
person.setId(1L); // Just a POJO
managedPerson = entityManager.merge(person); // Sync the state with the existing
                                             // persistence context
managedPerson.setName("New Name"); // Make a change which be eventually become
                                   // propagated to the DB
entityManager.detach(managedPerson); // Make "managedPerson" unmanaged
managedPerson.setName("Just a POJO");  // This state change will *not* be
                                       // propagated to the DB, as we're now
                                       // unmanaged
```

Use Cases and Requirements

This is the first chapter in which we'll be dealing with the companion GeekSeek example application for the book; its purpose is to highlight all layers working in concert to fulfill the *user requirements* dictated by each chapter. From here out, we'll be pointing to selections from the GeekSeek application in order to showcase how we wire together the domain, application, view, and test layers in a cohesive, usable project.

As we proceed, we'll note each file so that you can draw references between the text and the deployable example. We're firm believers that you best learn by doing (or at least exploring real code), so we invite you to dig in and run the examples as we go along.

Testing is a first-class citizen in verifying that our development is done correctly, so, for instance, in this chapter we'll be focusing on interactions with persistent data. Before we can hope to arrive at any solutions, it's important to clearly identify the problem domain. Each subsequent chapter will first outline the goals we're looking to address.

User Perspective

Our users are going to have to perform a series of *CRUD* (Create, Read, Update, Delete) operations upon the entities that drive our application's data. As such, we've defined a set of user-centric requirements:

```
As a User, I should be able to:
...add a Conference.
...add a Session.
...view a Conference.
...view a Session.
...change a Conference.
...change a Session.
...remove a Conference.
...remove a Session.
```

Quite simple (and maybe even redundant!) when put in these terms, especially for this persistence example. However, it's wise to get into the habit of thinking about features from a user perspective; this technique will come in quite handy later on when, in more complex cases, it'll be easy to get mired in the implementation specifics of providing a feature, and we don't want to lose track of the *real* goal we're aiming to deliver.

To state even more generally:

```
As a User, I should be able to Create, Read, Update,
and Delete Conference and Session types.
```

Of course, we have some other requirements that do not pertain to the user perspective.

Technical Concerns

As noted in the introduction, the issue of data persistence is not trivial. We must ensure that our solution will address:

- Concurrent access
- Multiuser access
- Fault-tolerance

These constraints upon the environment will help to inform our implementation choices. Again, explicitly stating these issues may seem obvious, but our experience teaches that sometimes we get so comfortable with an implementation choice that we may not first stop to think if it's even appropriate! For instance, a news or blogging site that has a high read-to-write ratio may not even need to worry about concurrency if the application can support stale data safely. In that case, we might not even need transactions, and bypassing that implementation choice can lead to great gains in performance.

In GeekSeek, however, we'll want to ensure that users are seeing up-to-date information that's consistent, and that implies a properly synchronized data source guarded by transactions.

Implementation

Given our user and technical concerns, the Java EE stack using JPA described earlier will do a satisfactory job toward meeting our requirements. And there's an added benefit: by using frameworks designed to relieve the application developer of complicated programming, we'll end up writing a lot less code. This will help us to reduce the *conceptual weight* of our code and ease maintenance over the long run. The slices of Java EE that we'll use specifically include:

- Java Transaction API (JTA)
- Enterprise JavaBeans (EJB, JSR 318 (*http://bit.ly/MAYJwZ*))
- JPA

Transactions are a wide subject that merits its own book when dealing with the mechanics of implementing a viable transactional engine. For us as users, however, the rules are remarkably simple. We'll imagine a transaction is a set of code that runs within a block. The instructions that are executed within this block must adhere to the *ACID* properties—Atomicity, Consistency, Isolation, and Durability:

Atomicity
> The instructions in the block act as one unit; they either succeed (*commit*) or fail (*rollback*) together.

Consistency
> All resources associated with the transaction (in this case, our database) will always be in a legal, viable state. For instance, a foreign key field will always point to a valid primary key. These rules are typically enforced by the transactional resource (again, our database).

Isolation
> Actions taken upon transactional resources within a Tx block will *not* be seen outside the scope of the current transaction until and unless the transaction has successfully committed.

Durability
> Once committed, the state of a transactional resource will not revert back or lose data.

Enterprise JavaBeans, or EJBs, enjoy close integration with JTA, so we won't have to touch much of the transactional engine directly. By managing our JPA entities through an `EntityManager` that is encapsulated inside a transactional EJB, we'll get the benefits of transaction demarcation and management for free.

Persistence is a case that's well-understood by and lives at the heart of most Java EE applications, and these standards have been built specifically with our kind of use case in mind. What's left for us is to sanely tie the pieces together, but not before we consider that the runtime is not the only thing with which we should be concerned.

Entity Objects

There are a few common fields we'll want from each of our entities and ultimately the tables they represent. All will have a primary key (ID), and a created and last modified `Date`. To avoid duplication of code, we'll create a base class from which our entities may extend; this is provided by `org.cedj.geekseek.domain.persistence.model.Base Entity`:

```
@MappedSuperclass
public abstract class BaseEntity
   implements Identifiable, Timestampable, Serializable {
```

The `@javax.persistence.MappedSuperclass` annotation signals that there will be no separate table strategy for this class; its fields will be reflected directly in the tables defined by its subclasses.

We'll also want to fulfill the contract of `org.cedj.app.domain.model.Identifiable`, which mandates we provide the following:

```
/**
 * @return The primary key, or ID, of this entity
 */
String getId();
```

Objects of type `Identifiable` simply have an ID, which is a primary key.

Similarly, we'll be `org.cedj.geekseek.domain.model.Timestampable`, which notes that we provide support for the following timestamps:

```
/**
 * @return the Date when this Entity was created
 */
Date getCreated();

/**
 * Returns the LastUpdated, or the Created Date
 * if this Entity has never been updated.
 *
 * @return the Date when this Entity was last modified
```

```
*/
Date getLastModified();
```

`BaseEntity` will therefore contain fields and JPA metadata to reflect these contracts:

```
@Id
private String id;

@Temporal(TemporalType.TIMESTAMP)
private Date created = new Date();

@Temporal(TemporalType.TIMESTAMP)
private Date updated;
```

You'll notice a few interesting bits in play here.

We denote the `id` field as our primary key by use of the `@javax.persistence.Id` annotation.

`@javax.persistence.Temporal` is required by JPA upon `Date` and `Calendar` fields that are persistent.

We're primarily concerned with the introduction of our `Conference` and `Session` entities; a `Conference` may have many `Session` objects associated with it. So `org.cedj.app.domain.conference.model.Conference` looks a bit like this:

```
@Entity
public class Conference extends BaseEntity {
```

Our class definition indicates that we'll be a JPA entity through use of the `@javax.per sistence.Entity` annotation. We'll extend the `Timestampable` and `Identifiable` support from our `BaseEntity`.

Next we can put in place the fields holding the state for `Conference`:

```
    private static final long serialVersionUID = 1L;

    private String name;

    private String tagLine;

    @Embedded
    private Duration duration;

    @OneToMany(fetch = FetchType.EAGER, orphanRemoval = true,
        mappedBy = "conference", cascade = CascadeType.ALL)
    private Set<Session> sessions;

    public Conference() {
        this.id = UUID.randomUUID().toString();
    }
```

The duration field is @javax.persistence.Embedded, which is used to signal a complex object type that will decompose into further fields (columns) when mapped to relational persistence. org.cedj.app.domain.conference.model.Duration looks like this:

```java
public class Duration implements Serializable {

    private static final long serialVersionUID = 1L;

    private Date start;

    private Date end;

    // hidden constructor for Persistence
    Duration() {
    }

    public Duration(Date start, Date end) {
        requireNonNull(start, "Start must be specified");
        requireNonNull(end, "End must be specified");
        if (end.before(start)) {
            throw new IllegalArgumentException("End can not be before Start");
        }
        this.start = (Date)start.clone();
        this.end = (Date)end.clone();
    }

    public Date getEnd() {
        return (Date) end.clone();
    }

    public Date getStart() {
        return (Date) start.clone();
    }

    public Integer getNumberOfDays() {
        return -1;
    }

    public Integer getNumberOfHours() {
        return -1;
    }
}
```

Conference also has a relationship with Session as denoted by the @OneToMany annotation. This is a bidirectional relationship; we perform the object association in both the Conference and Session classes.

Let's define the constructors that will be used to create new instances:

```java
// JPA
protected Conference() {}
```

```
    public Conference(String name, String tagLine, Duration duration) {
        super(UUID.randomUUID().toString());
        requireNonNull(name, "Name must be specified)");
        requireNonNull(tagLine, "TagLine must be specified");
        requireNonNull(duration, "Duration must be specified");
        this.name = name;
        this.tagLine = tagLine;
        this.duration = duration;
    }
```

A no-argument constructor is required by JPA, so we'll provide one, albeit with pro
tected visibility so we won't encourage users to call upon it.

Now we can flush out the accessors/mutators of this POJO entity, applying some intelligent defaults along the way:

```
    public String getName() {
        return name;
    }

    public Conference setName(String name) {
        requireNonNull(name, "Name must be specified)");
        this.name = name;
        return this;
    }

    public String getTagLine() {
        return tagLine;
    }

    public Conference setTagLine(String tagLine) {
        requireNonNull(tagLine, "TagLine must be specified");
        this.tagLine = tagLine;
        return this;
    }

    public Conference setDuration(Duration duration) {
        requireNonNull(duration, "Duration must be specified");
        this.duration = duration;
        return this;
    }

    public Duration getDuration() {
        return duration;
    }

    public Set<Session> getSessions() {
        if (sessions == null) {
            this.sessions = new HashSet<Session>();
        }
        return Collections.unmodifiableSet(sessions);
    }
```

```
public Conference addSession(Session session) {
    requireNonNull(session, "Session must be specified");
    if (sessions == null) {
        this.sessions = new HashSet<Session>();
    }
    sessions.add(session);
    session.setConference(this);
    return this;
}

public void removeSession(Session session) {
    if(session == null) {
        return;
    }
    if (sessions.remove(session)) {
        session.setConference(null);
    }
}
}
```

Similar in form to the Conference entity, `org.cedj.app.domain.conference.mod`
`el.Session` looks like this:

```
@Entity
public class Session extends BaseEntity {

    @Lob
    private String outline;

    @ManyToOne
    private Conference conference;

    // ... redundant bits omitted

    @PreRemove
    public void removeConferenceRef() {
        if(conference != null) {
            conference.removeSession(this);
        }
    }
}
```

We'll allow an outline for the session of arbitrary size, permitted by the @Lob annotation.

At this end of the relationship between Session and Conference, you'll see that a Session is associated with a Conference via the ManyToOne annotation.

We've also introduced a *callback handler* to ensure that before a Session entity is removed, we also remove the association it has with a Conference so that we aren't left with *orphan* references.

Repository EJBs

The "Repository" EJBs are where we'll define the operations that may be taken by the user with respect to our entities. Strictly speaking, they define the verbs "Store," "Get," and "Remove."

Because we want to completely decouple these persistent actions from JPA, we'll define an interface to abstract out the verbs from the implementations. Later on, we'll want to provide mechanisms that fulfill these responsibilities in both RDBMS and other NoSQL variants. Our contract is in `org.cedj.geekseek.domain.Repository`:

```
public interface Repository<T extends Identifiable> {

    Class<T> getType();

    T store(T entity);

    T get(String id);

    void remove(T entity);
}
```

This means that for any `Identifiable` type, we'll be able to obtain the concrete class type, store the entity, and get and remove it from the database. In JPA, we do this via an `EntityManager`, so we can write a base class to support these operations for all JPA entities. The following is from `org.cedj.geekseek.domain.persistence.Persisten ceRepository`:

```
public abstract class PersistenceRepository<T extends Identifiable>
        implements Repository<T> {

    @PersistenceContext
    private EntityManager manager;

    private Class<T> type;

    public PersistenceRepository(Class<T> type) {
        this.type = type;
    }

    @Override
    public Class<T> getType() {
        return type;
    }

    @Override
    public T store(T entity) {
        T merged = merge(entity);
        manager.persist(merged);
        return merged;
    }
}
```

```
    @Override
    public T get(String id) {
        return manager.find(type, id);
    }

    @Override
    public void remove(T entity) {
        manager.remove(merge(entity));
    }

    private T merge(T entity) {
        return manager.merge(entity);
    }

    protected EntityManager getManager() {
        return manager;
    }
}
```

An instance member of this class is our `EntityManager`, which is injected via the `@Per sistenceContext` annotation and will be used to carry out the public business methods `store` (Create), `remove` (Delete), and `get` (Read). Update is handled by simply reading in an entity, then making any changes to that object's state. The application server will propagate these state changes to persistent storage when the transaction commits (i.e., a transactional business method invocation completes successfully).

We can now extend this behavior with a concrete class and supply the requisite EJB annotations easily; for instance, `org.cedj.geekseek.domain.conference.Conferen ceRepository`:

```
@Stateless
@LocalBean
@Typed(ConferenceRepository.class)
@TransactionAttribute(TransactionAttributeType.REQUIRED)
public class ConferenceRepository extends PersistenceRepository<Conference> {

    public ConferenceRepository() {
        super(Conference.class);
    }
}
```

Despite the small amount of code here, there's a lot of utility going on.

The `Stateless` annotation defines this class as an EJB, a Stateless Session Bean, meaning that the application server may create and destroy instances at will, and a client should not count on ever receiving any particular instance. `@LocalBean` indicates that this EJB has no *business interface*; clients may call upon `ConferenceRepository` methods directly.

The `TransactionAttribute` annotation and its `REQUIRED` value on the class level notes that every method invocation upon one of the business methods exposed by the EJB will run in a transaction. That means that if a transaction does not exist one will be created, and if there's currently a transaction in flight, it will be used.

The `@Typed` annotation from CDI is explained best by the `ConferenceRepository` JavaDocs:

```
/**
 * This EJB is @Typed to a specific type to avoid being picked up by
 * CDI under Repository<Conference> due to limitations/error in the CDI EJB
 * interactions. A EJB Beans is always resolved as Repository<T>, which means
 * two EJBs that implements the Repository interface both respond to
 * the InjectionPoint @Inject Repository<X> and making the InjectionPoint
 * ambiguous.
 *
 * As a WorkAround we wrap the EJB that has Transactional properties in CDI bean
 * that can be used by the Type system. The EJB is to be considered a internal
 * implementation detail. The CDI Type provided by the
 * ConferenceCDIDelegateRepository is the real Repository api.
 */
```

Requirement Test Scenarios

Of course the runtime will be the executable code of our application. However, the theme of this book is *testable development*, and we'll be focusing on proof through automated tests. To that end, every user and technical requirement we identify will be matched to a test that will ensure that functions are producing the correct results during the development cycle.

In this case, we need to create coverage to ensure that we can:

- Perform CRUD operations on the `Conference` and `Session` entities
  - Execute operations against known data sets and validate the results
- Exercise our transaction handling
  - Commits should result in entity object state flushed to persistent storage.
  - Rollbacks (when a commit fails) result in no changes to persistent storage.

Test Setup

Our tests will be taking advantage of the *Arquillian Persistence Extension* (*http://bit.ly/MB0wCg*), which has been created to aid in writing tests where the persistence layer is involved. It supports the following features:

- Wrapping each test in the separated transaction.

- Seeding database using:
  - — DBUnit with XML, XLS, YAML, and JSON supported as data set formats.
  - — Custom SQL scripts.
- Comparing database state at the end of the test using given data sets (with column exclusion).

Creating ad hoc object graphs in the test code is often too verbose and makes it harder to read the tests themselves. The Arquillian Persistence Extension provides alternatives to set database fixtures to be used for the given test.

Adding transactional support to these tests is fairly straightforward. If that's all you need, simply put a @Transactional annotation either on the test you want to be wrapped in the transaction or on the test class (which will result in all tests running in their own transactions). The following modes are supported:

COMMIT
> Each test will be finished with a commit operation. This is default behavior.

ROLLBACK
> At the end of the test execution, rollback will be performed.

DISABLED
> If you have enabled transactional support at the test class level, marking a given test with this mode will simply run it without the transaction.

We'll start by defining the Arquillian Persistence Extension in the dependencyManagement section of our parent POM:

code/application/pom.xml:

```
<properties>
  <version.arquillian_persistence>1.0.0.Alpha6</version.arquillian_persistence>
  ...
</properties>

...

<dependencyManagement>
  <dependencies>
    <dependency>
      <groupId>org.jboss.arquillian.extension</groupId>
      <artifactId>arquillian-persistence-impl</artifactId>
      <version>${version.arquillian_persistence}</version>
      <scope>test</scope>
    </dependency>
    ...
  </dependencies>
</dependencyManagement>
```

And we'll also enable this in the dependencies section of the POMs of the projects in which we'll be using the extension:

code/application/domain/pom.xml:

```
<dependencies>
  <dependency>
    <groupId>org.jboss.arquillian.extension</groupId>
    <artifactId>arquillian-persistence-impl</artifactId>
    <scope>test</scope>
  </dependency>
  ...
</dependencies>
```

Database configuration for tests powered by the Persistence Extension is done via the same mechanism as is used for the runtime: the *persistence.xml* configuration file. For instance, we supply a persistence descriptor in org.cedj.geekseek.domain.persis tence.test.integration.PersistenceDeployments:

```
public static PersistenceDescriptor descriptor() {
        return Descriptors.create(PersistenceDescriptor.class)
                .createPersistenceUnit()
                    .name("test")
                    .getOrCreateProperties()
                        .createProperty()
                            .name("hibernate.hbm2ddl.auto")
                            .value("create-drop").up()
                        .createProperty()
                            .name("hibernate.show_sql")
                            .value("true").up().up()
                    .jtaDataSource("java:jboss/datasources/ExampleDS").up();
    }
```

CRUD Tests

With our setup and objectives clearly in place, we'd like to assert that the CRUD operations against our Repository implementations hold up. For instance, the org.cedj.geekseek.domain.conference.test.integration.ConferenceTestCase contains a series of tests that aim to do just that, and are backed by the Arquillian Persistence Extension.

First, the test class definition:

```
@Transactional(TransactionMode.COMMIT)
@RunWith(Arquillian.class)
public class ConferenceTestCase {
```

This is a plain class with no parent, and will be executed by Arquillian using the JUnit @RunWith annotation, passing along Arquillian.class as the test runner.

The `@Transactional` annotation from the Arquillian Transaction Extension (a dependency of the Persistence Extension) notes that we'll be running each test method in a transaction, and committing the result upon completion.

Next we'll define a ShrinkWrap `@Deployment` that will be deployed onto the backing server as our application under test:

```
@Deployment
public static WebArchive deploy() {
    return ShrinkWrap.create(WebArchive.class)
        .addAsLibraries(
            ConferenceDeployments.conference().addClasses(
            ConferenceTestCase.class,
            TestUtils.class)
                .addAsManifestResource(new StringAsset(
                    PersistenceDeployments.descriptor().exportAsString()),
                    "persistence.xml")
                .addAsManifestResource(
                    new File("src/main/resources/META-INF/beans.xml")))
        .addAsWebInfResource(EmptyAsset.INSTANCE, "beans.xml");
}
```

This will create a WAR of a structure similar to:

```
a23508c0-974e-4ae3-a609-cc532828e6c4.war:
/WEB-INF/
/WEB-INF/lib/
/WEB-INF/lib/c2c1eaf4-4f80-49ce-875b-5090cc6dcc7c.jar
/WEB-INF/beans.xml
```

The nested JAR in *WEB-INF/lib* are our own libraries under test, which include the core deployments, the `ConferenceRepository`, and their dependencies.

We'll now be able to use Arquillian to inject the `ConferenceRepository` right into the test instance, which will be executed inside the deployment on the server. This makes it a local reference to the runtime code:

```
@Inject
private Repository<Conference> repository;
```

Our tests will use this repository to interact with persistent storage.

We can also set a few flags to note whether our create and remove JPA events are fired:

```
// these fields are static because Events observed by this TestClass
// are not observed on the same TestClass instance as @Test is running.
private static boolean createdEventFired = false;
private static boolean removedEventFired = false;
```

And we'll put some methods in place to observe the JPA create events and set the flags. Because our test is *itself* a CDI bean, we can use the CDI `@Observes` annotation to listen in:

```
    public void createdEventFired(@Observes @Created Conference conference) {
        createdEventFired = true;
    }

    public void removedEventFired(@Observes @Removed Conference conference) {
        removedEventFired = true;
    }
```

@Created and @Removed are our own CDI qualifiers, defined like so:

```
@Qualifier
@Target({ElementType.FIELD, ElementType.PARAMETER})
@Retention(RetentionPolicy.RUNTIME)
public @interface Created {

    public static class Literal extends AnnotationLiteral<Created> {
        private static final long serialVersionUID = 1L;
    }
}
```

Now we're set to run some tests. The first one will ensure we can create a conference:

```
// Story: As a User I should be able to create a Conference
@Test
@ShouldMatchDataSet(value = { "conference.yml" }, excludeColumns = { "*id" })
public void shouldBeAbleToCreateConference() {

    Conference conference = createConference();

    repository.store(conference);
    Assert.assertTrue(createdEventFired);
}

public static Conference createConference() {
    Conference conference = new Conference(
        "Devoxx Belgium 2013",
        "We Code In Peace",
        new Duration(toDate(2013, 11, 11), toDate(2013, 11, 15)));
    return conference;
}
```

Because we'll check that the flag was set based upon the CDI @Observes support, we can be sure that the conference was in fact created. Additionally, we use the @Should MatchDataSet annotation from the Arquillian Persistence Extension to check that the values in the DB are in the expected form, given the contents of the *conference.xml* file, which looks like:

```
conference:
  - id: CA
    name: Devoxx Belgium 2013
    tagLine: We Code In Peace
    start: 2013-11-11 00:00:00.0
    end: 2013-11-15 00:00:00.0
```

In this manner, we can more easily check that data is making its way to and from the persistence layer intact, with an easier syntax to define the values we'll expect to find. This also frees us from writing a lot of assertions on each individual field of every entry in the DB, and makes for much easier automated checking of large data sets.

Our test class has similar methods to enforce related behaviors mandated by our requirements:

```java
// Story: As a User I should be able to create a Conference with a Session
@Test
@ShouldMatchDataSet(value = { "conference.yml", "session.yml" },
    excludeColumns = { "*id" })
public void shouldBeAbleToCreateConferenceWithSession(){...}


// Story: As a User I should be able to add a Session to an
// existing Conference
@Test
@UsingDataSet("conference.yml")
@ShouldMatchDataSet(value = { "conference.yml", "session.yml" },
    excludeColumns = { "*id" })
public void shouldBeAbleToAddSessionToConference() {...}

// Story: As a User I should be able to remove a Conference
@Test
@UsingDataSet("conference.yml")
@ShouldMatchDataSet("conference_empty.yml")
public void shouldBeAbleToRemoveConference() {...}


// Story: As a User I should be able to remove a Session from a Conference
@Test
@UsingDataSet({ "conference.yml", "session.yml" })
@ShouldMatchDataSet({ "conference.yml", "session_empty.yml" })
public void shouldBeAbleToRemoveConferenceWithSession(){...}

// Story: As a User I should be able to change a Conference
@Test
@UsingDataSet("conference.yml")
@ShouldMatchDataSet(value = { "conference_updated.yml" })
public void shouldBeAbleToChangeConference() {...}


// Story: As a User I should be able to change a Session
@Test
@UsingDataSet({ "conference.yml", "session.yml" })
@ShouldMatchDataSet(value = { "conference.yml", "session_updated.yml" })
public void shouldBeAbleToChangeSession() {...}
```

By using Arquillian's injection facilities along with the additional transactions and data-checking support offered by the Persistence Extension, we can, with very little test logic, perform powerful assertions which validate that our data is making its way to the real persistence layer without the use of mock objects.

CHAPTER 6

NoSQL: Data Grids and Graph Databases

I'm more of an adventurous type than a relationship type.

— Bob Dylan

Until relatively recently, the relational database (RDBMS) reigned over data in enterprise applications by a wide margin when contrasted with other approaches. RDBMSs follow a premise of storing heavily normalized data in relational structures such as tables, and are heavily based on rigorous mathematical set theory. Commercial offerings from Oracle (*http://www.oracle.com/index.html*) and established open source projects like MySQL (*http://www.mysql.com/*) (reborn as MariaDB (*https://mariadb.org/*)) and PostgreSQL (*http://www.postgresql.org/*) became de facto choices when it came to storing, archiving, retrieving, and searching for data. In retrospect, it's shocking that given the varying requirements from those operations, one solution was so widely lauded for so long.

In the late 2000s, a trend away from the strict ACID transactional properties could be clearly observed, given the emergence of data stores that organized information differently from the traditional row-based table model. In addition, many programmers were beginning to advocate for a release from strict transactions; in many use cases it appeared that this level of isolation wasn't enough of a priority to warrant the computational expense necessary to provide ACID guarantees, and the often severe performance penalties it imposed on storage systems distributed across more than one server.

In 2009, Amazon's Werner Vogels published Eventually Consistent (*http://bit.ly/MB2t1C*), an article that advocated for the tolerance of inconsistent data in large, distributed systems. He argued that this was central to providing a system that could continue to perform effectively under load and could withstand times when part of a distributed data model was effectively unavailable for use. In contrast with the rigid ACID properties, this system could be described as *BASE* (Basically Available, Soft state, Eventual consistency).

The tenets of *eventual consistency* are as the name implies: in a distributed system, updates to a data item will, over time, be reflected in all nodes. There is no guarantee of when, or that this will happen immediately, so it's possible that disparate nodes in a replicated database may not all be in sync at any given point in time. Vogels argued that this was a condition to embrace, not fear.

Thus began the rise of the newly coined *NoSQL* systems, an umbrella term that encompasses, very generally, data solutions that do not adhere to the ACID properties or store information in a relational format.

It's important to remember that as developers we're not bound to any set of solutions before we've fully analyzed the problem. The overwhelming dominance of RDBMS is a clear sign that as an industry we stopped focusing on the operations needed by *our* data model, and instead were throwing all persistent storage features into solutions that perhaps were not the most efficient at solving a particular storage or querying problem.

Let's have a look at a few scenarios in which an RDBMS might not be the best-suited solution.

RDBMS: Bad at Binary Data

An RDBMS is absolutely capable of storing binary data of arbitrary type. Typically done in a column of type BLOB (Binary Large OBject), CLOB (Character Large OBject), or some related variant, these fields can hold images, PDFs, or anything else we'd like to persist. There are a few caveats, however.

Most RDBMS engines have mechanisms to ensure that queries are executed quickly. One device is a *query cache*, a temporary location held in memory that remembers the result of recently or often-executed queries and holds them until the data changes, invalidating the cached result and evicting the result from the cache. This space is precious and valuable; it's typically limited by the amount of RAM available and configuration parameters supported by the vendor. When we add BLOB data into a query and it makes its way into the cache, this very quickly fills up space that's better used for holding references or other small bits of useful data. When a query is not available in the cache or an index is not available, a full table scan must be performed to attain the result. It's therefore best to ensure that our large bits of data stay clear of the cache.

The other issue with a traditional RDMBS is that its adherence to the ACID properties is, in most cases, overkill for fetching documents. It's entirely possible (and probable) in a distributed environment with many database nodes that the user can see data that's not entirely up-to-date. Consider the case of Twitter (*http://twitter.com/*) or Facebook (*http://www.facebook.com*); seeing the newest tweets or status updates in your feed is not a request that demands completely up-to-date information. *Eventually* you'll want to catch all the posts of your friends, but this doesn't need to be available to you immediately after the update is posted to the server. To provide complete consistency across the database implies that there is *locking* and *blocking* taking place; other writes and reads in this concurrent environment would have to wait until the new update is fully committed. Before long, we'd have requests queueing up at a rate likely to exceed that at which the writes could be committed, and the system could grind to a standstill. The mark of a functioning concurrent environment is to avoid blocking wherever possible.

Data Grids

In an era where *big data* is becoming more and more relevant, we're faced with the problem of *scaling*. Our systems are continually asked to store and query upon larger and larger data sets, and one machine is unlikely to be able to handle the load for a non-trivial, public application.

Traditional RDBMS implementations typically offer one or two approaches. First, *replication* involves a write-only *master* instance where a single machine is knighted as the authoritative instance. *Slaves* then pull data from the master's write operations and replay those writes locally, thus being able to serve read requests. This works well in an application where there is a low write-to-read ratio; the reads will scale out to new slaves while the writes remain centralized on the master.

Second, *clustering* is an option where a number of database instances keep state current over the network. This is generally a preferred approach in a write-heavy environment where scaling out only the read operations is unlikely to provide much performance benefit. Full clustering has significant overhead, however, so the costs should be weighed carefully.

Data grids work a little bit differently. They're designed to store pieces of data across available nodes; each node cannot contain the entire data set. Because of this arrangement, they're built to scale out by simply adding more nodes to the network. Configuration is typically available to control the amount of redundancy; should each piece of data live on two nodes, three, or four? If a node goes down, the system is built to re-distribute the information contained in the now-offline node. This makes data grids especially fault-tolerant and *elastic*; nodes can be provisioned at runtime. The key to a data grid lies in its capability to partition the data and distribute it across nodes on the network.

Infinispan

Infinispan (*http://www.jboss.org/infinispan/*) is an open source data grid from the JBoss Community. Its API centers around a `Cache`, a `Map` structure that provides a mapping between a key and value (this does not actually extend the `java.util.Map` interface from the Java Collections library). The full `javax.cache` API is defined by the Java Community Process in JSR-107 (*http://bit.ly/MB357k*), and although Infinispan is not a direct implementor of this specification, it contains many ideas adjacent to and inspiring JSR-107 and the newer Data Grids Specification JSR-347 (*http://bit.ly/*

MB31Ve). Infinispan bills itself as a "Transactional in-memory key/value NoSQL datastore & Data Grid."

 Readers keen on gaining better insight into Infinispan and data grids are urged to check out *Infinispan Data Grid Platform* (*http://bit.ly/ MB3l6r*) by Francesco Marchioni and Manik Surtani (Packt Publishing, 2012). A guide to the Infinispan User API is located at *http:// bit.ly/MB3ree*.

The general idea behind Infinispan is that it aims to provide unlimited heap to keep all objects available in memory. For instance, if we have an environment of 50 servers each with 2GB of available RAM, the total heap size is 100GB. When the data set becomes too large for the currently deployed nodes, new memory can be added in the form of new nodes. This keeps all data quickly accessible, though it may be partitioned across nodes. This is not an issue, because every item remains accessible from every node in the grid, even though the current node may not be the one storing the data.

This makes Infinispan well-suited to holding large objects that may have otherwise been baked into a traditional RDBMS model. Its implementation is versatile enough to be used in other applications (for instance, as a local cache), but for the purposes of our GeekSeek application we'll be leveraging it to handle the storage and retrieval of our binary data.

RDBMS: Bad at Relationships

The greatest irony of the *relational* database management system is that it starts to break down when we need to model complex *relationships*. As we've seen, a traditional RDBMS will associate data types by drawing pointers between tables using foreign-key relationships, as shown in Figure 6-1.

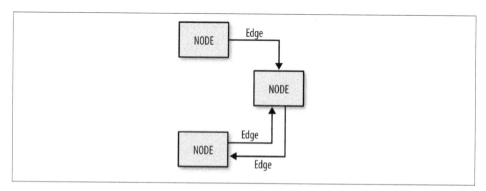

Figure 6-1. Foreign-key relationships in an RDBMS

When we go to query for these relationships, we often perform an operation called an SQL JOIN to return a result of rows from two or more tables. This process involves resolving any foreign keys to provide a *denormalized* view; one that combines all relevant data into a form that's useful for us as humans to interpret, but might not be the most efficient for storage or searching purposes.

The problem is that running joins between data types is an inherently expensive operation, and often we need to join more than two tables. Sometimes we even need to join *results*. Consider the following example, which has now become a commonplace feature in social media.

Andy has a set of friends. His friends also each have a set of friends. To find all of the people who are friends with both Andy and his friends, we might do something like:

- Find all of Andy's friends.
- For each of those friends, find their friends (third-degree friends).
- For each of the third-degree friends, determine who is also friends directly with Andy.

That amounts to a lot of querying and joining. What makes this approach unworkable from a computer science standpoint is the use of the term *for each*, which indicates a loop. The preceding example has two of these, creating a computational problem with *geometric complexity* at best. As the size of the friend network increases linearly, the time it will take to determine a result increases by factors of magnitude. Eventually (and it doesn't take a very large social network size), our system will be unable to perform these calculations in a reasonable amount of time, if at all.

Additionally, the approach outlined in the preceding example will need to either search entire tables for the correct foreign-key relationships or maintain a separate index for each type of query. Indexing adds some overhead to write operations; whenever a row is updated or added, the index must reflect that. And working devoid of an index will require the database to do a full table scan. If the size of the table is large enough that it cannot be contained in memory (RAM) or the query cannot be held in a cache, now we face another serious roadblock, because the system must resort to reading from physical disk, which is a far slower undertaking.

When it comes to complex relationships involving tables of any substantial size, the classic RDBMS approach is simply not the most intelligent way to model these resources.

Graph Theory

The preceding problem illustrates that we're simply using the wrong tool for the job. An RDBMS excels at storage of tabular data, and even does a passable job of drawing simple relationships.

What we want to do here is easily explore *transitive relationships* without a geometric complexity problem, so we need to tackle the problem from a different angle. Students of computer science will remember studying various data structures and their strengths and weaknesses. In this case, we benefit from turning to the writings of mathematician Leonhard Euler on the *Seven Bridges of Königsberg*, which in 1735 established the roots of *graph theory*.

Graphs are data structures comprised from *nodes* or *vertices* and edges; the node/vertex represents our data, while the edge defines the relationship.

Using this view of our data points and the relationships between them, we can apply much more efficient algorithms for:

• Calculating the shortest distance between two nodes

• Determining a path from one node to another

• Finding subgraphs and intersections based on query criteria

We'll be using a graph database to represent some of the relationships between the data held in our RDBMS; we can think of this as a "relationship layer" atop our pure data storage model.

Neo4j

Neo4j is is an open source, transactional graph database that *does* adhere to the ACID properties. Both its user view and its backing storage engine use underlying graph structures, so it achieves the performance we'd expect from applying graph theory to queries it's suited to serve. Because of this, the Neo4j documentation touts performance one thousand times faster than possible with an RDBMS for connected data problems.

 For those looking to understand graph databases and Neo4j in greater detail, we recommend *Graph Databases* (*http://graphdataba ses.com/*) by Robinson, Webber, and Eifrém (O'Reilly, 2013).

Because our GeekSeek application has a social component (who is attending which conferences, who is following speakers and attendees, etc.), we'd like to put in place a solution that will enable us to augment the data in our RDBMS to:

• Draw relationships between data unrelated in the RDBMS schema

• Quickly query recursive relationships

• Efficiently seek out information relevant to users based on relationship data

Use Cases and Requirements

We've already seen the domain model for our GeekSeek application in the previous chapter; this encompasses all of our Conference, Session, User, and Venue entities. The link between Conference and Session is fairly restricted, so we use an RBDMS relationship to handle this.

We'd also like to be able to introduce the notion of an Attachment; this can be any bit of supporting documentation that may be associated with a Conference or Session. Therefore we have the requirement:

    As a User I should be able to Add/Change/Delete an Attachment.

Because the Attachment is binary data (perhaps a PDF, *.doc*, or other related material), we'll store these in a data grid backend using Infinispan.

Additionally, we'd like to introduce some relationships atop our existing data model.

Adding an Attachment is wonderful, but it won't have much utility for us unless we somehow associate this information with the entity it represents. Therefore, we have the requirement:

    As a User I should be able to Add/Delete an Attachment to a Conference.

    As a User I should be able to Add/Delete an Attachment to a Session.

A User may attend or speak at a Conference, and it'll be useful to see who might be nearby while we're at the show. So we also have the general requirement:

    As a User I should be able to SPEAK at a Conference.

    As a User I should be able to ATTEND a Conference.

Because this represents a potentially recursive situation ("I want to see all the attendees at conferences in which I'm a speaker"), we'd be smart to use a graph structure to model these ties.

Implementation

We'll be introducing two domain objects here that are not reflected in our relational model: Attachment and Relation.

Attachment

We'll start by introducing the model for our Attachment. Because this will not be stored in our RDBMS engine, we'll create a value object to hold the data describing this entity, and it will not be an @Entity under the management of JPA. We can accomplish this

by making a simple class to hold our fields, `org.cedj.geekseek.domain.attach`
`ment.model.Attachment`:

```
public class Attachment implements Identifiable, Timestampable, Serializable {

    private static final long serialVersionUID = 1L;
    private final String id;
    private final String title;
    private final String mimeType;
    private final URL url;
    private final Date created;
    private final Date updated;
```

This class declaration will adhere to the contracts we've seen before in `Identifiable` and `Timestampable`, and it has no JPA annotations or metadata because we'll be delegating the persistent operations of this class to Infinispan.

We should also be sure that these `Attachment` objects are in a valid state, so we'll add some assertion checks and intelligent defaults along the way:

```
public Attachment(String title, String mimeType, URL url) {
    this(UUID.randomUUID().toString(),
       title, mimeType, url, new Date());
}

private Attachment(String id, String title, String mimeType,
       URL url, Date created) {
    requireNonNull(title, "Title must be specified)");
    requireNonNull(mimeType, "MimeType must be specified)");
    requireNonNull(url, "Url must be specified)");
    this.id = id;
    this.created = created;
    this.updated = new Date();
    this.title = title;
    this.mimeType = mimeType;
    this.url = url;
}

@Override
public String getId() {
    return id;
}

public String getTitle() {
    return title;
}

public Attachment setTitle(String title) {
    return new Attachment(this.id, title, this.mimeType, this.url,
       this.created);
}
```

```
    public String getMimeType() {
        return mimeType;
    }

    public Attachment setMimeType(String mimeType) {
        return new Attachment(this.id, this.title, mimeType, this.url,
        this.created);
    }

    public URL getUrl() {
        return url;
    }

    public Attachment setUrl(URL url) {
        return new Attachment(this.id, this.title, this.mimeType, url,
        this.created);
    }

    public Date getLastUpdated() {
        return updated == null ? null:(Date)updated.clone();
    }

    @Override
    public Date getCreated() {
        return created == null ? null:(Date)created.clone();
    }

    @Override
    public Date getLastModified() {
        return getLastUpdated() == null ? getCreated():getLastUpdated();
    }
}
```

Of note are the calls to our updated method, which will set the timestamp to the current time on any state change operation.

Recall that our persistence layer for objects, whether through JPA or other means, operates through the Repository abstraction; this provides hooks for all CRUD operations. The previous chapter illustrated a Repository backed by JPA and the EntityManager, but because we'll be storing Attachment objects in a data grid, we need an implementation that will delegate those operations to Infinispan. org.cedj.geekseek.domain.attachment.AttachmentRepository handles this for us:

```
@Stateless
@LocalBean
@Typed(AttachmentRepository.class)
@TransactionAttribute(TransactionAttributeType.REQUIRED)
public class AttachmentRepository implements Repository<Attachment> {
```

We're implementing this AttachmentRepository as a Stateless Session EJB, where all business methods are executed inside the context of a transaction. If a transaction is already in flight, it will be used; otherwise, a new one will be started at the onset of the method invocation and committed when complete.

Our storage engine will be accessed via the Infinispan API's `org.infinispan.Advan cedCache`, so we'll inject this using CDI:

```
@Inject
private AdvancedCache<String, Attachment> cache;
```

Armed with a hook to the Infinispan grid, we can then implement the methods of the `Repository` contract using the Infinispan API:

```
@Override
public Class<Attachment> getType() {
    return Attachment.class;
}

@Override
public Attachment store(Attachment entity) {
    try {
        cache.withFlags(Flag.SKIP_REMOTE_LOOKUP,
            Flag.SKIP_CACHE_LOAD,
            Flag.IGNORE_RETURN_VALUES)
            .put(entity.getId(), entity);
        return entity;
    } catch (Exception e) {
        throw new RuntimeException("Could not store Attachment with id " +
        entity.getId(), e);
    }
}

@Override
public Attachment get(String id) {
    try {
        return cache.get(id);
    } catch (Exception e) {
        throw new RuntimeException(
            "Could not retreive Attachment with id "
            + id, e);
    }
}

@Override
public void remove(Attachment entity) {
    cache.withFlags(Flag.SKIP_REMOTE_LOOKUP,
        Flag.SKIP_CACHE_LOAD,
        Flag.IGNORE_RETURN_VALUES)
        .remove(entity.getId());
}
```

Our `AttachmentRepository` relies upon an Infinispan `AdvancedCache`, so we must make a CDI producer to create the cache instance to be injected. This is handled by `org.cedj.geekseek.domain.attachment.infinispan.CacheProducer`:

```
public class CacheProducer {

    @Produces @ApplicationScoped
    public EmbeddedCacheManager create() {
        GlobalConfiguration global = new GlobalConfigurationBuilder()
            .globalJmxStatistics().cacheManagerName("geekseek")
            .build();

        Configuration local = new ConfigurationBuilder()
            .clustering()
                .cacheMode(CacheMode.LOCAL)
            .transaction()
                .transactionMode(TransactionMode.TRANSACTIONAL)
                .transactionManagerLookup(new GenericTransactionManagerLookup())
            .autoCommit(false)
            .build();
        return new DefaultCacheManager(global, local);
    }

    @Produces @ApplicationScoped
    public AdvancedCache<String, Attachment> createAdvanced(
        EmbeddedCacheManager manager) {
        Cache<String, Attachment> cache =
          manager.getCache();
        return cache.getAdvancedCache();
    }

    public void destroy(@Disposes Cache<?, ?> cache) {
        cache.stop();
    }

    ...
}
```

`CacheProducer` does the business of creating and configuring the Infinispan `Advan cedCache` instance and makes it a valid injection source by use of CDI's (technically `javax.enterprise.inject`) `@Produces` annotation.

This should be enough to fulfill our requirements to perform CRUD operations on an `Attachment`, and does so in a way that won't bog down our RDBMS with binary data.

Relation

With our `Attachment` now modeled and capable of persistence in the data grid, we can move on to the task of associating it with a `Session` or `Conference`. Because we'll handle relationships in a separate layer over the RDBMS, we can do this in a generic fashion that will also grant us the ability to let a User attend or speak at a Conference. The model for a relationship is reflected by org.cedj.geekseek.domain.relation.model. Relation:

```
public class Relation {
    private Key key;
    private Date created;
```

Relation is another standalone class with no additional metadata or dependencies. It contains a Date of creation and a Reference.Key:

```
private static class Key implements Serializable {

        private static final long serialVersionUID = 1L;
        private String sourceId;
        private String targetId;
        private String type;

        private Key(String sourceId, String targetId, String type) {
            this.sourceId = sourceId;
            this.targetId = targetId;
            this.type = type;
        }

        @Override
        public int hashCode() {
            final int prime = 31;
            int result = 1;
            result = prime * result + ((sourceId == null) ? 0 :
                sourceId.hashCode());
            result = prime * result + ((targetId == null) ? 0 :
                targetId.hashCode());
            result = prime * result + ((type == null) ? 0 : type.hashCode());
            return result;
        }

        @Override
        public boolean equals(Object obj) {
            if (this == obj)
                return true;
            if (obj == null)
                return false;
            if (getClass() != obj.getClass())
                return false;
            Key other = (Key) obj;
            if (sourceId == null) {
                if (other.sourceId != null)
                    return false;
            } else if (!sourceId.equals(other.sourceId))
                return false;
            if (targetId == null) {
                if (other.targetId != null)
```

```
                return false;
        } else if (!targetId.equals(other.targetId))
            return false;
        if (type != other.type)
            return false;
        return true;
    }
}
```

The Reference.Key very simply draws a link between a source primary key and a target primary key, the IDs of the entities it is linking. Additionally, we assign a type to note what the relationship is reflecting. Because we want to determine *value equality* using the Object.equals method, we override the equals and hashCode methods (by Object contract, objects with equal values *must* have equal hashCodes).

The rest of the Relation class is straightforward:

```
    public Relation(String sourceId, String targetId, String type) {
        this.key = new Key(sourceId, targetId, type);
        this.created = new Date();
    }

    public String getSourceId() {
        return key.sourceId;
    }

    public String getTargetId() {
        return key.targetId;
    }

    public String getType() {
        return key.type;
    }

    public Date getCreated() {
        return (Date) created.clone();
    }
}
```

Now we need a mechanism to persist and remove Relation instances. Our Reposito ry interface used on other objects doesn't really fit the operations we need; relationships are not true entities, but are instead pointers from one entity to another. So in org.cedj.geekseek.domain.relation.RelationRepository we'll define a more fitting contract:

```
public interface RelationRepository {

    Relation add(Identifiable source, String type, Identifiable target);

    void remove(Identifiable source, String type, Identifiable target);
```

```
    <T extends Identifiable> List<T> findTargets(Identifiable source,
        String type, Class<T> targetType);
}
```

The RelationRepository will be used by the services layer, and acts as an abstraction above the data store provider persisting the relationships (a graph database in this case).

Now we're free to implement RelationRepository with a Neo4j backend in org.cedj.geekseek.domain.relation.neo.GraphRelationRepository:

```
@ApplicationScoped
public class GraphRelationRepository implements RelationRepository {

    private static final String PROP_INDEX_NODE = "all_nodes";
    private static final String PROP_INDEX_REL = "all_relations";
    private static final String PROP_ID = "id";
    private static final String PROP_NODE_CLASS = "_classname";
    private static final String PROP_CREATED = "created";
    private static final String REL_TYPE_ALL = "all";

    @Inject
    private GraphDatabaseService graph;

    @Inject
    private BeanManager manager;
```

GraphRelationRepository is implemented as an application-scoped CDI bean; it contains a few constants, a hook to the backend graph database (Neo4j API's GraphDatabaseService), and a reference to the CDI BeanManager.

The RelationRepository contract implementation looks like this:

```
@Override
public Relation add(Identifiable source, final String type,
    Identifiable target) {

    Transaction tx = graph.beginTx();
    try {
        Node root =graph.getNodeById(0);
        String sourceTypeName = source.getClass().getSimpleName();
        String targetTypeName = target.getClass().getSimpleName();
        Node sourceTypeNode = getOrCreateNodeType(sourceTypeName);
        Node targetTypeNode = getOrCreateNodeType(targetTypeName);
        getOrCreateRelationship(root, sourceTypeNode,
            Named.relation(sourceTypeName));
        getOrCreateRelationship(root, targetTypeNode,
            Named.relation(targetTypeName));

        Node sourceNode = getOrCreateNode(source, sourceTypeName);
        getOrCreateRelationship(sourceTypeNode, sourceNode,
            Named.relation(REL_TYPE_ALL));
        Node targetNode = getOrCreateNode(target, targetTypeName);
```

```
            getOrCreateRelationship(targetTypeNode, targetNode,
                Named.relation(REL_TYPE_ALL));

            getOrCreateRelationship(sourceNode, targetNode, Named.relation(type));

            tx.success();
        } catch(Exception e) {
            tx.failure();
            throw new RuntimeException(
                "Could not add relation of type " + type + " between " + source +
                " and " + target, e);
        } finally {
            tx.finish();
        }
        return new Relation(source.getId(), target.getId(), type);
    }


    @Override
    public void remove(Identifiable source, String type, Identifiable target) {

        Transaction tx = graph.beginTx();
        try {
            Index<Node> nodeIndex = graph.index().forNodes(PROP_INDEX_NODE);
            Index<Relationship> relationIndex = graph.index().forRelationships(
                PROP_INDEX_REL);

            Node sourceNode = nodeIndex.get(PROP_ID, source.getId()).getSingle();
            Node targetNode = nodeIndex.get(PROP_ID, target.getId()).getSingle();
            for(Relationship rel : sourceNode.getRelationships(
                Named.relation(type))) {
                if(rel.getEndNode().equals(targetNode)) {
                    rel.delete();
                    relationIndex.remove(rel);
                }
            }

            tx.success();
        } catch(Exception e) {
            tx.failure();
            throw new RuntimeException(
                "Could not add relation of type " + type + " between " + source +
                " and " + target, e);
        } finally {
            tx.finish();
        }
    }


    @Override
    public <T extends Identifiable> List<T> findTargets(Identifiable source,
        final String type, final Class<T> targetType) {

        Repository<T> repo = locateTargetRepository(targetType);
```

```
        if(repo == null) {
            throw new RuntimeException("Could not locate a " +
                Repository.class.getName() + " instance for Type " +
                targetType.getName());
        }

        List<T> targets = new ArrayList<T>();
        Index<Node> index = graph.index().forNodes(PROP_INDEX_NODE);
        Node node = index.get(PROP_ID, source.getId()).getSingle();
        if(node == null) {
            return targets;
        }
        Iterable<Relationship> relationships = node.getRelationships(
            Named.relation(type));
        List<String> targetIds = new ArrayList<String>();
        for(Relationship relation : relationships) {
            targetIds.add(relation.getEndNode().getProperty(PROP_ID).toString());
        }

        for(String targetId : targetIds) {
            targets.add(repo.get(targetId));
        }
        return targets;
    }
```

As shown, this is a fairly simple undertaking given a little research into proper use of
the Neo4j API. We'll also need a little help to resolve the proper Repository types from
the types of the entities between which we're drawing relationships. So we'll add some
internal helper methods to GraphRelationRepository to contain this logic:

```
/**
 * Helper method that looks in the BeanManager for a Repository that
 * matches signature Repository<T>.
 *
 * Used to dynamically find repository to load targets from.
 *
 * @param targetType Repository object type to locate
 * @return Repository<T>
 */
private <T extends Identifiable> Repository<T> locateTargetRepository(
    final Class<T> targetType) {
    ParameterizedType paramType = new ParameterizedType() {
        @Override
        public Type getRawType() {
            return Repository.class;
        }
        @Override
        public Type getOwnerType() {
            return null;
        }
        @Override
        public Type[] getActualTypeArguments() {
```

```java
                return new Type[] {targetType};
            }
        };

        Set<Bean<?>> beans = manager.getBeans(paramType);
        Bean<?> bean = manager.resolve(beans);
        CreationalContext<?> cc = manager.createCreationalContext(null);

        @SuppressWarnings("unchecked")
        Repository<T> repo = (Repository<T>)manager.getReference(bean,
            paramType, cc);
        return repo;
}

private Node getOrCreateNodeType(String type) {
    UniqueFactory<Node> factory = new UniqueFactory.UniqueNodeFactory(
        graph, PROP_INDEX_NODE) {
        @Override
        protected void initialize(Node created, Map<String, Object>
            properties) {
            created.setProperty(PROP_ID, properties.get(PROP_ID));
        }
    };
    return factory.getOrCreate(PROP_ID, type);
}

private Node getOrCreateNode(Identifiable source,
    final String nodeClassType) {
    UniqueFactory<Node> factory = new UniqueFactory.UniqueNodeFactory(
      graph, PROP_INDEX_NODE) {
        @Override
        protected void initialize(Node created, Map<String, Object>
        properties) {
            created.setProperty(PROP_ID, properties.get(PROP_ID));
            created.setProperty(PROP_NODE_CLASS, nodeClassType);
        }
    };
    return factory.getOrCreate(PROP_ID, source.getId());
}

private Relationship getOrCreateRelationship(final Node source,
    final Node target, final RelationshipType type) {
    final String key = generateKey(source, target, type);

    UniqueFactory<Relationship> factory =
      new UniqueFactory.UniqueRelationshipFactory(
        graph, PROP_INDEX_REL) {

        @Override
        protected Relationship create(Map<String, Object> properties) {
            Relationship rel = source.createRelationshipTo(target, type);
            rel.setProperty(PROP_ID, properties.get(PROP_ID));
```

```
                    return rel;
                }

                @Override
                protected void initialize(Relationship rel,
                    Map<String, Object> properties) {
                    rel.setProperty(PROP_CREATED, System.currentTimeMillis());
                }
            };
            return factory.getOrCreate(PROP_ID, key);
        }

        /**
         * Generate some unique key we can identify a relationship with.
         */
        private String generateKey(Node source, Node target,
            RelationshipType type) {
            return source.getProperty(PROP_ID, "X") + "-" + type.name() + "-" +
            target.getProperty(PROP_ID, "X");
        }

        private static class Named implements RelationshipType {

            public static RelationshipType relation(String name) {
                return new Named(name);
            }

            private String name;

            private Named(String name) {
                this.name = name;
            }

            @Override
            public String name() {
                return name;
            }
        }
    }
```

Again, we've made an implementation class that depends upon injection of a backend provider's API. To enable injection of the Neo4j GraphDatabaseService, we'll create another CDI producer in org.cedj.geekseek.domain.relation.neo.GraphDataba seProducer:

```
@ApplicationScoped
public class GraphDatabaseProducer {

    private String DATABASE_PATH_PROPERTY = "neo4j.path";

    private static Logger log = Logger.getLogger(
        GraphDatabaseProducer.class.getName());
```

```
@Produces
public GraphDatabaseService createGraphInstance() throws Exception {
    String databasePath = getDataBasePath();
    log.info("Using Neo4j database at " + databasePath);
    return new GraphDatabaseFactory().newEmbeddedDatabase(databasePath);
}

public void shutdownGraphInstance(@Disposes GraphDatabaseService service)
    throws Exception {
    service.shutdown();
}

private String getDataBasePath() {
    String path = System.clearProperty(DATABASE_PATH_PROPERTY);
    if(path == null || path.isEmpty()) {
        try {
            File tmp = File.createTempFile("neo", "geekseek");
            File parent = tmp.getParentFile();
            tmp.delete();
            parent.mkdirs();
            path = parent.getAbsolutePath();
        }catch (IOException e) {
            throw new RuntimeException(
                "Could not create temp location for Nepo4j Database. " +
                "Please provide system property " + DATABASE_PATH_PROPERTY +
                " with a valid path", e);
        }
    }
    return path;
}
```

With this in place we can inject a `GraphDataBaseService` instance into our `GraphRela tionRepository`.

Our implementation is almost complete, though it's our position that nothing truly exists until it's been proven through tests.

Requirement Test Scenarios

Given our user requirements and the implementation choices we've made, it's important we assert that a few areas are working as expected:

- CRUD operations on `Attachment` objects
- Transactional integrity of CRUD operations on `Attachment` objects
- Create, Delete, and Find relationships between entities

Attachment CRUD Tests

First we'll need to ensure that we can Create, Read, Update, and Delete `Attachment` instances using the data grid provided by Infinispan. To ensure these are working, we'll use `org.cedj.geekseek.domain.attachment.test.integration.AttachmentRepo sitoryTestCase`:

```
@RunWith(Arquillian.class)
public class AttachmentRepositoryTestCase {

    // Given
    @Deployment
    public static WebArchive deploy() {
        return ShrinkWrap.create(WebArchive.class)
            .addAsLibraries(
                CoreDeployments.core(),
                AttachmentDeployments.attachmentWithCache())
            .addAsLibraries(AttachmentDeployments.resolveDependencies())
            .addClass(TestUtils.class)
            .addAsWebInfResource(EmptyAsset.INSTANCE, "beans.xml");
    }
```

Here we have a simple Arquillian test defined with no additional extensions. We'll deploy an `attachmentWithCache`, as defined by:

```
public static JavaArchive attachment() {
    return ShrinkWrap.create(JavaArchive.class)
        .addPackage(Attachment.class.getPackage())
        .addAsManifestResource(EmptyAsset.INSTANCE, "beans.xml");
}

public static JavaArchive attachmentWithCache() {
    return attachment()
        .addPackage(AttachmentRepository.class.getPackage())
        .addPackage(CacheProducer.class.getPackage());
}
```

This will give us our `Attachment` domain entity, the `AttachmentRepository`, and the CDI producer to inject hooks into an Infinispan `Cache` as shown before. Additionally, we'll need to deploy the Infinispan API and implementation as a library, so `Attach mentDeployments.resolveDependencies` will bring this in for us:

```
public static File[] resolveDependencies() {
    return Maven.resolver()
        .offline()
        .loadPomFromFile("pom.xml")
        .resolve("org.infinispan:infinispan-core")
        .withTransitivity()
        .asFile();
}
```

This uses the *ShrinkWrap Maven Resolver* to pull the `groupId:artifactId` of `org.infinispan:infinispan-core` and all of its dependencies in from the Maven repository, returning the artifacts as files. We don't need to define the version explicitly here; that will be configured from the definition contained in the project's *pom.xml* file because we've told the resolver to `loadPomFromFile("pom.xml")`.

Also as part of the deployment we'll throw in a `TestUtils` class, which will let us easily create `Attachment` objects from the tests running inside the container:

```
public static Attachment createAttachment() {
    try {
        return new Attachment(
        "Test Attachment",
        "text/plain",
        new URL("http://geekseek.org"));
    } catch(MalformedURLException e) {
        throw new RuntimeException(e);
    }
}
```

The resulting deployment should have structure that looks similar to this:

```
749e9f51-d858-42a6-a06e-3f3d03fc32ad.war:
/WEB-INF/
/WEB-INF/lib/
/WEB-INF/lib/jgroups-3.3.1.Final.jar
/WEB-INF/lib/43322d61-32c4-444c-9681-079ac34c6e87.jar
/WEB-INF/lib/staxmapper-1.1.0.Final.jar
/WEB-INF/lib/jboss-marshalling-river-1.3.15.GA.jar
/WEB-INF/lib/56201983-371f-4ed5-8705-d4fd6ec8f936.jar
/WEB-INF/lib/infinispan-core-5.3.0.Final.jar
/WEB-INF/lib/jboss-marshalling-1.3.15.GA.jar
/WEB-INF/lib/jboss-logging-3.1.1.GA.jar
/WEB-INF/beans.xml
/WEB-INF/classes/
/WEB-INF/classes/org/
/WEB-INF/classes/org/cedj/
/WEB-INF/classes/org/cedj/geekseek/
/WEB-INF/classes/org/cedj/geekseek/domain/
/WEB-INF/classes/org/cedj/geekseek/domain/attachment/
/WEB-INF/classes/org/cedj/geekseek/domain/attachment/test/
/WEB-INF/classes/org/cedj/geekseek/domain/attachment/test/TestUtils.class
```

As we can see, Infinispan and all of its dependencies have made their way to *WEB-INF/lib*; our own libraries are not explicitly named, so they're assigned a UUID filename.

It's useful to debug your deployments by simply printing out a listing of your archive; this is easily accomplished by throwing a statement like System.out.println(archive.toString(true)); in your @Deployment method before returning the archive. If you want to debug the content of the final deployment as seen by the container, you can set the deploymentExportPath property under the engine element in *arquillian.xml* to the path where you want Arquillian to output the deployments. This is useful if you're having deployment problems that you suspect are related to how Arquillian enriches the deployment, or if you're generating file content dynamically.

Now let's give our test a hook to the Repository we'll use to perform CRUD operations on our Attachment objects:

```
@Inject
private Repository<Attachment> repository;
```

With the deployment and injection of the Repository done, we're now free to implement our tests:

```
// Story: As a User I should be able to create an Attachment

@Test
public void shouldBeAbleToCreateAttachment() throws Exception {
    Attachment attachment = createAttachment();
    repository.store(attachment);

    Attachment stored = repository.get(attachment.getId());
    Assert.assertNotNull(stored);

    Assert.assertEquals(attachment.getId(), stored.getId());
    Assert.assertEquals(attachment.getTitle(), stored.getTitle());
    Assert.assertEquals(attachment.getUrl(), stored.getUrl());
    Assert.assertEquals(attachment.getMimeType(), stored.getMimeType());
    Assert.assertNotNull(stored.getCreated());
}

// Story: As a User I should be able to update an Attachment

@Test
public void shouldBeAbleToUpdateAttachment() throws Exception {
    String updatedTitle = "Test 2";
    Attachment attachment = createAttachment();
    attachment = repository.store(attachment);

    attachment = attachment.setTitle(updatedTitle);
    attachment = repository.store(attachment);

    Attachment updated = repository.get(attachment.getId());
```

```
        Assert.assertEquals(updated.getTitle(), updatedTitle);
        Assert.assertNotNull(attachment.getLastUpdated());
    }

    // Story: As a User I should be able to remove an Attachment

    @Test
    public void shouldBeAbleToRemoveAttachment() throws Exception {
        Attachment attachment = createAttachment();
        attachment = repository.store(attachment);

        repository.remove(attachment);

        Attachment removed = repository.get(attachment.getId());
        Assert.assertNull(removed);
    }

    @Test
    public void shouldNotReflectNonStoredChanges() throws Exception {
        tring updatedTitle = "Test Non Stored Changes";
        Attachment attachment = createAttachment();
        String originalTitle = attachment.getTitle();

        Attachment stored = repository.store(attachment);

        // tile change not stored to repository
        stored = stored.setTitle(updatedTitle);

        Attachment refreshed = repository.get(attachment.getId());

        Assert.assertEquals(refreshed.getTitle(), originalTitle);
    }
}
```

So here we have our CRUD tests using the injected `Repository` to perform their persistence operations. In turn, we've implemented the `Repository` with an Infinispan backend (which in this case is running in local embedded mode). We can now be assured that our repository layer is correctly hooked together and persistence to the data grid is working properly.

Transactional Integrity of Attachment Persistence

While we're confident that the CRUD operations of our `Attachment` entity are in place, we should ensure that the transactional semantics are upheld if a transaction is in flight. This will essentially validate that Infinispan is respectful of the *Java Transactions API* (*JTA*), a specification under the direction of the JSR-907 (*http://jcp.org/en/jsr/detail? id=907*) Expert Group.

To accomplish this, we're going to directly interact with JTA's `UserTransaction` in our test. In fact, the `Attachment` entity is not the only one we should be verifying, so we'll code this test in a way that will enable us to extend it to ensure that `Conference`, `Session`, and other entities can be exercised for transactional compliance.

Our goals are to assert that for any entity type T:

- T is Stored on commit and can be read from another transaction.
- T is Updated on commit and can be read from another transaction.
- T is Removed on commit and cannot be read by another transaction.
- T is not Stored on rollback and cannot be read by another transaction.
- T is not Updated on rollback and cannot be read by another transaction.
- T is not Removed on rollback and can be read by another transaction.

Therefore we'll attempt to centralize these operations in a base test class that will, when provided a T and a `Repository<T>`, verify that T is committed and rolled back as required. Thus we introduce `org.cedj.geekseek.domain.test.integration.BaseTran sactionalSpecification`:

```
public abstract class BaseTransactionalSpecification<
    DOMAIN extends Identifiable,
    REPO extends Repository<DOMAIN>> {
```

We define some generic variables for easy extension; this test will deal with entity objects of type `Identifiable` and the `Repository` that interacts with them. Next we'll gain access to the JTA `UserTransaction`:

```
@Inject
private UserTransaction tx;
```

Because this class is to be extended for each entity type we'd like to test, we'll make a contract for those implementations to supply:

```
/**
 * Get the Repository instance to use.
 */
protected abstract REPO getRepository();

/**
 * Create a new unique instance of the Domain Object.
 */
protected abstract DOMAIN createNewDomainObject();

/**
 * Update some domain object values.
 */
protected abstract void updateDomainObject(
  DOMAIN domain);

/**
```

```
 * Validate that the update change has occurred.
 * Expecting Assert error when validation does not match.
 */
protected abstract void validateUpdatedDomainObject(
  DOMAIN domain);
```

And now we're free to write the tests backing the points listed earlier; we want to validate that objects are either accessible or not based on commit or rollback operations to the transaction in play. For instance, this test ensures that an object is stored after a commit:

```
@Test
public void shouldStoreObjectOnCommit() throws Exception {
    final DOMAIN domain = createNewDomainObject();

    commit(Void.class, new Store(domain));

    DOMAIN stored = commit(new Get(domain.getId()));
    Assert.assertNotNull(
        "Object should be stored when transaction is committed",
        stored);
}

protected DOMAIN commit(Callable<DOMAIN> callable) throws Exception {
    return commit(getDomainClass(), callable);
}

protected <T> T commit(Class<T> type, Callable<T> callable)
    throws Exception {
    try {
        tx.begin();
        return callable.call();
    } finally {
        tx.commit();
    }
}

private class Store implements Callable<Void> {
    private DOMAIN domain;

    public Store(DOMAIN domain) {
        this.domain = domain;
    }

    @Override
    public Void call() throws Exception {
        getRepository().store(domain);
        return null;
    }
}

private class Get implements Callable<DOMAIN> {
    private String id;
```

```
        public Get(String id) {
            this.id = id;
        }

        @Override
        public DOMAIN call() throws Exception {
            return getRepository().get(id);
        }
    }
```

Here we see that we manually manipulate the `UserTransaction` to our liking in the test method; the mechanics of this interaction are handled by the `commit` method.

We have similar tests in place to validate the other conditions:

```
@Test public void shouldUpdateObjectOnCommit() throws Exception {...}

@Test public void shouldRemoveObjectOnCommmit() throws Exception {...}

@Test public void shouldNotStoreObjectOnRollback() throws Exception {...}

@Test public void shouldNotUpdateObjectOnRollback() throws Exception {...}

@Test public void shouldNotRemoveObjectOnRollback() throws Exception {...}

@Test public void shouldSetCreatedDate() throws Exception {...}

@Test public void shouldSetUpdatedDate() throws Exception {...}
```

With our base class containing most of our support for the transactional specification tests, now we can provide a concrete implementation for our `Attachment` entities. We do this in `org.cedj.geekseek.domain.attachment.test.integration.Attachment` `RepositoryTransactionalTestCase`:

```
@RunWith(Arquillian.class)
public class AttachmentRepositoryTransactionalTestCase
    extends
        BaseTransactionalSpecification<Attachment, Repository<Attachment>> {
```

We'll extend `BaseTransactionalSpecification` and close the generic context to be relative to `Attachment`. By implementing the parent abstract methods of the parent class, we'll then be done and able to run transactional tests on `Attachment` types:

```
    private static final String UPDATED_TITLE = "TEST UPDATED";
    ...
    @Inject
    private Repository<Attachment> repository;

    @Override
    protected Attachment createNewDomainObject() {
        return createAttachment();
```

```
    }

    @Override
    protected Attachment updateDomainObject(
      Attachment domain) {
        return domain.setTitle(UPDATED_TITLE);
    }

    @Override
    protected void validateUpdatedDomainObject(Attachment domain) {
        Assert.assertEquals(UPDATED_TITLE, domain.getTitle());
    }

    @Override
    protected Repository<Attachment> getRepository() {
        return repository;
    }
```

With these tests passing, we're now satisfied that our Infinispan backend is complying with the semantics of a backing application transaction. We therefore have nicely abstracted the data grid from the perspective of the caller; it's just another transactionally aware persistence engine representing itself as a `Repository`.

Validating Relationships

Armed with our Neo4j-backed `RelationRepository`, we're able to draw relationships between entities that are not otherwise related in the schema, or may even be in separate data stores. Let's construct a test to validate that our `Relation` edges in the graph are serving us well. We'll do this in `org.cedj.geekseek.domain.relation.test.integra tion.RelationTestCase`:

```
@RunWith(Arquillian.class)
public class RelationTestCase {
```

This will be another relatively simple Arquillian test case, running inside the container. We'll again define a deployment, this time including Neo4j as a dependency in place of Infinispan:

```
@Deployment
public static WebArchive deploy() {
    return ShrinkWrap.create(WebArchive.class)
        .addAsLibraries(
            RelationDeployments.relationWithNeo(),
            CoreDeployments.core())
        .addAsLibraries(RelationDeployments.neo4j())
        .addPackage(SourceObject.class.getPackage())
        .addAsWebInfResource(EmptyAsset.INSTANCE, "beans.xml");
}
```

This deployment will include our `GraphDatabaseProducer`, so we'll be able to inject a `GraphRelationRepository` in our test case to create, remove, and find `Relation` edges. We'll obtain this easily via injection into the test instance:

```
@Inject
private GraphRelationRepository repository;
```

Now we'll set up some constants and instance members, then populate them before each test runs using a JUnit lifecycle annotation:

```
private static final String SOURCE_ID = "11";
private static final String TARGET_ID = "1";

private SourceObject source;
private TargetObject target;
private String type;

@Before
public void createTypes() {
    source = new SourceObject(SOURCE_ID);
    target = new TargetObject(TARGET_ID);
    type = "SPEAKING";
}
```

`SourceObject` and `TargetObject` are test-only objects we've introduced to represent entities. Again, we only care about *relationships* here, so there's no sense tying this test to one of our real entities at this level of integration. At this point we want to test the `Relation` and its persistence mechanisms in as much isolation as possible, so it's appropriate to tie together test-only entities.

Now we'll want to run our tests to:

- Create a relationship
- Find the created relationship
- Delete the relationship
- Only find valid targets remaining

Rather than do this in one large test, we'll make separate tests for each case. There are dependencies however, because the state of the system will change after each test is run. Therefore we need to make sure that these tests run in the proper order using Arquillian's `@InSequence` annotation:

```
@Test @InSequence(0)
public void shouldBeAbleToCreateRelation() {

    Relation relation = repository.add(source, type, target);

    Assert.assertEquals("Verify returned object has same source id",
        relation.getSourceId(), source.getId());
```

```
    Assert.assertEquals("Verify returned object has same target id",
        relation.getTargetId(), target.getId());
    Assert.assertEquals("Verify returned object has same type",
        relation.getType(), type);

    Assert.assertNotNull("Verify created date was set",
        relation.getCreated());
}

@Test @InSequence(1)
public void shouldBeAbleToFindTargetedRelations(
    Repository<TargetObject> targetRepo,
    Repository<SourceObject> sourceRepo) {...}

@Test @InSequence(2)
public void shouldBeAbleToDeleteRelations() {...}

@Test @InSequence(3)
public void shouldOnlyFindGivenRelation() {...}
```

With these passing, it's now proven that we can perform all the contracted operations of `RelationRepository` against a real Neo4j graph database backend.

Our GeekSeek application now has many database layers at its disposal: CRUD operations in an RDBMS for most entities, a key/value store to hold onto `Attachment` objects, and a graph to draw ties among the entities such that their relationships can be explored in an efficient manner.

CHAPTER 7

Business Logic and the Services Layer

The best way to find yourself is to lose yourself in the service of others.

— Mahatma Gandhi

The code we've developed and tested up to this point has dealt with data: organizing, accessing, mutating, and transforming it into formats more comfortable to us as application developers. We've mentioned that these are the nouns of our GeekSeek project; now it's time to put these to some good use and take *action*.

Business logic governs the behaviors that power our applications. As compared with more generic (and *cross-cutting*) concerns that can be abstracted—security, transactions, object-relational mapping, resource management—business logic lies at the heart of our projects. It is unique to our needs, and no one else can write it for us.

That said, the cross-cutting concerns just mentioned (and many more!) are all commonly demanded by our business needs. For instance, imagine we have a series of services, each of which needs to be accessed by an authenticated and authorized user, and in the context of a transaction. If we were diligently applying proper modularization and encapsulation, we might implement separate functions for the transactional and security enforcement, and then call these from our services.

A glaring problem with this approach is that, although we've nicely extracted out the logic for our security and transactions for reuse, we must still manually *invoke* them, sprinkling these method calls at the head and foot of every function requiring their use. Additionally, we may have to pass around contextual objects that know about the state of the current user or transactional registration (though in practice, these are commonly associated with a Thread, and thus are able to fly under the visible API radar in an obfuscated context).

Things get more complicated when we introduce *dependent* services. A UserRegistra tion function may in turn call many finer-grained services like SendEmail, PutUserIn

Database, and `GenerateHashOfPassword`. This composition is desirable because it separates concerns, but we're left with the problem of *looking up* or locating each of these disparate services from `UserRegistration`. Ultimately this adds to the "plumbing" code, which provides no benefit to us aside from hooking our cleanly decoupled modules together. Although this has historically been addressed by employing a technique known as the *Service Locator Pattern*, for reasons we'll soon see, this is a largely outdated and inferior approach.

A more subtle, yet very important, issue that arises with pure POJO programming in a multiuser environment is one of *shared state*. Consider the following code:

```
public class UserService {

  /** Cached flag denoting if our current user has logged in **/
  private boolean isLoggedIn;

  public boolean authenticate(final String userName,
    final String password){

    // First check if we're already logged in
    if(isLoggedIn){
      return true;
    }

    // Else hash the password, check against the hash
    // in the database, and return true if and
    // only if they match
    /** Omitted for brevity **/

  }
}
```

This `UserService` is clearly meant to be associated with a current user session, and thus has what we call *conversational scope* confined to that session. When writing manual POJO services, the onus is upon us as developers to ensure that this is enforced; imagine if UserB were to come along and receive the object for which UserA had already set `isLoggedIn` to `true`? Scope confinement is vitally important to the integrity of our system, and we have to be very careful when rolling our own solutions.

In this chapter we'll be examining each of these complications and a proposed solution when tackling the testable development of a common, and seemingly innocuous, business requirement: sending email from a Java EE-based application.

Use Cases and Requirements

As always, before digging into the implementation, we'll define some requirements based on our desired use cases.

Send Email on New User Signup

Web-based applications offer few avenues to push information to their users once off-line; perhaps the most prevalent is through the use of email. We see this in a variety of user stories: "Confirm Email Address," "Reset Password," and "Welcome New User" are all subject lines we've grown to expect from the sites we use. It's fitting, then, that we devise a simple strategy to send email from our application that can be easily reused by the more coarsely grained operations.

Our GeekSeek application will therefore introduce the requirement: "Send an Email to the New User Upon Successful Signup."

At first blush, this seems like a fairly trivial problem to solve. The JavaMail (*http://bit.ly/ 1noNtRq*) API is straightforward enough to use (though a bit dated), and is included as part of the Java EE Platform.

Unfortunately, there are many issues to consider beyond the boilerplate code required to send the email itself:

Should we block (wait) while the mail message is sent to the SMTP server?
> Connecting to an external service can take some time, depending on how it handles open connections. The delivery of the email isn't designed to be immediate, so there's not much sense forcing the user to wait while we connect to an SMTP server, construct a MimeMessage, and send.

What if sending the email fails? Should the enclosing user registration action that called the email service fail, too?
> Sending the email is, in our case, part of a welcome operation. A new user registration doesn't strictly *need* this to succeed because we won't be relying on email to validate the user's identity. Still, we'd like to make every available effort to ensure that the email goes through, independent of the user registration action. And we'd like to have some notification and options to handle emails that were attempted to be sent, but have failed.

How do we test to ensure that the emails we've sent are received? How do we validate that the email's contents are correct?
> Even if we don't dispatch the communication with the SMTP server to a new Thread, interacting with this external process makes for an asynchronous action. Asynchronous testing is not always the simplest process to set up, but this does not excuse us from the responsibility of ensuring that our email service works as designed.

Implementation

We'll begin our example with the construction of a generic `SMTPMailService`. As the name implies, its job will be to act as our Java interface to perform SMTP operations. Specifically, we'll write this to send email.

First we'll make a self-explanatory value object to encapsulate the fields needed to send an email message. This is implemented as a mutable builder for ease of use:

```java
public class MailMessageBuilder implements Serializable {

    private static final long serialVersionUID = 1L;

    private static final String[] EMPTY = new String[]{};
    private String from;
    private String subject;
    private String body;
    private String contentType;
    private final Collection<String> toAddresses = new HashSet<String>();

    public MailMessageBuilder from(final String from)
        throws IllegalArgumentException {
        if (from == null || from.length() == 0) {
            throw new IllegalArgumentException("from address must be specified");
        }
        this.from = from;
        return this;
    }
    // Other fluent API methods omitted for brevity; see full source for details
```

`MailMessageBuilder` has a `build` method that can then return an immutable view:

```java
public MailMessage build() throws IllegalStateException {

    // Validate
    if (from == null || from.length() == 0) {
        throw new IllegalStateException("from address must be specified");
    }
    if (toAddresses.size() == 0) {
        throw new IllegalStateException(
            "at least one to address must be specified");
    }
    if (subject == null || subject.length() == 0) {
        throw new IllegalStateException("subject must be specified");
    }
    if (body == null || body.length() == 0) {
        throw new IllegalStateException("body must be specified");
    }
    if (contentType == null || contentType.length() == 0) {
        throw new IllegalStateException("contentType must be specified");
    }
```

```
// Construct immutable object and return
return new MailMessage(from, toAddresses.toArray(EMPTY),
    subject, body, contentType);

}
```

It's this immutable MailMessageBuilder.MailMessage that will be safely passed between our services.

With our value object defined, we can now create our SMTPMailService. We know that we'll need to connect to some external SMTP server via the JavaMail API, and Java EE allows injection of these via the @Resource annotation (though the mechanics of exactly where some services are bound is vendor-dependent). Also, we know that this SMTPMail Service is meant to be shared by all users running the application, and won't have any session-specific state. For these reasons, we'll implement the SMTPMailService as a Singleton Session EJB. Note that a Stateless Session Bean (for use of a pool of instances) might work in an equally appropriate fashion:

```
@Singleton
@LocalBean
@TransactionAttribute(value = TransactionAttributeType.SUPPORTS)
public class SMTPMailService {
```

This is our Singleton bean declaration. Of particular note is the TransactionAttribu teType.SUPPORTS value for @TransactionAttribute, which will apply to all business methods of this EJB.

An SMTP server is an external resource that is not transactionally aware. Therefore, we'll have to make note of any exceptions and ensure that if we want a transaction rolled back, we either explicitly tell that to the TransactionManager or throw an unchecked exception, which will signal the EJB container to mark any currently executing transaction for rollback.

We're making a general-purpose SMTP service here, so we may not always know the appropriate actions to take with regard to transactions. The default for EJB is @Trans actionAttributeType.MANDATORY, which creates a transaction if one is not already in flight. That's not really appropriate here: the SMTP server with which we interact is not transactional; it would be silly to sacrifice the overhead of starting a transaction when we're not even dealing with a resource that will respect its semantics! @TransactionAt tributeType.SUPPORTS, which we've used here, will accept existing transactions if one is in play, or do nothing if the service is invoked outside of a transactional context.

Now we need to define a method to do the dirty work: accept our MailMessage as a parameter and send it along to the SMTP server. The JavaMail API will act as our conduit to connect to the SMTP server, so we'll take advantage of Java EE's @Resource annotation to inject some relevant supporting services into our SMTPMailService.

With our service and class declaration handled, we're now ready to inject the external hooks we'll need to send email. The Java EE container will provide these for us:

```
@Resource(lookup = SMTPMailServiceConstants.JNDI_BIND_NAME_MAIL_SESSION)
private javax.mail.Session mailSession;

@Resource(lookup = "java:/ConnectionFactory")
private javax.jms.ConnectionFactory connectionFactory;

@Resource(lookup = SMTPMailServiceConstants.JNDI_BIND_NAME_SMTP_QUEUE)
private javax.jms.Queue smtpQueue;
```

The @Resource.lookup attribute has vendor-specific function but most often maps to a JNDI name. This use case has been coded to run specifically on the JBoss family of application servers, so some adjustment to these values may be necessary in your environment. To that end we've centralized some JNDI names in a small interface:

```
public interface SMTPMailServiceConstants {

    /**
     * Name in JNDI to which the SMTP {@link javax.mail.Session} will be bound
     */
    String JNDI_BIND_NAME_MAIL_SESSION = "java:jboss/mail/GeekSeekSMTP";

    /**
     * Name in JNDI to which the SMTP Queue is bound
     */
    String JNDI_BIND_NAME_SMTP_QUEUE = "java:/jms/queue/GeekSeekSMTP";
}
```

Note that we have put into place a field called smtpQueue, of type javax.jms.Queue. This is how we'll handle two of the "hidden" problems with testable development of sending email raised earlier.

First, sending a message to a JMS Queue is a "fire and forget" operation. Once the message is received by the queue (which is in process, unlike our production SMTP server), control is returned to the caller and the handling of the message is processed asynchronously. If we create a listener to pull messages off the queue and send emails, we won't have to wait for this process to complete. This gives us asynchrony for free.

The other tangible benefit to using a JMS Queue to send messages is in the guaranteed processing afforded by JMS. If there's a temporary error in sending the email, for instance a connection problem with the remote SMTP server, the messaging server will dutifully retry (as configured) a number of times. This process will even survive server restarts; if for some reason all of these retries fail to yield a successful result (again, after some configured number of tries or timeout), messages can be forwarded to the DLQ (dead-letter queue) for manual inspection by system administrators later. This gives us some assurance that we won't lose messages we intended to send, and we also won't have to fail our user registration process entirely if there's some issue with sending the welcome email.

In WildFly/JBoss AS7/JBoss EAP, we deploy a JMS Queue with the deployment descriptor *geekseek-smtp-queue-jms.xml* (the filename may be anything located in the EJB JAR's META-INF and ending with the suffix *-jms.xml*):

```xml
<?xml version="1.0" encoding="UTF-8"?>
<messaging-deployment xmlns="urn:jboss:messaging-deployment:1.0">
    <hornetq-server>
        <jms-destinations>
            <jms-queue name="GeekSeekSMTP">
                <entry name="jms/queue/GeekSeekSMTP"/>
            </jms-queue>
        </jms-destinations>
    </hornetq-server>
</messaging-deployment>
```

This will bind a new JMS Queue to the JNDI address *java:/jms/queue/GeekSeekSMTP*, which we referenced earlier in the @Resource.lookup attribute.

With our supporting services and resources hooked in and available to our EJB, we can code the sendMail method. As noted before, this is likely the least interesting part of the use case, even though it's technically the code that drives the entire feature:

```java
public void sendMail(final MailMessageBuilder.MailMessage mailMessage)
    throws IllegalArgumentException {

    // Precondition check
    if (mailMessage == null) {
        throw new IllegalArgumentException("Mail message must be specified");
    }

    try {
        // Translate
        final MimeMessage mime = new MimeMessage(mailSession);
        final Address from = new InternetAddress(mailMessage.from);
        final int numToAddresses = mailMessage.to.length;
        final Address[] to = new InternetAddress[numToAddresses];
        for (int i = 0; i < numToAddresses; i++) {
            to[i] = new InternetAddress(mailMessage.to[i]);
        }
        mime.setFrom(from);
        mime.setRecipients(Message.RecipientType.TO, to);
        mime.setSubject(mailMessage.subject);
        mime.setContent(mailMessage.body, mailMessage.contentType);
        Transport.send(mime);
    } // Puke on error
    catch (final javax.mail.MessagingException e) {
        throw new RuntimeException("Error in sending " + mailMessage, e);
    }
}
```

There's nothing special going on here: we translate our own value object MailMessage Builder.MailMessage into fields required by JavaMail's MimeMessage, and send. We'll wrap any errors in a RuntimeException to be handled by the EJB container (resulting in transaction rollback if one is being used).

This method, of course, is synchronous up until the mail message is delivered to the SMTP server. We noted earlier that it's likely better in a multiuser environment to queue the mail for sending such that we don't have to wait on interaction with this external resource, so we'll also supply a queueMailForDelivery method to send our desired message to a JMS Queue:

```
public void queueMailForDelivery(
    final MailMessageBuilder.MailMessage mailMessage)
        throws IllegalArgumentException {

    // Precondition check
    if (mailMessage == null) {
        throw new IllegalArgumentException("Mail message must be specified");
    }

    try {
        final Connection connection = connectionFactory.createConnection();
        final javax.jms.Session session = connection
          .createSession(false, javax.jms.Session.AUTO_ACKNOWLEDGE);
        final MessageProducer producer = session.createProducer(smtpQueue);
        final ObjectMessage jmsMessage =
            session.createObjectMessage(mailMessage);
        producer.send(jmsMessage);
    } catch (final JMSException jmse) {
        throw new RuntimeException(
            "Could not deliver mail message to the outgoing queue", jmse);
    }
}
```

Sending the JMS message doesn't fully get our mail delivered, however; it just sends it to a JMS Queue. We still need a component to pull this JMS message off the queue, unwrap the MailMessage it contains, and call upon our sendMail method to send the mail. For this we can again turn to EJB, which provides listeners to any JCA (Java Connector Architecture) backend by means of the *Message-Driven Bean* (MDB). Our MDB will be configured as a JMS Queue listener, and is defined as:

org.cedj.geekseek.service.smtp.SMTPMessageConsumer

```
@MessageDriven(activationConfig = {
        @ActivationConfigProperty(propertyName = "acknowledgeMode",
            propertyValue = "Auto-acknowledge"),
        @ActivationConfigProperty(propertyName = "destinationType",
            propertyValue = "javax.jms.Queue"),
        @ActivationConfigProperty(propertyName = "destination",
```

```
              propertyValue = SMTPMailServiceConstants.JNDI_BIND_NAME_SMTP_QUEUE)})
    public class SMTPMessageConsumer implements MessageListener {
```

The `ActivationConfigProperty` annotations are in place to tell the EJB container how to connect to the backing JCA resource, in this case our queue. Because MBDs are business components just like EJB Session Beans, we have injection at our disposal, which we'll use to obtain a reference back to the `SMTPMailService`:

```
@EJB
private SMTPMailService mailService;
```

Now, our `SMTPMessageConsumer` is registered by the EJB container as a listener on our queue; when a new message arrives, we'll receive a callback to the `onMessage` method. By implementing this, we can unwrap the `MailMessage` and send it directly to the `SMTPMailService` to be sent:

```
@Override
public void onMessage(final javax.jms.Message message) {

    // Casting and unwrapping
    final ObjectMessage objectMessage;
    try {
        objectMessage = ObjectMessage.class.cast(message);
    } catch (final ClassCastException cce) {
        throw new RuntimeException(
           "Incorrect message type sent to object message consumer; got:"
           + message.getClass().getSimpleName(), cce);
    }
    final MailMessageBuilder.MailMessage mailMessage;
    try {
        final Object obj = objectMessage.getObject();
        mailMessage = MailMessageBuilder.MailMessage.class.cast(obj);
    } catch (final JMSException jmse) {
        throw new RuntimeException("Could not unwrap JMS Message", jmse);
    } catch (final ClassCastException cce) {
        throw new RuntimeException("Expected message contents of type "
                + MailMessageBuilder.MailMessage.class.getSimpleName(), cce);
    }

    // Send the mail
    mailService.sendMail(mailMessage);
}
```

These comprise all the working pieces of the business logic supporting this feature. However, the true challenge lies in verifying that everything works as expected.

Requirement Test Scenarios

Testing the SMTP service will involve a few moving pieces.

A Test-Only SMTP Server

The JavaMail API nicely abstracts out connections to an SMTP server, and we've built our `SMTPMailService` to pull *any* configured JavaMail `Session` from JNDI. This gives us the option to provide a test-only SMTP server for use in development and staging environments with only configuration changes differing between these and the production setup. Although it's true that this text has generally discouraged the use of mock objects and services, that's a guideline. In this instance, we'll absolutely need a hook that differs from production in order to validate that emails are being delivered as expected. Otherwise, we'd be using a real SMTP service that could send emails out to real email addresses.

For our own testing, we'll aim not to change the code in our `SMTPMailService`, but to configure it to point to an embeddable SMTP server: one that will allow us to see which messages were received and do some assertion checking to be sure the contents are as expected. For this we look to the SubEtha project (*https://code.google.com/p/subetha/*), an open source Java SMTP server that fulfills our requirements nicely.

We'll let our SMTP server run in the same process as our application server and tests; this will allow us to use shared memory and set guards to handle the asynchrony implicit in dispatching messages to an SMTP server.

A nice technique is to install SubEtha to come up alongside our application. In Java EE, the mechanism for creating application-start events is to implement a `PostConstruct` callback on a Singleton Session EJB that's configured to eagerly load. We do this by defining a new service:

`org.cedj.geekseek.service.smtp.SMTPServerService`

```java
import javax.ejb.LocalBean;
import javax.ejb.Singleton;
import javax.ejb.Startup;
import javax.ejb.TransactionAttribute;

/**
 * Test fixture; installs an embedded SMTP Server on startup, shuts it down on
 * undeployment. Allows for pluggable handling of incoming messages for use in
 * testing.
 */
@Singleton
@Startup
@LocalBean
@TransactionAttribute(TransactionAttributeType.SUPPORTS)
public class SMTPServerService {
```

The `@Startup` annotation will trigger this EJB bean instance to be created alongside application start, which in turn will lead to the container invoking the `PostConstruct` method:

```
private SMTPServer server;
private final PluggableReceiveHandlerMessageListener listener =
  new PluggableReceiveHandlerMessageListener();

@javax.annotation.PostConstruct
public void startup() throws Exception {
  server = new SMTPServer(new SimpleMessageListenerAdapter(listener));
  server.setBindAddress(InetAddress.getLoopbackAddress());
  server.setPort(BIND_PORT);
  server.start();
}
```

This gives us an opportunity to create a new SMTPServer instance, register a handler (which defines what will be done when a new message is received), and start it on our configured port on localhost. The companion PreDestroy callback method provides for graceful shutdown of this server when the application is undeployed and the Singleton EJB instance is brought out of service:

```
@javax.annotation.PreDestroy
public void shutdown() throws Exception {
  server.stop();
}
```

In our test SMTPServerService, we also define an inner TestHandler interface; the simple type our tests can implement, containing one method called handle(String):

```
interface TestReceiveHandler {
    void handle(String data) throws AssertionFailedError;
}
```

The TestReceiveHandler will serve as our extension point for tests to apply behavior fitting their requirements. We do this via the setHandler(TestReceiveHandler) method on our test EJB:

```
public void setHandler(final TestReceiveHandler handler) {
    this.listener.setHandler(handler);
}
```

Pluggable handling in our SMTP server can then be set up on the fly by tests. When a new message is received by the SMTP server, our listener will read in the contents, log them for our convenience, then call upon our TestReceiveHandler:

```
private class PluggableReceiveHandlerMessageListener
    implements SimpleMessageListener {

    private TestReceiveHandler handler;

    @Override
    public boolean accept(String from, String recipient) {
        return true;
    }
```

```
    @Override
    public void deliver(final String from,
      final String recipient, final InputStream data)
      throws TooMuchDataException, IOException {

        // Get contents as String
        byte[] buffer = new byte[4096];
        int read;
        final StringBuilder s = new StringBuilder();
        while ((read = data.read(buffer)) != -1) {
            s.append(new String(buffer, 0, read, CHARSET));
        }
        final String contents = s.toString();
        if (log.isLoggable(Level.INFO)) {
            log.info("Received SMTP event: " + contents);
        }

        // Pluggable handling
        if (handler == null) {
            log.warning("No SMTP receive handler has been associated");
        } else {
            handler.handle(contents);
        }
    }
    void setHandler(final TestReceiveHandler handler) {
        this.handler = handler;
    }
}
```

The Test

Our test will again use Arquillian for the container interaction as we've seen before, but it will require no extra extensions. Therefore, the declaration here is fairly simple:

`org.cedj.geekseek.service.smtp.SMTPMailServiceTestCase`

```
@RunWith(Arquillian.class)
public class SMTPMailServiceTestCase {
```

Unlike in previous examples, this time we'll handle deployment and undeployment operations manually. This is because we'd first like to configure the server *before* deployment, but *after* it has started. Because Arquillian currently does not provide for a lifecycle operation between the server startup and deployment, we'll use ordered test methods to clearly delineate which actions should be handled when. This is what we'd like to see:

- Server start (handled automatically by Arquillian)
- Server configuration
- Deployment

- Test methods
- Undeployment
- Reset server configuration
- Server shutdown

We do manual deployment in Arquillian by associating a name with the deployment, then creating a @Deployment method just like we've seen before.

The following code is used to define the deployment:

```
/**
 * Name of the deployment for manual operations
 */
private static final String DEPLOYMENT_NAME = "mailService";

/**
 * Deployment to be tested; will be manually deployed/undeployed
 * such that we can configure the server first
 *
 * @return
 */
@Deployment(managed = false, name = DEPLOYMENT_NAME)
public static WebArchive getApplicationDeployment() {
    final File[] subethamailandDeps = Maven.resolver().
      loadPomFromFile("pom.xml").resolve("org.subethamail:subethasmtp")
      .withTransitivity().asFile();
    final WebArchive war = ShrinkWrap.create(WebArchive.class)
      .addAsLibraries(subethamailandDeps)
      .addClasses(SMTPMailService.class, MailMessageBuilder.class,
        SMTPMailServiceConstants.class,
        SMTPMessageConsumer.class, SMTPServerService.class)
      .addAsWebInfResource(EmptyAsset.INSTANCE, "beans.xml")
      .addAsWebInfResource("META-INF/geekseek-smtp-queue-jms.xml");
    System.out.println(war.toString(true));
    return war;
}
```

Of special note is the Deployment.managed attribute, which when set to false will tell Arquillian that we'll handle the act of deployment on our own. The preceding method constructs a deployment with the following layout:

```
/WEB-INF/
/WEB-INF/geekseek-smtp-queue-jms.xml
/WEB-INF/lib/
/WEB-INF/lib/subethasmtp-3.1.7.jar
/WEB-INF/lib/slf4j-api-1.6.1.jar
/WEB-INF/lib/activation-1.1.jar
/WEB-INF/lib/mail-1.4.4.jar
/WEB-INF/lib/jsr305-1.3.9.jar
/WEB-INF/beans.xml
```

```
/WEB-INF/classes/
/WEB-INF/classes/org/
/WEB-INF/classes/org/cedj/
/WEB-INF/classes/org/cedj/geekseek/
/WEB-INF/classes/org/cedj/geekseek/service/
/WEB-INF/classes/org/cedj/geekseek/service/smtp/
/WEB-INF/classes/org/cedj/geekseek/service/smtp/SMTPMessageConsumer.class
/WEB-INF/classes/org/cedj/geekseek/service/smtp/SMTPMailServiceConstants.class
/WEB-INF/classes/org/cedj/geekseek/service/smtp/SMTPMailService.class
/WEB-INF/classes/org/cedj/geekseek/service/smtp/SMTPServerService$1.class
/WEB-INF/classes/org/cedj/geekseek/service/smtp/
    MailMessageBuilder$MailMessage.class
/WEB-INF/classes/org/cedj/geekseek/service/smtp/
    SMTPServerService$TestReceiveHandler.class
/WEB-INF/classes/org/cedj/geekseek/service/smtp/SMTPServerService.class
/WEB-INF/classes/org/cedj/geekseek/service/smtp/
    SMTPServerService$PluggableReceiveHandlerMessageListener.class
/WEB-INF/classes/org/cedj/geekseek/service/smtp/MailMessageBuilder.class
```

As you can see, the SubEtha project and its dependencies are dutifully added to the *WEB-INF/lib* folder because we've requested ShrinkWrap Resolver to fetch these as configured from the project POM.

With the deployment accounted for, we can inject both the SMTPMailService EJB and our test SMTPServerService EJB into the test:

```
/**
 * Service which sends email to a backing SMTP Server
 */
@Inject
private SMTPMailService mailService;

/**
 * Hook into the embeddable SMTP server so we can customize its handling from
 * the tests
 */
@Inject
private SMTPServerService smtpServerService;
```

We can also inject a hook to manually deploy and undeploy our deployment, such that we can configure the server before our @Deployment is sent to the server. We do this with the @ArquillianResource annotation:

```
@ArquillianResource
private Deployer deployer;
```

At this point, Arquillian is set to run and start the server, and the deployment is defined but not yet deployed. Next on our agenda is to configure the server; we'll ensure this is done in the proper order by creating a test method to run first by using Arquillian's @InSequence annotation. Also, we don't want this test method running inside the container (as is the default), but rather on the client process, so we'll flag this method with @RunAsClient:

```
/*
 * Lifecycle events; implemented as tests, though in truth they perform no
 * assertions.  Used to configure the server and deploy/undeploy the @Deployment
 * archive at the appropriate times.
 */

@RunAsClient
@InSequence(value = 1)
@Test
public void configureAppServer() throws Exception {

    /*
     * First configure a JavaMail Session for the Server to bind into JNDI; this
     * will be used by our MailService EJB.  In a production environment, we'll
     * likely have configured the server before it was started to point to a real
     * SMTP server.
     */
    // Code omitted for brevity, not really relevant to
    // our objectives here

    /*
     * With the config all set and dependencies in place, now we can deploy
     */
    deployer.deploy(DEPLOYMENT_NAME);

}
```

Yes, the preceding code is technically implemented as a test method, and it'd be much cleaner to fully separate out our tests from our harness. Future versions of Arquillian may provide more fine-grained handling of lifecycle events to accommodate that kind of separation, but for the time being, this is our mechanism to configure running servers before issuing a deployment.

Now with server configuration completed and our application deployed, we're free to write our test logic.

The test is fairly simple from a conceptual standpoint, though the steps we've taken to achieve it have admittedly involved some more work. We'd like to:

- Construct a mail message
- Set a handler on the test SMTP service to ensure the email is in the proper form, then signal to the test that we're ready to proceed
- Send the email asynchronously
- Wait on the handler to let us know that the message was received and that we can now proceed

The test logic looks like this:

```java
@InSequence(value = 2)
@Test
public void testSmtpAsync() {

    // Set the body of the email to be sent
    final String body = "This is a test of the async SMTP Service";

    // Define a barrier for us to wait upon while email is sent through the
    // JMS Queue
    final CyclicBarrier barrier = new CyclicBarrier(2);

    // Set a handler which will ensure the body was received properly
    smtpServerService.setHandler(new SMTPServerService.TestReceiveHandler() {
        @Override
        public void handle(final String contents) throws
        AssertionFailedError {
            try {

                // Perform assertion
                Assert.assertTrue(
                    "message received does not contain body sent in email",
                    contents.contains(body));

                // Should probably be the second and last to arrive, but this
                // Thread can block indefinitely w/ no timeout needed.  If
                // the test waiting on the barrier times out, it'll trigger a
                // test failure and undeployment of the SMTP Service
                barrier.await();
            } catch (final InterruptedException e) {
                // Swallow, this would occur if undeployment were triggered
                // because the test failed (and we'd get a proper
                // AssertionFailureError on the client side)
            } catch (final BrokenBarrierException e) {
                throw new RuntimeException("Broken test setup", e);
            }
        }
    });

    // Construct and send the message async
    final MailMessageBuilder.MailMessage message =
            new MailMessageBuilder().from("alr@continuousdev.org")
            .addTo("alr@continuousdev.org")
                .subject("Test").body(body).contentType("text/plain")
                    .build();
    mailService.queueMailForDelivery(message);

    // Wait on the barrier until the message is received by the SMTP
    // server (pass) or the test times out (failure)
    try {
        barrier.await(5, TimeUnit.SECONDS);
    } catch (final InterruptedException e) {
```

```
        throw new RuntimeException("Broken test setup", e);
    } catch (final BrokenBarrierException e) {
        throw new RuntimeException("Broken test setup", e);
    } catch (final TimeoutException e) {
        // If the SMTP server hasn't processed the message in the allotted
        // time
        Assert.fail(
            "Test did not receive confirmation message in the allotted time");
    }
}
```

Walking through this, we see that first we define the subject of the email to be sent. Then we create a `java.util.concurrent.CyclicBarrier` initialized to a count of 2; this will be the mutual waiting point between the test and the SMTP server to coordinate that both parties have completed their actions and that control should not continue until each caller (`Thread`) has arrived at this waiting point.

The handler will perform our assertions to validate the message contents, then wait at the barrier until the test is done with its processing.

Meanwhile, the test will send the email via the `SMTPMailService`, then wait for the handler to receive the mail message and carry through the logic we put in place.

When both the test client and the handler arrive at the `CyclicBarrier` and no `Asser tionErrors` or other issues have cropped up, we know that we're free to proceed; the test method can continue its execution until invocation is complete and it reports a success.

Finally, we need to be sure to undeploy the archive (remember, we opted for manual deployment this time around) and reset the server's configuration. Again, we'll run this code in the client/test process:

```
@RunAsClient
@InSequence(value = 3)
@Test
public void resetAppServerConfig()
        throws Exception
{
    deployer.undeploy(DEPLOYMENT_NAME);

    // Server config code omitted for brevity,
    // not really relevant to our objectives here
}
```

This example serves to illustrate a common and often undertested aspect of enterprise development. Though the techniques we've applied here deal with external, non-transactional resources, asynchronous calling, and server configurations, this should serve as proof that even difficult cases can be adequately tested given a little thought and effort. It's our belief that this will pay dividends in avoiding production runtime errors and peace of mind in being armed with one more weapon in the battle to maintain a comprehensive, automated test suite.

CHAPTER 8

REST and Addressable Services

Rest and be thankful.

— Inscription at a rest stop along
Scotland's Highway A83

The concepts guiding the makeup of the modern Web could be considered a happy accident, or at least an implementation of ideas that had general applicability far beyond their initial design criteria. In the late 1980s we had the hardware and software necessary for networking; these were low-level tools for transmitting data from one computer to another. We even had some payload protocols and application layers available including IRC for chat, POP for email, and Usenet for general discussions. We were communicating, albeit over relatively constrained channels.

Out of necessity for his own research, Tim Berners-Lee of the European Organization for Nuclear Research (CERN) concocted a small recipe for publishing documents in a manner that would make his findings more accessible between departments and encourage updates over time. Called the "WorldWideWeb" (WWW), this project proposed a series of simple constructs (*http://bit.ly/1e8h4rh*):

Addressable resources
    A unique key or address assigned to each document

Hypertext
    A unidirectional pointer to an addressable resource

Browser
    A client program capable of reading hypertext-enabled documents

We take these concepts lightly now, but it's worthwhile considering the paradigm shift this evoked in the early 1990s; in only 10 years' time, most of the world's university students and many homes were connected to a Web that contained a marketing presence for an overwhelming majority of the Fortune 500. These ideas ushered innovation and communication at a rate never before seen in the history of mankind. This was instant, global publishing, and it was free.

Central to the makeup of the WWW was the introduction of the *Uniform Resource Identifier*, or URI. The URI defined by RFC 3986 (*http://bit.ly/1e8haPu*) forms the basis of an addressable resource, and has the following makeup:

```
scheme ":" hierarchical-part ["?" query] ["#" fragment]
```

Examples from the RFC include:

```
foo://example.com:8042/over/there?name=ferret#nose
```

and:

```
urn:example:animal:ferret:nose
```

In a short time, Berners-Lee introduced the first version of the *HyperText Markup Language* (HTML), aimed at providing a more concise vernacular for incorporating links into a common markup that browsers could format for viewing. The WWW was built as a mechanism for *document exchange*, sharing of published material over a commonly understood protocol and payload format (commonly HTML).

In 2000, University of California at Irvine's Roy Fielding published his dissertation "Architectural Styles and the Design of Network-based Software Architectures" (*http://bit.ly/1e8hbTD*), which expanded the notion of addressing documents to include *services* among the data exchanged on the Web, and defined a system of *REpresentational State Transfer* (REST). With his background in coauthoring RFC-2616 (*http://bit.ly/1e8he1T*), which defined the HTTP/1.1 protocol, Fielding was in a position of expertise to rethink how the principles of the Web might be applied to services.

By addressing services and applying a set of conventions to these URIs, we're able to compose a wide array of operations on services with the following key benefits:

- Loose coupling
- Interoperability
- Encapsulation
- Distributed programming
- Modularization

Clearly the study of REST is worthy of its own text, and we'll recommend *REST in Practice* by Webber, et al. (O'Reilly, 2010) to those looking to explore in greater depth.

REST is certainly not the first distributed architecture: *Remote Procedure Call* (RPC) variants have been used in various forms (i.e., SOAP, XML-RPC) for a long while. In recent years, the trend toward REST has been largely attributed to its ease of use and slim profile when coupled with the *HyperText Transfer Protocol* (HTTP), an established communication protocol providing for *methods*, *headers*, and *return status codes* that map well to the objectives of the caller. In practice, the success of the WWW is inherently linked to HTTP, though this is only one protocol (scheme) that can be applied to the general guidelines of the Web. Due to its widespread usage and versatility, we'll be employing HTTP throughout this chapter.

Because of its success, REST has become an abused buzzword in some circles. It's helpful for us to clarify the stages of compliance with a truly RESTful system, and a maturity model developed by Leonard Richardson (*http://www.crummy.com/self/*) presents four rungs of evolution. Martin Fowler aptly sums these up in a blog post (*http://bit.ly/1fh2AGt*), and we'll outline them here:

Stage 0   Using HTTP as a transport system for arbitrary payloads; typically used in plain RPC where a caller may wish to invoke upon a server over a network.

Stage 1   Addressable Resources; each domain object may be assigned to an address, and client requests contain all the necessary metadata needed to carry out the invocation.

Stage 2   HTTP Verbs; in addition to assigning each domain object or service an address, we use the conventions of the HTTP methods to differentiate between a "Create," "Update," "Delete," or other actions.

Stage 3   *HATEOAS*, or "Hypermedia As The Engine Of Application State"; a request upon a resource can return a list of links to the client in order to proceed to the next available actions. For instance, after "creating a user," the client may be given a success confirmation and shown links to "view the user," "edit the user," "view all users." Additionally, projects with Stage 3 maturity will utilize media types (content types) as part of content negotiation; an XML-based request should likely yield an XML-based response, while a JSON request might imply a JSON response. With media types set in the request, these can all take place using the same URI. Stage 3 is about *workflow* and *transition*; it guides the client through the stages of the application.

A RESTful system is always Stage 3, though this is an often-misunderstood and neglected understanding of the REST architecture, particularly for newcomers. In layman's terms, a Stage 3 exchange may sound a little like this:

Server
     You've just created an order. Do you want to pay? Do you want to add more items? Do you want to save your cart for later? Here are the links for each of these actions.

Client
     I'm following the link to save my cart, here is the request.

Server
     Your cart is saved. Do you want to continue shopping? Do you want to view your cart? Here are the links for these actions.

It's important to consider that REST is an *architectural style*, agnostic of any particular programming model or language. At its core, REST is most simply explained as an API for accessing services and domain objects over the Web.

As the Java community has come to understand the REST principles, it has provided a mapping layer between requests and backend services: *JAX-RS*.

REST in Enterprise Java: The JAX-RS Specification

The *Java API for RESTful Web Services*, or JAX-RS, is a specification under the direction of the Java Community Process, defined by JSR-339 (*http://bit.ly/1e8hjT0*) in its latest 2.0 version. Java EE6 incorprates the 1.1 revision, as defined by JSR-311 (*http://bit.ly/ 1e8hkXe*); this is the version we'll be covering here. From the specification document, its goals are to be/have:

POJO-based
   API will provide a set of annotations and associated classes/interfaces that may be used with POJOs in order to expose them as web resources. The specification will define object lifecycle and scope.

HTTP-centric
   The specification will assume HTTP is the underlying network protocol and will provide a clear mapping between HTTP and URI elements and the corresponding API classes and annotations. The API will provide high-level support for common HTTP usage patterns and will be sufficiently flexible to support a variety of HTTP applications, including WebDAV and the Atom Publishing Protocol.

Format independence
   The API will be applicable to a wide variety of HTTP entity body content types. It will provide the necessary pluggability to allow additional types to be added by an application in a standard manner.

Container independence
   Artifacts using the API will be deployable in a variety of web-tier containers. The specification will define how artifacts are deployed in a Servlet container and as a JAX-WS Provider.

Inclusion in Java EE
   The specification will define the environment for a web resource class hosted in a Java EE container and will specify how to use Java EE features and components within a web resource class.

Because it's not our aim to provide a comprehensive overview of JAX-RS, we recommend *RESTful Java with JAX-RS* by Bill Burke (O'Reilly, 2009), a member of the JSR-339 Expert Group and lead of the JBoss Community's RESTEasy implementation (*http://www.jboss.org/rest easy*). The second revision of the book (*http://oreil.ly/ restful_java_jax-rs_2_0*), covering the latest 2.0 version of the specification, is now on sale.

The JAX-RS Specification API (*http://jsr311.java.net/nonav/javadoc/*) provides a set of annotations helpful to developers seeking to map incoming HTTP-based requests to backend services. From the docs, these include:

Application Path	Identifies the application path that serves as the base URI for all resource URIs provided by Path.
Consumes	Defines the media types that the methods of a resource class or MessageBodyReader can accept.
CookieParam	Binds the value of an HTTP cookie to a resource method parameter, resource class field, or resource class bean property.
DefaultValue	Defines the default value of request metadata that is bound using one of the following annotations: PathParam, QueryParam, MatrixParam, CookieParam, FormParam, or HeaderParam.
DELETE	Indicates that the annotated method responds to HTTP DELETE requests.
Encoded	Disables automatic decoding of parameter values bound using QueryParam, PathParam, FormParam, or MatrixParam.
FormParam	Binds the value(s) of a form parameter contained within a request entity body to a resource method parameter.
GET	Indicates that the annotated method responds to HTTP GET requests.
HEAD	Indicates that the annotated method responds to HTTP HEAD requests.
HeaderParam	Binds the value(s) of an HTTP header to a resource method parameter, resource class field, or resource class bean property.
HttpMethod	Associates the name of an HTTP method with an annotation.
MatrixParam	Binds the value(s) of a URI matrix parameter to a resource method parameter, resource class field, or resource class bean property.
OPTIONS	Indicates that the annotated method responds to HTTP OPTIONS requests.
Path	Identifies the URI path that a resource class or class method will serve requests for.
PathParam	Binds the value of a URI template parameter or a path segment containing the template parameter to a resource method parameter, resource class field, or resource class bean property.
POST	Indicates that the annotated method responds to HTTP POST requests.
Produces	Defines the media type(s) that the methods of a resource class or MessageBodyWriter can produce.
PUT	Indicates that the annotated method responds to HTTP PUT requests.
QueryParam	Binds the value(s) of an HTTP query parameter to a resource method parameter, resource class field, or resource class bean property.

These can be composed together to define the mapping between a business object's methods and the requests it will service, as shown in the API documentation:

```
@Path("widgets/{widgetid}")
@Consumes("application/widgets+xml")
@Produces("application/widgets+xml")
public class WidgetResource {

    @GET
    public String getWidget(@PathParam("widgetid") String id) {
        return getWidgetAsXml(id);
    }

    @PUT
    public void updateWidget(@PathParam("widgetid") String id,Source update) {
        updateWidgetFromXml(id, update);
    }
    ...
}
```

This defines an example of a business object that will receive requests to $application Root/widgets/$widgetid, where $widgetid is the identifier of the domain object to be acted upon. HTTP GET requests will be serviced by the getWidget method, which will receive the $widgetid as a method parameter; HTTP PUT requests will be handled by the updateWidget method. The class-level @Consumes and @Produces annotations designate that all business methods of the class will expect and return a media type (content type) of application/widgets+xml.

Because the specification supplies only a contract by which JAX-RS implementations must behave, the runtime will vary between application server vendors. For instance, the Reference Implementation, Jersey (*http://jersey.java.net/*), can be found in the GlassFish Application Server (*http://glassfish.java.net/*), while WildFly (*http://www.wildfly.org/*) from the JBoss Community uses RESTEasy (*http://www.jboss.org/resteasy*).

Use Cases and Requirements

Thus far, we've visited and described the internal mechanisms with which we interact with data. Now we're able to work on building an API for clients to access the domain state in a self-describing fashion, and RESTful design coupled with JAX-RS affords us the tools to expose our application's capabilities in a commonly understood way.

We'd like to encourage third-party integrators—clients about whom we may not have any up-front knowledge—to view, update, and create domain objects within the Geek-Seek application. Therefore, our use case requirements will be simply summed up as the following:

- As a third-party integrator, I should be able to perform CRUD operations upon:
  — A Conference
  — Sessions within Conferences
  — Attachments within Sessions
  — Attachments within Conferences
  — A Venue (and associate with a Conference and/or Session)

Additionally, we want to lay out a map of the application as the client navigates through state changes. For instance, at the root, a client should know what operations it's capable of performing. Once that operation is complete, a series of possible next steps should be made available to the client such that it may continue execution. This guide is known as the *Domain Application Protocol* (DAP), and it acts as a slimming agent atop the wide array of possible HTTP operations in order to show the valid business processes that are available to a client as it progresses through the application's various state changes. It's this DAP layer that grants us the final HATEOAS step of the Richardson Maturity Model. Our DAP will define a series of addressable resources coupled with valid HTTP methods and media types to determine what actions are taken, and what links are to come next in the business process:

- / application/vnd.ced+xml;type=root
  — GET → Links
  — Link → conference application/vnd.ced+xml;type=conference
  — Link → venue application/vnd.ced+xml;type=venue
- /conference application/vnd.ced+xml;type=conference
  — GET → List
  — POST → Add
- /conference/[c_id] application/vnd.ced+xml;type=conference
  — GET → Single
  — PUT → Update
  — DELETE → Remove
  — Link → session application/vnd.ced+xml;type=session
  — Link → venue application/vnd.ced+xml;type=venue
  — Link → attachments application/vnd.ced+xml;type=attachment
- /conference/[c_id]/session application/vnd.ced+xml;type=session
  — GET → List

— POST → Add

- /conference/[c_id/session/[s_id]   application/vnd.ced+xml;type=session

    — GET → Single

    — PUT → Update

    — DELETE → Remove

    — Link → venue application/vnd.ced+xml;type=room

    — Link → attachments application/vnd.ced+xml;type=attachment

    — Link → parent application/vnd.ced+xml;type=conference

- /venue application/vnd.ced+xml;type=venue

    — GET → List

    — POST → Add

- /venue/[v_id] application/vnd.ced+xml;type=venue

    — GET → Single

    — PUT → Update

    — DELETE → Remove

    — Link → room application/vnd.ced+xml;type=room

- /venue/[v_id]/room application/vnd.ced+xml;type=room

    — GET → List

    — POST → Add

    — Link → attachments application/vnd.ced+xml;type=attachment

- /venue/[v_id]/room/[r_id] application/vnd.ced+xml;type=room

    — GET → Single

    — PUT → Update

    — DELETE → Remove

    — Link → attachments application/vnd.ced+xml;type=attachment

- /attachment application/vnd.ced+xml;type=attachment

    — GET → List

    — POST → Add

- /attachment/[a_id] application/vnd.ced+xml;type=attachment

    — GET → List

— POST → Add

The preceding DAP can be conceptually understood as a site map for services, and it defines the API for users of the system. By designing to the DAP, we provide clients with a robust mechanism by which the details of attaining each resource or invoking the application's services can be read as the client navigates from state to state.

Implementation

With our requirements defined, we're free to start implementation. Remember that our primary goal here is to create HTTP endpoints at the locations defined by our DAP, and we want to ensure that they perform the appropriate action and return the contracted response. By using JAX-RS we'll be making business objects and defining the mapping between the path, query parameters, and media types of the request before taking action and supplying the correct response.

The first step is to let the container know that we have a JAX-RS component in our application; we do this by defining a `javax.ws.rs.ApplicationPath` annotation atop a subclass of `javax.ws.rs.core.Application`. Here we provide this in `org.geek seek.rest.GeekSeekApplication`:

```
import javax.ws.rs.ApplicationPath;
import javax.ws.rs.core.Application;

@ApplicationPath("api")
public class GeekSeekApplication extends Application {

}
```

This will be picked up by the container and signal that requests to paths under the `$applicationRoot/api` pattern will be serviced by JAX-RS.

Repository Resources

Looking over our requirements, we see that all paths in our DAP are capable of performing CRUD operations. Therefore, it makes sense for us to define a base upon which individual resources can build, while giving persistence capabilities to create, read, update, and delete. In GeekSeek, we'll handle this by making a generic `RepositoryRe source` base to give us a hook into the `Repository` abstractions detailed in Chapter 5. Let's walk through `org.cedj.geekseek.web.rest.core.RepositoryResource`:

```
public abstract class RepositoryResource<
  DOMAIN extends Identifiable&Timestampable,
  REP extends Representation<DOMAIN>>
    implements Resource {
```

Simple enough; an abstract class notes we'll be extending this later for more specific resources that interact with a `Respository`. Let's define the base media types our application will be using. Remember, media types are a key part of the maturity model in handling the types of responses to be returned, given the input from the request. For example, a JSON request should yield a JSON response in our known format:

```
protected static final String BASE_XML_MEDIA_TYPE = "application/vnd.ced+xml";
protected static final String BASE_JSON_MEDIA_TYPE = "application/vnd.ced+json";
```

Next up, some fields that will be set later by subclasses; this composes our abstraction point, which will need specialization later:

```
private Class<? extends Resource> resourceClass;
private Class<DOMAIN> domainClass;
private Class<REP> representationClass;
```

We'll also use some instance members to be injected by either the CDI (`@Inject`) or JAX-RS (`@Context`) containers:

```
@Context
private UriInfo uriInfo;

@Context
private HttpHeaders headers;

@Inject
private Repository<DOMAIN> repository;

@Inject
private RepresentationConverter<REP, DOMAIN> converter;
```

The `@Context` annotation will help us gain access to the context of the request in flight: information about the URI or HTTP headers. The `Repository` is how we'll access the persistence layer, and the `RepresentationConverter` will be responsible for mapping between the client payload and our own entity object model.

Now let's make sure that subclasses set our extension fields properly:

```
public RepositoryResource(Class<? extends Resource> resourceClass,
    Class<DOMAIN> domainClass,
    Class<REP> representationClass) {
        this.resourceClass = resourceClass;
        this.domainClass = domainClass;
        this.representationClass = representationClass;
    }
```

That should do it for the fields needed by our `RepositoryResource`. Time to do something interesting; we want to map HTTP `POST` requests of our JSON and XML media types defined earlier to create a new entity. With a couple of annotations and a few lines of logic in a business method, JAX-RS can handle that for us:

```
@POST
@Consumes({ BASE_JSON_MEDIA_TYPE, BASE_XML_MEDIA_TYPE })
public Response create(REP representation) {
    DOMAIN entity = getConverter().to(
      uriInfo, representation);
    getRepository().store(entity);
    return Response.created(
      UriBuilder.fromResource(
        getResourceClass())
          .segment("{id}")
          .build(entity.getId())).build();
}
```

The @POST annotation defines that this method will service HTTP POST requests, and the @Consumes annotation designates the valid media types. The JAX-RS container will then map requests meeting those criteria to this create method, passing along the Representation of our Domain object. From there we can get a hook to the Repository, store the entity, and issue an HTTP Response to the client. Of importance is that we let the client know the ID of the entity that was created as part of the response; in this case, the ID is the URI to the newly created resource, which may take a form similar to Response: 201 Location: resource-uri.

We'll handle the other CRUD operations in similar fashion:

```
@DELETE
@Path("/{id}")
public Response delete(@PathParam("id") String id) {
    DOMAIN entity = getRepository().get(id);
    if (entity == null) {
        return Response.status(Status.NOT_FOUND).build();
    }
    getRepository().remove(entity);
    return Response.noContent().build();
}

@GET
@Path("/{id}")
@Produces({ BASE_JSON_MEDIA_TYPE, BASE_XML_MEDIA_TYPE })
public Response get(@PathParam("id") String id) {
    DOMAIN entity = getRepository().get(id);
    if (entity == null) {
        return Response.status(Status.NOT_FOUND).type(
            getMediaType()).build();
    }

    return Response.ok(
      getConverter().from(uriInfo, entity))
          .type(getMediaType())
          .lastModified(entity.getLastModified())
          .build();
}
```

```
@PUT
@Path("/{id}")
@Consumes({ BASE_JSON_MEDIA_TYPE, BASE_XML_MEDIA_TYPE })
public Response update(@PathParam("id") String id,
    REP representation) {
    DOMAIN entity = getRepository().get(id);
    if (entity == null) {
        return Response.status(Status.BAD_REQUEST)
           .build();
    }

    getConverter().update(
        uriInfo, representation, entity);
    getRepository().store(entity);

    return Response.noContent().build();
}
```

Note that for GET, PUT, and DELETE operations we must know which entity to work with, so we use the @Path annotation to define a path parameter as part of the request, and pass this along as a PathParam to the method when it's invoked. We also are sure to use the correct HTTP response codes when the situation warrants:

- OK(200) on GET of an entity
- NotFound(404) on GET of an entity with an ID that does not exist
- Created(201) with Header: "Location $resourceUri" on successful POST and creation of a new entity
- NoContent(204) on DELETE or successful update
- BadRequest(400) on attemped PUT of a missing resource

With this base class in place, we have effectively made a nice mapping between the DAP API as part of our requirements and the backend Repository and JPA. Incoming client requests are mapped to business methods, which in turn delegate the appropriate action to the persistence layer and supply a response.

Let's have a look at a concrete implementation of the RepositoryResource, one that handles interaction with User domain objects. We've aptly named this the org.cedj. geekseek.web.rest.user.UserResource:

```
@ResourceModel
@Path("/user")
public class UserResource
    extends RepositoryResource<User, UserRepresentation> {

    private static final String USER_XML_MEDIA_TYPE =
        BASE_XML_MEDIA_TYPE + "; type=user";
```

```
    private static final String USER_JSON_MEDIA_TYPE =
        BASE_JSON_MEDIA_TYPE + "; type=user";

    public UserResource() {
        super(UserResource.class, User.class, UserRepresentation.class);
    }

    @Override
    public String getResourceMediaType() {
        return USER_XML_MEDIA_TYPE;
    }

    @Override
    protected String[] getMediaTypes() {
        return new String[]{USER_XML_MEDIA_TYPE, USER_JSON_MEDIA_TYPE};
    }
}
```

Because we inherit all the support to interact with JPA from the parent `RepositoryRe`
`source`, this class needs to do little more than:

- Note that we are an `@ResourceModel`, a custom type that is a CDI `@Stereotype` to
  add interceptors. We explain this in greater depth in "The @ResourceModel" on
  page 163.
- Define a path for the resource, in this case, "/user" under the JAX-RS application
  root.
- Supply the custom media types for user representations.
- Set the resource type, the domain object type, and the representation type in the
  constructor.

Now we can handle CRUD operations for `User` domain objects; similar implementations
to this are also in place for `Conference`, `Session`, etc.

The Representation Converter

We've seen that the underlying domain model implemented in JPA is not the same as
the REST model we're exposing to clients. Although EE allows us to annotate JPA models
with JAX-B bindings etc., we likely would like to keep the two models separate because
the REST model may:

- Contain less data
- Combine JPA models into one unified view
- Link resources
- Render itself in multiple different representations and formats

Additionally, some resources act as proxies and have no representation on their own. To allow these resources to operate in a modular fashion, we need a way to describe conversion—for example, the relation resource links users to a conference (attendees, speakers). The relation itself knows nothing about the source or target types, but it knows how to get a converter that supports converting between these types. To handle this, we supply the org.cedj.geekseek.web.rest.core.RepresentationConverter:

```
public interface RepresentationConverter<REST, SOURCE> {

    Class<REST> getRepresentationClass();

    Class<SOURCE> getSourceClass();

    REST from(UriInfo uriInfo, SOURCE source);

    Collection<REST> from(UriInfo uriInfo, Collection<SOURCE> sources);

    SOURCE to(UriInfo uriInfo, REST representation);

    SOURCE update(UriInfo uriInfo, REST representation, SOURCE target);

    Collection<SOURCE> to(UriInfo uriInfo, Collection<REST> representations);
```

Inside the preceding interface is also a base implementation to handle the conversion, RepresentationConverter.Base:

```
public abstract static class Base<REST, SOURCE>
        implements RepresentationConverter<REST, SOURCE> {

    private Class<REST> representationClass;
    private Class<SOURCE> sourceClass;

    protected Base() {}

    public Base(Class<REST> representationClass,
        Class<SOURCE> sourceClass) {
        this.representationClass = representationClass;
        this.sourceClass = sourceClass;
    }

    @Override
    public Collection<REST> from(UriInfo uriInfo,
        Collection<SOURCE> ins) {
        Collection<REST> out = new ArrayList<REST>();
        for(SOURCE in : ins) {
            out.add(from(uriInfo, in));
        }
        return out;
    }

    @Override
    public Collection<SOURCE> to(UriInfo uriInfo,
```

```
            Collection<REST> ins) {
            Collection<SOURCE> out = new ArrayList<SOURCE>();
            for(REST in : ins) {
                out.add(to(uriInfo, in));
            }
                return out;
        }


        ...

    }
```

CDI will dutifully inject the appropriate instance of this converter where required; for instance, in this field of the `org.cedj.geekseek.web.rest.conference.Conference Resource`:

```
@Inject
private RepresentationConverter<SessionRepresentation,
    Session> sessionConverter;
```

Through these converters we can easily delegate the messy business of parsing the media-type payload formats to and from our own internal domain objects.

The @ResourceModel

Because JAX-RS 1.x does not define an interceptor model, we need to apply these on our own to activate cross-cutting concerns such as security, validation, and resource linking to our JAX-RS endpoints. This is easily enough accomplished using the stereotype feature of CDI, where we can create our own annotation type (which itself has annotations): wherever our custom type is applied, the metadata we specify upon the stereotype will propagate. So we can create an annotation to apply all of the features we'd like upon a `RepositoryResource`, and we call it `org.cedj.geekseek.web.rest. core.annotation.ResourceModel`:

```
@REST
@RequestScoped
@Stereotype
@Retention(RetentionPolicy.RUNTIME)
@Target(ElementType.TYPE)
public @interface ResourceModel {

}
```

By placing this `@ResourceModel` annotation atop, for instance, `UserResource` as we've done here, this JAX-RS resource will now be marked as `@REST` via the CDI `@Stereo type`. This is a nice shortcut provided by CDI to compose behaviors together in one definition.

The `@org.cedj.geekseek.web.rest.core.annotation.REST` annotation is defined as a CDI `@InterceptorBinding`:

```
@InterceptorBinding
@Retention(RetentionPolicy.RUNTIME)
@Target(ElementType.TYPE)
public @interface REST {

}
```

To avoid having to define the entire interceptor chain for the REST layer in piecemeal fashion for each module that wants to use it, we create only one CDI Interceptor and define our own chain using pure CDI beans, which is handled in org.cedj.geek seek.web.rest.core.interceptor.RESTInterceptorEnabler:

```
@REST
@Interceptor
public class RESTInterceptorEnabler {

    @Inject
    private Instance<RESTInterceptor> instances;

    @AroundInvoke
    public Object intercept(final InvocationContext context) throws Exception {
        final List<RESTInterceptor> interceptors = sort(instances);
        InvocationContext wraped = new InvocationContext() {
            // Omitted for brevity
        }
        return wraped.proceed();
    }

    ...
}
```

Marking the RESTInterceptorEnabler with @REST and @Interceptor binds the RESTI nterceptorEnabler to the use of the @REST annotation; then we can inject all valid RESTInterceptor instances and invoke them according to a sorted order in the intercept method annotated with @AroundInvoke. With our custom chain, we can rely on CDI to provide an Instance<X> of our desired custom interceptor type dynamically based on what is deployed rather then what is configured.

In practice, this means that our SecurityInterceptor, LinkedInterceptor, and Vali datedInterceptor (our implementations of type RESTInterceptor) will all be invoked for business methods on classes marked @ResourceModel.

LinkableRepresentation

As you may have noticed from our DAP, we have a series of paths that accept a source media type and return another media type representing the data in question. These are modeled by our org.cedj.geekseek.web.rest.core.Representation:

```
public interface Representation<X> {

    Class<X> getSourceType();

    String getRepresentationType();
}
```

Some paths are linkable; they contain pointers to resources that aren't in the domain model itself. For example, a `Session` in a `Conference` is in the `Conference` domain, because a `Conference` contains N `Session` entities. A `Conference` may have a tracker (`User`), someone "following" the `Conference` for updates; this further links into the `User` domain via a `Relation` domain. Although each domain entity is separate, once we start to draw relationships between them, it's helpful to consider a mechanism to link together these bonds.

So while domain model links are handled directly by JPA, the `Representation`, and a `RepresentationConverter` into the target formats, the relationships need to be addressed slightly differently.

For this we can introduce the notion of a `org.cedj.geekseek.web.rest.core.LinkableRepresentation`; a `Representation` type capable of coupling a source type with a series of links:

```
public abstract class LinkableRepresentation<X>
  implements Representation<X> {

    private List<ResourceLink> links;
    private Class<X> sourceType;
    private String representationType;
    private UriInfo uriInfo;

    protected LinkableRepresentation() {}

    public LinkableRepresentation(Class<X> sourceType,
      String representationType, UriInfo uriInfo) {
        this.sourceType = sourceType;
        this.representationType = representationType;
        this.uriInfo = uriInfo;
    }

    @XmlElement(name = "link", namespace = "urn:ced:link")
    public List<ResourceLink> getLinks() {
        if (this.links == null) {
            this.links = new ArrayList<ResourceLink>();
        }
        return links;
    }

    public void addLink(ResourceLink link) {
        getLinks().add(link);
```

```
    }

    public boolean doesNotContainRel(String rel) {
        return !containRel(rel);
    }

    public boolean containRel(String rel) {
        if(links == null || links.size() == 0) {
            return false;
        }
        for(ResourceLink link : links) {
            if(rel.equals(link.getRel())) {
                return true;
            }
        }
        return false;
    }

    @Override @XmlTransient
    public Class<X> getSourceType() {
        return sourceType;
    }

    @Override @XmlTransient
    public String getRepresentationType() {
        return representationType;
    }

    @XmlTransient
    public UriInfo getUriInfo() {
        return uriInfo;
    }
}
```

In "The @ResourceModel" on page 163, we see that our @ResourceModel stereotype is marked with @REST. This implies that we'll apply an interceptor called org.cedj.geek seek.web.rest.core.interceptor.LinkedInterceptor to anything with this annotation. LinkedInterceptor has the responsibility of determining if the invocation has a linkable representation, and if so, link all of the LinkableRepresentation views together, as demonstrated in the preceding code sample. Anything with the @REST annotation will run this interceptor.

The reasoning behind this approach is: some Representation objects are linkable. Via the @ResourceModel (which contains @REST), a link provider can link a given resource to some other resource. This way, we can draw relationships between resources (entities) that are not described by JPA. The interceptor is implemented like so:

```
public class LinkedInterceptor implements RESTInterceptor {

    @Inject
```

```
    private Instance<LinkProvider> linkProviers;

    @Override
    public int getPriority() {
        return -10;
    }

    @Override
    public Object invoke(InvocationContext ic) throws Exception {
        Object obj = ic.proceed();
        if(hasLinkableRepresentations(obj)) {
            linkAllRepresentations(obj);
        }
        return obj;
    }

    private boolean hasLinkableRepresentations(Object obj) {
        return locateLinkableRepresentations(obj) != null;
    }

    private LinkableRepresentation<?> locateLinkableRepresentations(
        Object obj) {
        if(obj instanceof Response) {
            Object entity = ((Response)obj).getEntity();
            if(entity instanceof LinkableRepresentation) {
                return (LinkableRepresentation<?>)entity;
            }
        }
        return null;
    }

    private void linkAllRepresentations(Object obj) {
        LinkableRepresentation<?> linkable = locateLinkableRepresentations(obj);
        for(LinkProvider linker : linkProviers) {
            linker.appendLinks(linkable);
        }
    }
}
```

ResourceLink

Recall from our DAP that many requests are to return a link to other resources as the client makes its way through state changes in the application. A link is really a value object to encapsulate a media type, href (link), and relation. We provide this in org.cedj.geekseek.web.rest.core.ResourceLink:

```
public class ResourceLink {

    private String rel;
    private URI href;
    private String type;
```

```java
    public ResourceLink(String rel, URI href, String media) {
        this.rel = rel;
        this.href = href;
        this.type = media;
    }

    @XmlAttribute
    public String getHref() {
        if (href == null) {
            return null;
        }
        return href.toASCIIString();
    }

    @XmlAttribute
    public String getRel() {
        return rel;
    }

    @XmlAttribute
    public String getMediaType() {
        return type;
    }

    public void setHref(String href) {
        this.href = URI.create(href);
    }

    public void setRel(String rel) {
        this.rel = rel;
    }

    public void setType(String type) {
        this.type = type;
    }
}
```

LinkableRepresentation will use this value object in particular to handle its linking
strategy between disparate entities that are not related in the JPA model.

Requirement Test Scenarios

With our implementation in place, leveraging JAX-RS to map our DAP to business
methods, we're set to test our endpoints. The core areas we want to assert are the expected
responses from requests to:

- PUT data
- GET data

- POST data
- DELETE data
- Obtain the appropriate links

A Black-Box Test

The general flow of our first test will be to model a user's actions as she navigates through the site. To accomplish execution of the test methods in sequence, we'll use Arquillian's `@InSequence` annotation to signal the order of test execution. This will really position the test class as more of a "test scenario," with each test method acting as the separate tests that must maintain a proper order. In this fashion, we will follow the normal REST client flow from point A to B to C and so on. We're going to execute requests to:

- GET the Root resource
- Locate the `Conference` link
- POST to create a new `Conference`
- GET to read the created `Conference`
- Locate the `Session` link
- POST to create a new `Session`
- GET to read the created `Session`
- PUT to update the `Session`
- DELETE to delete the `Session`
- PUT to update the `Conference`
- DELETE to delete the `Conference`

This will be a pure client-side test; it requires *something* deployed that will talk to the REST APIs. We have provided this logic in `org.cedj.geekseek.web.rest.confer` `ence.test.integration.story.CreateConferenceAndSessionStory`:

```
@RunWith(Arquillian.class)
public class CreateConferenceAndSessionStory {

    private static String uri_conference = null;
    private static String uri_conferenceInstance = null;
    private static String uri_session = null;
    private static String uri_sessionInstance = null;

    @ArquillianResource
    private URL base;
```

```
@BeforeClass
public static void setup() {
    RestAssured.filters(
            ResponseLoggingFilter.responseLogger(),
            new RequestLoggingFilter());
}
```

The @RunWith annotation should be familiar by now; Arquillian will be handling the
test lifecycle for us. As noted previously, it's good practice to allow Arquillian to inject
the base URL of the application by using @ArquillianResource. And because we're not
bound to any frameworks in particular, we can also use the REST-assured project
(*https://code.google.com/p/rest-assured/*) to provide a clean DSL to validate our REST
services.

Notably missing from this declaration is the @Deployment method, which we supply in
CreateConferenceAndSessionStoryTestCase so we can decouple the test scenario
from the test deployment logic; this encourages re-use for running the same tests with
different deployments, so we can further integrate other layers later. The deployment
method for our purposes here looks like this:

```
@Deployment(testable = false)
public static WebArchive deploy() {
    return ConferenceRestDeployments.conference()
      .addAsWebInfResource(new File("src/main/resources/META-INF/beans.xml"));
}
```

Because this is a black-box test, we set `testable` to `false` to tell Arquillian not to equip
the deployment with any additional test runners; we don't want to test in-container here,
but rather run requests from the outside of the server and analyze the response. The
test should verify a behavior, not any internal details. We could likely write a test where
we employ sharing of objects, and this might be easier to code and update, but it could
also sneak in unexpected client changes that should have been caught by the tests. We're
interested only in testing the contract between the client and the server, which is specified by our DAP. Thus, black-box testing is an appropriate solution in this case.

In this deployment, we'll also use "fake" implementations for the Repository/JPA layer;
these are provided by the `TestConferenceRepository` and `TestSessionRepository`
test classes, which simulate the JPA layer for testing purposes. We won't be hitting the
database for the tests at this level of integration. Later on, when we fully integrate the
application, we'll bring JPA back into the picture:

```
@ApplicationScoped
public abstract class TestRepository<T extends Identifiable>
    implements Repository<T> { .. }

public class TestConferenceRepository extends
  TestRepository<Conference> { .. }
```

On to the tests:

```
// Story: As a 3rd party Integrator I should be able to locate
// the Conference root Resource
@Test @InSequence(0)
public void shouldBeAbleToLocateConferenceRoot() throws Exception {
        //uri_conference = new URL(base, "api/conference").toExternalForm();
        uri_conference =
                given().
                then().
                    contentType(BASE_MEDIA_TYPE).
                    statusCode(Status.OK.getStatusCode()).
                    root("root").
                        body(
                            "link.find {it.@rel == 'conference'}.size()",
                            equalTo(1)).
                when().
                    get(new URL(base, "api/").toExternalForm()).
                body().
                    path("root.link.find {it.@rel == 'conference'}.@href");
    }
```

Our first test is charged with locating the conference root at the base URL + "api" (as we configured the path using the @ApplicationPath annotation in our application). We set the media type and expect to have our links for the conference returned to the client matching the @Path annotation we have sitting atop our ConferenceResource class (baseURL + "api" + "conference"). The @InSequence annotation set to a value of 0 will ensure that this test is run first.

Assuming that's successful, we can move on to our next test, creating a conference:

```
// Story: As a 3rd party Integrator I should be able to create a Conference
@Test @InSequence(1)
public void shouldBeAbleToCreateConference() throws Exception { .. }
...
```

The rest of the test class contains test logic to fulfill our test requirements.

Validating the HTTP Contracts with Warp

We've ensured that the responses from the server are in expected form. We'd additionally like to certify that our service is obeying the general contracts of HTTP. Because by definition this will involve a lot of client-side requests and parsing of server responses, it'll be helpful for us to avoid writing a lot of custom code to negotiate the mapping. For these tasks, we introduce an extension to Arquillian that is aimed at making this type of testing easier.

Arquillian Warp

Arquillian Warp fills the void between client- and server-side testing.

Using Warp, we can initiate an HTTP request using a client-side testing tool such as WebDriver and, in the same request cycle, execute in-container server-side tests. This powerful combination lets us cover integration across client and server.

Warp effectively removes the need for mocking and opens new possibilities for debugging. It also allows us to know as little or as much of the application under test as we want.

Gray-box testing

Initially, Warp can be used from any black-box testing tool (like HttpClient, REST client, Selenium WebDriver, etc.). But it allows us to hook into the server request lifecycle and verify what happens inside the box (referred to as white-box testing). Thus, we identify Warp as a hybrid "gray-box" testing framework.

Integration testing

No matter the granularity of our tests, Warp fits the best integration level of testing with an overlap to functional testing. We can either test components, application API, or functional behavior.

Technology independence

Whatever client-side tools we use for emitting an HTTP request, Warp allows us to assert and verify logic on the most appropriate place of client-server request lifecycle.

Use cases

Warp can:

- Send a payload to a server
- Verify an incoming request
- Assert the state of a server context
- Verify that a given event was fired during request processing
- Verify a completed response
- Send a payload to a client

Deploying Warp

Thanks to an ability to bring an arbitrary payload to a server and hook into server lifecycles, we can use Warp in partially implemented projects. We do not require the database layer to be implemented in order to test UI logic. This is especially useful for projects based on loosely coupled components (e.g., CDI).

Supported tools and frameworks

Cross-protocol. Warp currently supports only the HTTP protocol, but conceptually it can be used with any protocol where we are able to intercept client-to-server communication on both the client and the server.

Client-side testing tools. Warp supports any client-side tools if you are using them in a way that requests can be intercepted (in the case of an HTTP protocol, you need to communicate through a proxy instead of direct communication with a server).

Examples of such libraries/frameworks include:

- `URL#openStream()`
- Apache HTTP Client
- Selenium WebDriver

 To use Warp, you should inject an `@ArquillianResource` URL into the test case, which points to the proxy automatically.

Frameworks

Warp currently focuses on frameworks based on the Servlets API, but it provides special hooks and additional support for:

- JSF
- JAX-RS (REST)
- Spring MVC

For more information about Warp, visit *http://arquillian.org/*.

Test Harness Setup

We'll start by enabling the Arquillian Warp in the POM's `dependencyManagement` section:

```
<dependency>
    <groupId>org.jboss.arquillian.extension</groupId>
    <artifactId>arquillian-warp-bom</artifactId>
    <version>${version.arquillian_warp}</version>
    <scope>import</scope>
```

```
            <type>pom</type>
    </dependency>
```

This will lock down the versions correctly such that all Warp modules are of the expected version. A `dependency` declaration in the `dependencies` section will make Warp available for our use:

```
<dependency>
    <groupId>org.jboss.arquillian.extension</groupId>
    <artifactId>arquillian-warp-impl</artifactId>
    <scope>test</scope>
</dependency>
```

The HTTP Contracts Test

Now we'd like to test details of the REST service behavior; we'll use Warp to allow easy control over permutations of data. Again, we'll be swapping out alternate `Repository` implementations to bypass JPA and real peristence; we're just interested in the HTTP request/response interactions at this stage.

What we'd like to do in this test is create `Conference` domain objects on the client side and transfer them to the server. Warp will allow us to control which data to fetch through the JAX-RS layer. We can look at the abstract base class of `ConferenceResourceSpeci ficationTestCase` as an example:

```
@Test
public void shouldReturnOKOnGETResource() throws Exception {
    final DOMAIN domain = createDomainObject();

    Warp.initiate(new Activity() {
        @Override
        public void perform() {
            responseValidation(
                given().
                then().
                    contentType(getTypedMediaType())
            , domain).when().
                get(createRootURL() + "/{id}",
                    domain.getId()).body();
        }
    }).inspect(
        new SetupRepository<DOMAIN>(
            getDomainClass(), domain));
}
```

Here we use Warp to produce the data we want the REST layer to receive, and validate that we obtain the correct HTTP response for a valid `GET` request.

Running this test locally, we'll see that Warp constructs an HTTP `GET` request for us:

```
GET /9676980f-2fc9-4103-ae28-fd0261d1d7c3/api/conference/
ac5390ad-5483-4239-850c-62efaeee7bf1 HTTP/1.1[\r][\n]
Accept: application/vnd.ced+xml; type=conference[\r][\n]
Host: 127.0.1.1:18080[\r][\n]
Connection: Keep-Alive[\r][\n]
Accept-Encoding: gzip,deflate[\r][\n]
```

Because we've coded our JAX-RS endpoints and backing business objects correctly, we'll receive the expected reply (an HTTP 200 OK status):

```
HTTP/1.1 200 OK
X-Arq-Enrichment-Response=3778738317992283532
Last-Modified=Wed, 21 Aug 2013 04:14:44 GMT
Content-Type=application/vnd.ced+xml; type=conference
Content-Length=564
Via=1.1.overdrive.home

<ns3:conference xmlns:ns3="urn:ced:conference">
  <ns2:link xmlns:ns2="urn:ced:link"
    href="http://127.0.1.1:18080/9676980f-2fc9-4103-ae28-fd0261d1d7c3/api/
    conference/ac5390ad-5483-4239-850c-62efaeee7bf1"
    rel="self"/>
  <ns2:link xmlns:ns2="urn:ced:link"
    href="http://127.0.1.1:18080/9676980f-2fc9-4103-ae28-fd0261d1d7c3/api/
    conference/ac5390ad-5483-4239-850c-62efaeee7bf1/session"
    rel="session"/>
  <end>
    2013-08-21T00:14:44.159-04:00
  </end>
  <name>
    Name
  </name>
  <start>
    2013-08-21T00:14:44.159-04:00
  </start>
  <tagLine>
    TagLine
  </tagLine>
</ns3:conference>
```

The response will contain our links to related resources, as well as information about the requested Conference object in the XML xmlns:ns3="urn:ced:conference" format. Using Warp, we can interact with and perform validations upon these types of payloads with ease.

There are plenty of other detailed Warp examples throughout the tests of the REST modules in the GeekSeek application code; we advise readers to peruse the source for additional ideas on using this very powerful tool for white-box testing of the request/response model.

CHAPTER 9

Security

There is no real security except for whatever you build inside yourself.

— Gilda Radner

In a utopian society, we'd leave our homes unlocked in the morning. We'd park our cars at the office with the windows open, and after dark we'd be free to walk unlit alleyways without concern.

Unfortunately, the small percentage of those looking to take advantage of others necessitates taking some measures to protect ourselves. We look after our belongings and each other. In the digital arena, our vulnerable currency is *data*—not everyone is entitled to see or edit everything. Although our systems are built to support a large number of users, we cannot simply allow anyone to take any action they please. In software and life, security amounts to controlling access.

The process by which we grant or restrict access is reflected in our *security model*; this defines the criteria by which we judge access attempts. If someone is asking to enter the office, should we ensure he's an employee? Is it after business hours, and how does that affect our decision? Access may be permitted or denied based on *contextual* information, and the way we value those contexts is what comprises our security model.

When we permit access to a resource, this is the process of *authorization*. A commonly employed approach involves *role-based security*, where functions and actions on the system are linked to a *role*. For instance, the task of unlocking an office's front doors may be permitted to someone with the "janitor" role. A staffer, Jim, may in turn be assigned to the "janitor" role; thus Jim will have permission to unlock the office's front doors. Role-based security decouples the *user* from the *task*; if Jim leaves the company and no longer is noted as the janitor, the permissions he'd had when assigned to that role would disappear as well.

Coupled with authorization, which is the act of granting or denying access, is ensuring that the requesting party is who they say they are. Surely the CEO of a company is privy to all sorts of details that wouldn't be available to the general public; if anyone could claim to be CEO, they'd be permitted to browse the whole system! The process of validating identity is called *authentication*.

Use Cases and Requirements

Because GeekSeek is intended to communicate its users' conference schedules publicly, we're not concerned with locking down read operations. However, it's still important that writes are done by authorized users, so our requirements will generally state "limit unauthorized users' access to create or change data":

- As a third-party integrator, I should not be able to:
  — Add/Change/Delete a Conference without being authorized
  — Add/Change/Delete a Session of a Conference without being authorized
  — Add/Change/Delete an Attachment to Sessions and Conferences without being authorized
  — Add/Change/Delete a Venue (and associate with a Conference and Session) without being authorized

In practice, this means we'll need to lock down the resources for these actions with a layer to inspect incoming requests, analyze the calling user and other contextual information, and determine whether or not we allow the invocation to proceed.

Implementation

Our security solution will rely on some third-party assistance to provide the implementation pieces.

Supporting Software

It likely doesn't benefit us much to build bespoke solutions for generalized and important layers such as security, so we'll be relying on integration with a few frameworks to help us fulfill our requirements.

PicketLink: application-level security

PicketLink (*http://www.picketlink.org*) is an umbrella project for security and identity management for Java applications. It provides the backbone of security for a variety of JBoss products, but it also can be used standalone, as we'll do with GeekSeek. PicketLink components are available to support the following:

IDM (http://www.jboss.org/picketlink/IDM.html)
Universal identity management with pluggable backends like LDAP or RDBMS

Federation (http://www.jboss.org/picketlink/Fed)
Federated Identity and Single-Sign-On (SSO)

XACML (http://www.jboss.org/picketlink/XACML.html)
Oasis XACML v2.0–compliant access control engine

We'll be leveraging PicketLink in GeekSeek to supply us with an *identity manager* that we can use for authentication. This comes in the form of the PicketLink API's `org.pick etlink.Identity`, which has operations to support checking the current login state, logging in, logging out, and checking access permission:

```
public interface Identity extends Serializable
{
    public enum AuthenticationResult {
        SUCCESS, FAILED
    }

    boolean isLoggedIn();

    Account getAccount();

    AuthenticationResult login() throws AuthenticationException;

    void logout();

    boolean hasPermission(Object resource, String operation);

    boolean hasPermission(Class<?> resourceClass, Serializable identifier,
        String operation);
}
```

We can use the `Identity` API to lock down all requests that match the URL pattern `/auth` via our `org.cedj.geekseek.service.security.oauth.AuthServlet`:

```
@WebServlet(urlPatterns={"/auth"})
public class AuthServlet extends HttpServlet {
```

The `@WebServlet` annotation and `urlPatterns` attribute assign this servlet to handle all requests to context paths matching the `/auth` pattern:

```
    private static final long serialVersionUID = 1L;

    private static final String SESSION_REDIRECT = "auth_redirect";
    private static final String REFERER = "Referer";
    private static final String LOCATION = "Location";

    @Inject
    private HttpObjectHolder holder;
```

```
    @Inject
    private Identity identity;
```

Here we define some constants and inject the PicketLink @Identity. We can then use these in our servlet's `service` method, called by the container on incoming client requests:

```
    @Override
    public void service(ServletRequest req, ServletResponse resp)
        throws IOException, ServletException {

        HttpServletRequest request = (HttpServletRequest)req;
        HttpServletResponse response = (HttpServletResponse)resp;
        HttpSession session = request.getSession();
        holder.setup(request, response);

        if(!identity.isLoggedIn()) {
            if(session.getAttribute(SESSION_REDIRECT) == null) {
                session.setAttribute(SESSION_REDIRECT,
                request.getHeader(REFERER));
            }

            try {
                AuthenticationResult status = identity.login();
                if(status == AuthenticationResult.FAILED) {
                    if(response.getStatus() == 302) { // Authenticator is
                                                      // requesting a redirect
                        return;
                    }
                    response.setStatus(400);
                    response.getWriter().append("FAILED");
                } else {
                    String url = String.valueOf(
                        request.getSession().getAttribute(SESSION_REDIRECT));
                    response.setStatus(302);
                    response.setHeader(LOCATION, url);
                    request.getSession().removeAttribute(SESSION_REDIRECT);
                }
            } catch(AuthenticationException e) {
                response.setStatus(400);
                response.getWriter().append(e.getMessage());
                e.printStackTrace();
            }
        }
        else {
            response.setStatus(302);
            response.setHeader("Location", request.getHeader("Referer"));
            response.getWriter().append("ALREADY_LOGGED_IN");
        }
    }
}
```

By using the operations permitted by the `Identity` API to check the login state and perform a login if necessary, we can set the appropriate HTTP status codes and authentication redirect attributes.

CDI beans will also be interested in knowing the current logged-in `User`. A PicketLink `Identity` is associated with an implementation of `org.picketlink.idm.model.Ac count`, and we link an `Identity` to a `User` via our `org.cedj.geekseek.service.secu rity.picketlink.UserAccount`:

```
public class UserAccount implements Account {

    private User user;

    public UserAccount(User user) {
        Validate.requireNonNull(user, "User must be specified");
        this.user = user;
    }

    public User getUser() {
        return user;
    }
    ...
```

With the line between an `Identity` and our own `User` object now drawn, we can make the current `User` available as an injection target by supplying a CDI producer method, scoped to the current request. This is handled by `org.cedj.geekseek.service.secu rity.CurrentUserProducer`:

```
import javax.enterprise.context.RequestScoped;
import javax.enterprise.inject.Produces;
import javax.inject.Inject;

import org.cedj.geekseek.domain.Current;
import org.cedj.geekseek.domain.user.model.User;
import org.cedj.geekseek.service.security.picketlink.UserAccount;
import org.picketlink.Identity;

@RequestScoped
public class CurrentUserProducer {

    @Inject
    private Identity identity;

    @Produces @Current
    public User getCurrentUser() {
        if(identity.isLoggedIn()) {
            return ((UserAccount)identity.getAccount()).getUser();
        }
        return null;
    }
}
```

This class will supply a `User` to fields annotated with `@Current`, or `null` if no one is logged in. As we've seen, our `UserAccount` implementation will allow us to call `getUser()` on the current `Identity`.

Here we've shown the use of PicketLink as a handy security abstraction, but we haven't done any real authentication or authorization yet. For that, we'll need to implement a provider that will power the IDM requirements we have to enable social login via Twitter.

Agorava and social authentication

Agorava (*http://agorava.org/*) is a library consisting of CDI beans and extensions for interaction with the predominant social networks. Its featureset touts:

- A generic and portable REST client API
- A generic API to work with OAuth 1.0a and 2.0 services
- A generic API to interact with JSON serialization and deserialization
- A generic identification API to retrieve basic user information from a social service
- Specific APIs for Twitter, Facebook, and LinkedIn

In short, we'll be using Agorava to handle our *authentication* process and do the behind-the-scenes interaction with Twitter, powering our sign-in integration.

Because the Twitter authentication mechanism is via OAuth, it'll benefit us to produce an Agorava `OAuthSession` to represent the current user. Again, we turn to a CDI producer method to handle the details in `org.cedj.geekseek.service.security.oauth.SessionProducer`:

```
import javax.enterprise.context.SessionScoped;
import javax.enterprise.inject.Default;
import javax.enterprise.inject.Produces;

import org.agorava.Twitter;
import org.agorava.core.api.oauth.OAuthSession;
import org.agorava.core.cdi.Current;

public class SessionProducer implements Serializable {
    @SessionScoped
    @Produces
    @Twitter
    @Current
    public OAuthSession produceOauthSession(
        @Twitter @Default OAuthSession session) {
        return session;
    }
}
```

The @Twitter annotation from Agorava supplies us with an injection point to map the OAuthSession into the @Produces method.

We also need a mechanism to initialize Agorava's settings for the OAuth application, so we have org.cedj.geekseek.service.security.oauth.SettingsProducer to provide these:

```
import javax.annotation.PostConstruct;
import javax.ejb.Singleton;
import javax.ejb.Startup;
import javax.enterprise.context.ApplicationScoped;
import javax.enterprise.inject.Produces;

import org.agorava.Twitter;
import org.agorava.core.api.oauth.OAuthAppSettings;
import org.agorava.core.oauth.SimpleOAuthAppSettingsBuilder;

@ApplicationScoped
@Startup @Singleton
public class SettingsProducer implements Serializable {

    private static final long serialVersionUID = 1L;

    private static final String PROP_API_KEY = "AUTH_API_KEY";
    private static final String PROP_API_SECRET = "AUTH_API_SECRET";
    private static final String PROP_API_CALLBACK = "AUTH_CALLBACK";

    @Produces @Twitter @ApplicationScoped
    public static OAuthAppSettings createSettings() {
        String apiKey = System.getenv(PROP_API_KEY);
        String apiSecret = System.getenv(PROP_API_SECRET);
        String apiCallback = System.getenv(PROP_API_CALLBACK);
        if(apiCallback == null) {
            apiCallback = "auth";
        }

        SimpleOAuthAppSettingsBuilder builder =
            new SimpleOAuthAppSettingsBuilder();
        builder.apiKey(apiKey).apiSecret(apiSecret).callback(apiCallback);

        return builder.build();
    }

    @PostConstruct
    public void validateEnvironment() {
        String apiKey = System.getenv(PROP_API_KEY);
        if(apiKey == null) {
            throw new IllegalStateException(
                PROP_API_KEY + " env variable must be set");
        }
        String apiSecret = System.getenv(PROP_API_SECRET);
        if(apiSecret == null) {
```

```
            throw new IllegalStateException(
                PROP_API_SECRET + " env variable must be set");
        }
    }
}
```

This @Singleton EJB is scoped application-wide and available to all sessions needing configuration to create OAuth sessions. We store the config data in environment variables to not couple secrets into our application, and allow our various deployment targets (local dev, staging, production, etc.) to have independent configurations.

Now we can move to the business of authenticating a user via the Twitter OAuth service via Agorava. We can extend PicketLink's BaseAuthenticator to provide the necessary logic in org.cedj.geekseek.service.security.picketlink.OAuthAuthenticator:

```
@ApplicationScoped
@PicketLink
public class OAuthAuthenticator extends BaseAuthenticator {

    private static final String AUTH_COOKIE_NAME = "auth";
    private static final String LOCATION = "Location";

    @Inject @PicketLink
    private Instance<HttpServletRequest> requestInst;

    @Inject @PicketLink
    private Instance<HttpServletResponse> responseInst;

    @Inject
    private Repository<User> repository;

    @Inject
    private OAuthService service;

    @Inject @Twitter @Current
    private OAuthSession session;

    @Inject
    private Event<SuccessfulAuthentication> successful;

    @Override
    public void authenticate() {
        HttpServletRequest request = requestInst.get();
        HttpServletResponse response = responseInst.get();

        if(request == null || response == null) {
            setStatus(AuthenticationStatus.FAILURE);
        } else {
            if(session.isConnected()) { // already got an active session going
                OAuthSession session = service.getSession();
                UserProfile userProfile = session.getUserProfile();
```

```
            User user = repository.get(userProfile.getId());
            if(user == null) {  // can't find a matching account, shouldn't
                                // really happen
                setStatus(AuthenticationStatus.FAILURE);
            } else {
                setAccount(new UserAccount(user));
                setStatus(AuthenticationStatus.SUCCESS);
            }
        } else {
            // Callback
            String verifier = request.getParameter(
                service.getVerifierParamName());
            if(verifier != null) {
                session.setVerifier(verifier);
                service.initAccessToken();

                // https://issues.jboss.org/browse/AGOVA-53
                successful.fire(new SuccessfulAuthentication(
                    service.getSession().getUserProfile(),
                    service.getAccessToken()));

                String screenName = ((TwitterProfile)service.
                    getSession().getUserProfile()).getScreenName();
                User user = repository.get(screenName);
                if(user == null) { // can't find a matching account
                    setStatus(AuthenticationStatus.FAILURE);
                } else {
                    setAccount(new UserAccount(user));
                    setStatus(AuthenticationStatus.SUCCESS);
                    response.addCookie(new Cookie(
                        AUTH_COOKIE_NAME, user.getApiToken()));
                }

            } else {
                // initiate redirect request to 3. party
                String redirectUrl = service.getAuthorizationUrl();

                response.setStatus(302);
                response.setHeader(LOCATION, redirectUrl);
                setStatus(AuthenticationStatus.DEFERRED);
            }
        }
    }
  }
}
```

Annotating the OAuthAuthenticator with @PicketLink denotes that this is the authenticator instance to be used by PicketLink.

The authenticate method uses the current (injected) OAuthSession to determine whether or not we have a logged-in user, and further may extract profile information from there. If the session is not yet connected, we can issue the redirect to the provider for access.

Upon a `SuccessfulAuthentication` event, we can take further action to store this user's information from Twitter in our data store by observing the event in `org.cedj.geek seek.service.security.user.UserRegistration`:

```
import javax.enterprise.event.Observes;
import javax.inject.Inject;

import org.agorava.core.api.oauth.OAuthToken;
import org.agorava.twitter.model.TwitterProfile;
import org.cedj.geekseek.domain.Repository;
import org.cedj.geekseek.domain.user.model.User;
import org.cedj.geekseek.service.security.oauth.SuccessfulAuthentication;

public class UserRegistration {

    @Inject
    private Repository<User> repository;

    public void registerUser(@Observes SuccessfulAuthentication event) {
        TwitterProfile profile = (TwitterProfile)event.getProfile();

        User user = repository.get(profile.getScreenName());
        if(user == null) {
            user = new User(profile.getScreenName());
        }
        user.setName(profile.getFullName());
        user.setBio(profile.getDescription());
        user.setAvatarUrl(profile.getProfileImageUrl());
        OAuthToken token = event.getToken();
        user.setAccessToken(token.getSecret() + "|" + token.getToken());
        if(user.getApiToken() == null) {
            user.setApiToken(UUID.randomUUID().toString());
        }

        repository.store(user);
    }
}
```

When the `SuccessfulAuthentication` event is fired from the `OAuthAuthenticator`, our `UserRegistration` bean will set the appropriate fields in our own data model, then persist via the injected `Repository`.

Requirement Test Scenarios

With our resources secured by URL patterns, it's time to ensure that the barriers we've put in place are protecting us as we'd expect.

Overview

We must validate that for each of the operations we invoke upon secured resources, we're getting back the appropriate response. As we've seen before, in Chapter 8, this will pertain to:

- PUT data
- GET data
- POST data
- PATCH data
- DELETE data
- OPTIONS filtered
- Login
  — Handling exceptional cases

Setup

By making use of CDI's producers, we can swap in some test-only implementations to provide our tests with a logged-in User; this will mimic the true @CurrentUser behavior we'll see in production. For instance, org.cedj.geekseek.service.security.test.model.TestCurrentUser contains:

```
public class TestCurrentUserProducer {

    @Produces @Current
    private static User current;

    public void setCurrent(User current) {
        TestCurrentUserProducer.current = current;
    }
}
```

This setCurrent method is invoked by Warp during our test execution via a class called org.cedj.geekseek.service.security.test.model.SetupAuth:

```
public class SetupAuth extends Inspection {

    private User user;

    public SetupAuth(User user) {
        this.user = user;
    }

    @BeforeServlet
    public void setup(TestCurrentUserProducer producer) {
```

```
        producer.setCurrent(this.user);
    }
}
```

Security Tests

Secured options

The whole picture comes together in `org.cedj.geekseek.service.security.test.`
`integration.SecuredOptionsTestCase`. This will test that the `Allow` HTTP header is
not returned for unauthorized users issuing state-changing requests upon a protected
URL. Additionally, it'll ensure that if a user *is* logged in, the state-changing methods will
be allowed and the `Allow` header will be present:

```
@RunAsClient
@WarpTest
@RunWith(Arquillian.class)
public class SecuredOptionsTestCase {

    @Deployment
    public static WebArchive deploy() {
        return ShrinkWrap.create(WebArchive.class)
            .addClasses(
                SecuredOptionsExceptionMapper.class,
                SecuredOptionsTestCase.class,
                SetupAuth.class,
                TestResource.class,
                TestApplication.class,
                TestCurrentUserProducer.class)
            .addAsLibraries(RestCoreDeployments.root())
            .addAsLibraries(UserDeployments.domain())
            .addAsWebInfResource(EmptyAsset.INSTANCE, "beans.xml");
    }

    @ArquillianResource
    private URL baseURL;
```

We start by defining a `@WarpTest` to run from the client side (as denoted by `@RunA`
`sClient`), and provide an `@Deployment` with test-double elements like our `TestCurren`
`tUserProducer`, as explained earlier. Arquillian will inject the `baseURL` of our deployment because we've annotated it with `@ArquillianResource`:

```
@Test
public void shouldNotContainStateChangingMethodsForUnauthorizedAccess()
    throws Exception {
    final URL testURL = createTestURL();
    Warp.initiate(new Activity() {
        @Override
        public void perform() {
            given().
                then().
                    statusCode(Status.OK.getStatusCode()).
                    header("Allow", allOf(
                        not(containsString("POST")),
                        not(containsString("PUT")),
                        not(containsString("DELETE")),
                        not(containsString("PATCH")))).
            when().
            options(testURL.toExternalForm());
        }
    }).inspect(new SetupAuth(null));
}
```

Warp's fluent syntax allows us to construct a test to ensure that the Allow header is not returned for the state-changing HTTP requests POST, PUT, DELETE, and PATCH. The use of a null user in SetupAuth is where we set no current user.

Conversely, we can ensure that we do obtain the Allow header for all methods when we are logged in:

```
@Test
public void shouldContainStateChangingMethodsForAuthorizedAccess()
    throws Exception {
    final URL testURL = createTestURL();
    Warp.initiate(new Activity() {
        @Override
        public void perform() {
            given().
                then().
                    statusCode(Status.OK.getStatusCode()).
                    header("Allow", allOf(
                        containsString("GET"),
                        containsString("OPTIONS"),
                        containsString("POST"),
                        containsString("PUT"),
                        containsString("DELETE"),
                        containsString("PATCH"))).
            when().
                options(testURL.toExternalForm());
        }
    }).inspect(new SetupAuth(new User("testuser")));
}
}
```

Here we use `SetupAuth` to set ourselves a `testuser` for use in this test.

We can take a similar approach to validating that we receive an HTTP Unauthorized 401 status response when attempting to POST, PUT, PATCH, or DELETE a resource if we're not an authorized user; we do this in `org.cedj.geekseek.service.security.test.in tegration.SecuredMethodsTestCase`:

```
@Test
public void shouldNotAllowPUTForUnauthorizedAccess() throws Exception {
    final URL testURL = createTestURL();
    Warp.initiate(new Activity() {
        @Override
        public void perform() {
            given().
                then().
                    statusCode(Status.UNAUTHORIZED.getStatusCode()).
                when().
                    put(testURL.toExternalForm());
        }
    }).inspect(new SetupAuth(null));
}

@Test
public void shouldAllowPUTForAuuthorizedAccess() throws Exception {
    final URL testURL = createTestURL();
    Warp.initiate(new Activity() {
        @Override
        public void perform() {
            given().
                then().
                    statusCode(Status.OK.getStatusCode()).
                when().
                    put(testURL.toExternalForm());
        }
    }).inspect(new SetupAuth(new User("testuser")));
}
...
```

We accomplish the requirements to lock down access to unauthorized users via our own `org.cedj.geekseek.service.security.interceptor.SecurityInterceptor`:

```
public class SecurityInterceptor implements RESTInterceptor {

    @Inject @Current
    private Instance<User> user;

    @Override
    public int getPriority() {
        return 0;
    }

    @Override
```

```
public Object invoke(InvocationContext ic) throws Exception {

    Method target = ic.getMethod();
    if(isStateChangingMethod(target)) {
        if(user.get() != null) {
            return ic.proceed();
        }
        else {
            return Response.status(Status.UNAUTHORIZED).build();
        }
    }
    return ic.proceed();
}

private boolean isStateChangingMethod(Method target) {
    return target.isAnnotationPresent(PUT.class) ||
        target.isAnnotationPresent(POST.class) ||
        target.isAnnotationPresent(DELETE.class) ||
        target.isAnnotationPresent(PATCH.class);
}
}
```

This interceptor prohibits access and returns an HTTP 401 if the request is for a state-changing method and there is no currently logged-in user.

Testing the current user

Our user interface will be using the WhoAmIResource to determine the login information; it issues an HTTP 302 redirect to a User resource if authorized and an HTTP 401 "Unauthorized" response if not. The org.cedj.geekseek.service.security.test.integration.WhoAmIResourceTestCase asserts this behavior, with test methods:

```
@Test
public void shouldReponseWithNotAuthorizedWhenNoUserFound()
    throws Exception {
      final URL whoAmIURL = createTestURL();
      Warp.initiate(new Activity() {
          @Override
          public void perform() {
              given().
                  then().
                      statusCode(Status.UNAUTHORIZED.getStatusCode()).
                  when().
                      get(whoAmIURL.toExternalForm());
          }
      }).inspect(new SetupAuth(null));
}

@Test
public void shouldReponseSeeOtherWhenUserFound() throws Exception {
    final URL whoAmIURL = createTestURL();
    Warp.initiate(new Activity() {
```

```
        @Override
        public void perform() {
            given().
                redirects().
                    follow(false).
            then().
                statusCode(Status.SEE_OTHER.getStatusCode()).
            when().
                get(whoAmIURL.toExternalForm());
        }
    }).inspect(new SetupAuth(new User("testuser")));
}

private URL createTestURL() throws MalformedURLException {
    return new URL(baseURL, "api/security/whoami");
}
```

Again we use Warp in the shouldReponseWithNotAuthorizedWhenNoUserFound and shouldReponseSeeOtherWhenUserFound test methods to execute a request and ensure that the response fits our requirements.

OAuth

Assuming a successful OAuth login, we should redirect back to the user's initial entry point. Additionally, we must handle exceptional cases and authorization responses from our PicketLink Authenticator implementation.

Our test case will use a custom Authenticator to control the various scenarios; we implement these in org.cedj.geekseek.service.security.test.integration.Con trollableAuthenticator:

```
@RequestScoped
@PicketLink
public class ControllableAuthenticator extends BaseAuthenticator {

    private boolean wasCalled = false;
    private boolean shouldFailAuth = false;

    @Override
    public void authenticate() {
        wasCalled = true;
        if(shouldFailAuth) {
            setStatus(AuthenticationStatus.FAILURE);
        } else {
            setStatus(AuthenticationStatus.SUCCESS);
            setAccount(new User());
        }
    }

    public boolean wasCalled() {
        return wasCalled;
```

```
        }

        public void setShouldFailAuth(boolean fail) {
            this.shouldFailAuth = fail;
        }

    }
```

This gives us a hook to programmatically control whether or not this `Authenticator` type will permit success via a call to the `setShouldFailAuth` method.

Our `org.cedj.geekseek.service.security.test.integration.AuthServletTest` `Case` can then use this `ControllableAuthenticator` in testing to ensure our *handling* of various authentication outcomes is correct, independently of the authentication process itself:

```
@RunAsClient
@WarpTest
@RunWith(Arquillian.class)
public class AuthServletTestCase {

    @Deployment
    public static WebArchive deploy() {
        return ShrinkWrap.create(WebArchive.class)
            .addClasses(AuthServlet.class, HttpObjectHolder.class,
                ControllableAuthenticator.class)
            .addAsWebInfResource(EmptyAsset.INSTANCE, "beans.xml")
            .addAsLibraries(
                Maven.resolver()
                    .loadPomFromFile("pom.xml")
                    .resolve("org.picketlink:picketlink-impl")
                        .withTransitivity()
                        .asFile());
    }

    @ArquillianResource
    private URL baseURL;

    @Test
    public void shouldRedirectToRefererOnAuthSuccess() throws Exception {
        Warp.initiate(new Activity() {

            @Override
            public void perform() {
                try {
                    final HttpURLConnection conn = (HttpURLConnection)new URL(
                        baseURL, "auth").openConnection();
                    conn.setRequestProperty("Referer", "http:/geekseek.com");
                    conn.setInstanceFollowRedirects(false);
                    Assert.assertEquals(302, conn.getResponseCode());
                    Assert.assertEquals(
                        conn.getHeaderField("Location"), "http:/geekseek.com");
```

```
                } catch(Exception e) {
                    throw new RuntimeException(e);
                }
            }
        }).inspect(new Inspection() {
            private static final long serialVersionUID = 1L;

            @Inject @PicketLink
            private ControllableAuthenticator auth;

            @BeforeServlet
            public void setup() {
                auth.setShouldFailAuth(false);
            }

            @AfterServlet
            public void validate() {
                Assert.assertTrue(auth.wasCalled());
            }
        });
    }

    @Test
    public void shouldReturnUnAuthorizedOnAuthFailure() throws Exception {
        Warp.initiate(new Activity() {

            @Override
            public void perform() {
                try {
                    final HttpURLConnection conn = (HttpURLConnection)new URL(
                        baseURL, "auth").openConnection();
                    conn.setInstanceFollowRedirects(false);
                    Assert.assertEquals(400, conn.getResponseCode());
                } catch(Exception e) {
                    throw new RuntimeException(e);
                }
            }
        }).inspect(new Inspection() {
            private static final long serialVersionUID = 1L;

            @Inject @PicketLink
            private ControllableAuthenticator auth;

            @BeforeServlet
            public void setup() {
                auth.setShouldFailAuth(true);
            }

            @AfterServlet
            public void validate() {
                Assert.assertTrue(auth.wasCalled());
            }
```

```
                });
        }
    }
```

Here we have two test methods, shouldRedirectToRefererOnAuthSuccess and shoul
dReturnUnAuthorizedOnAuthFailure, which issue plain HTTP requests and assert that
the response code returned is correct depending on how we've configured the Control
lableAuthenticator.

Although it's thematic that this text does not promote the usage of mocks in situations
where real runtime components may be used, these test fixtures give us a hook into the
greater runtime and allow tests to control backend responses normally out of their reach.
In this case, we advocate on behalf of their utility.

CHAPTER 10

The User Interface

Beauty is a sign of intelligence.

— Andy Warhol

To this point, we've focused entirely on elements that cannot be seen. In this chapter we bring everything home by exposing our backend services to the end user.

When it comes to Enterprise Java, we have our fill of options for display technologies. The Java EE Specification provides *JavaServer Faces* (JSF), a component-based framework for web applications. This approach takes advantage of *server-side rendering*: that is, the final response returned to the client is created on the server from source templates (typically *Facelets*).

In our GeekSeek example, however, we'll be going off the beaten path a bit and rolling our own single-page application in pure HTML. The dynamic elements backed by data will be supplied via JavaScript calls to the backend via the RESTful interface we exposed earlier.

In general, our requirements remain simply to expose our operations in a human-consumable format.

Use Cases and Requirements

On a high level, we're looking to allow a user to take advantage of the application's primary purpose: we'd like to modify the state of our domain objects in a consistent fashion. We can state these:

- As a User I should be able to Add/Change/Delete a Conference
- As a User I should be able to Add/Change/Delete a Session to Conferences

- As a User I should be able to Add/Change/Delete an Attachment to Sessions and Conferences
- As a User I should be able to Add/Change/Delete a Venue (and attach to Conferences and Sessions)

Implementation

Our frontend is written using the popular JavaScript framework AngularJS (*http://angularjs.org/*): a framework that lets us extend the HTML syntax, write client-side components in the familiar Model, View, Controller (MVC) pattern, and allow for a two-way binding of our data models.

AngularJS has a built-in abstraction to work with Resources like REST, but it lacks built-in support for HATEOAS. The AngularJS Resource can easily operate on a single Resource, but with no automatic link support or knowledge of the OPTIONS that the Resource might support. For our frontend view to be completely driven by the backend services, we need this extra layer of support.

To address HATEOAS in the client view we've created a simple object we call Rest Graph. The main responsibility of this object is to discover linked Resources in the Response and determine what we're allowed to do with the given Resource.

Without exposing too much of how exactly the RestGraph is implemented, we'll just give you a short overview of what it can do and how it is useful.

To start, the RestGraph requires you to define a root Resource URL, the top-level Resource of the graph:

```
var root = RestGraph('http://geekseek.continuousdev.org/api').init();
```

This is similar to how it's done when you visit a web page in a web browser; you give yourself and the browser a starting point by typing an address (URL) in the address bar.

Based on the Response from the root Resource we can determine what can be done next:

```
{
    "link": [
        {
            "rel": "conference",
            "href": "http://geekseek.continuousdev.org/api/conference",
            "mediaType": "application/vnd.ced+json; type=conference"
        },
        {
            "rel": "whoami",
            "href": "http://geekseek.continuousdev.org/api/security/whoami",
            "mediaType": "application/vnd.ced+json; type=user"
```

```
        }
    ]
}
```

In this example the start Resource only contains links to other resources and contains no data itself. We can choose to discover where to go next by looking at all available links. Maybe let the user decide what path to take?

```
var paths = root.links
```

Or choose to follow the graph down a desired path by fetching a named relation:

```
var conference = root.getLink('conference')
```

Some function calls on the conference instance can be mapped directly to the REST verbs for the given Resource: GET, DELETE, PATCH, PUT:

```
conference.get()
conference.remove()
conference.add({})
conference.update({})
```

Now we have the basics. But, we still don't know if we're allowed to perform all of those operations on all discovered Resources. Certain security constraints and possible other limitations are implemented on the server side that we need to take into consideration before/when we make a Request. In the same way we can discover related Resources and Actions via links in the Response, we can query the Resource for the OPTIONS it supports:

```
> OPTIONS /api/conference

< Allow: GET, OPTIONS, HEAD
```

If the user performing the Request is authenticated, the Response to the OPTIONS query might look like this:

```
> OPTIONS /api/conference

< Allow: GET, PATCH, OPTIONS, HEAD
```

The server just told us that an authenticated user is allowed to perform a PATCH operation on this Resource as well as a GET operation. Now the user is no longer restricted to a read-only view, but has full read/write access.

The RestGraph hides the usage of OPTIONS to query the server for allowed actions behind a meaningful API:

```
conference.canGet()
conference.canUpdate()
conference.canRemove()
conference.canCreate()
```

This gives us the complete picture of what the API and the backend, under the current circumstances, will allow us to do. While the communication with the backend is up and running, the user still can't see anything. We need to convert the raw data into a suitable user interface.

We choose to map the MediaTypes described in the DAP to HTML templates in the UI:

```
{
  "rel": "conference",
  "href": "http://geekseek.continuousdev.org/api/conference",
  "mediaType": "application/vnd.ced+json; type=conference"
}
```

By combining the current Action (View, Update, Create) with the MediaType subtype argument, we can identify a unique template for how to represent the current Resource as HTML.

As an example, the Conference MediaType in View mode could look like this:

```
<div class="single" data-ng-if="isSingle">
   <div class="well">
      <div class="pull-right">
         <a data-ng-show="resource.canUpdate()" data-ng-click="edit()">
            <i class="icon-edit-sign"></i></a>
         <a data-ng-show="resource.canRemove()" data-ng-click="remove()">
            <i class="icon-remove-sign"></i></a>
      </div>

      <h1>{{resource.data.name}} <small>{{resource.data.tagLine}}</small></h1>

      <p class="date">
         <abbr title="{{resource.data.start|date:medium}}" class="start">
            <span class="day">{{resource.data.start|date:'d'}}</span>
         </abbr>
         <span class="sep">-</span>
         <abbr title="{{resource.data.end|date:medium}}" class="end">
            <span class="day">{{resource.data.end|date:'d'}}</span>
            <span class="month">{{resource.data.end|date:'MMMM'}}</span>
            <span class="year">{{resource.data.end|date:'yyyy'}}</span>
         </abbr>
      </p>
      <div class="attendees pull-right">
         <subresource parent="resource" link="attendees" />
      </div>
   </div>
   <subresource parent="resource" link="session" />
</div>
```

Requirement Test Scenarios

The UI for our GeekSeek application is based on a JavaScript frontend talking to a REST backend. In this scenario, there are some different approaches and types of testing we can do: one is for the pure JavaScript code (e.g., client controllers) and the other part is the interaction with the browser and REST endpoints on the backend.

Pure JavaScript

For the pure client JavaScript we're going to use QUnit (*http://qunitjs.com/*), a JavaScript Unit Testing framework. And handily enough, Arquillian has an extension that can invoke QUnit execution within our normal Java build system.

Although the QUnit tests themselves do not require any Java code, the Arquillian QUnit extension uses a normal JUnit test class to configure and report on the QUnit execution.

Our UI code contains a graph that can hold the state of the various REST responses and their links. In this test scenario we want to test that the graph can understand the response returned from a REST service given an OPTIONS request.

We start by configuring the QUnit Arquillian runner in a simple JUnit Java class:

```
@RunWith(QUnitRunner.class)
@QUnitResources("src")
public class GraphTestCase {

    @QUnitTest("test/resources/assets/tests/graph/graph-assertions.html")
    public void testGraph() {
        // empty body
    }
}
```

In this example we introduce two new annotations that are specific to the Arquillian QUnit extension:

- @QUnitResources defines the root source of the JavaScript files.
- @QUnitTest defines which HTML page to *run* for this @Test.

The *graph-assertions.html* referenced in the @QUnitTest annotation is the HTML page that contains the <script> tag, which includes the QUnit JavaScript tests and any other JavaScript dependencies we might need:

```
<html>
<head>
<title>QUnit Test Suite</title>
<link rel="stylesheet" href="http://code.jquery.com/qunit/qunit-1.12.0.css"
    type="text/css" media="screen">
```

```
<script src="http://code.jquery.com/jquery-1.8.2.min.js"></script>
<script type="text/javascript"
  src="http://code.jquery.com/qunit/qunit-1.12.0.js"></script>
<script type="text/javascript"
  src="http://ajax.googleapis.com/ajax/libs/angularjs/1.2.0rc1/angular.js">
  </script>
<script type="text/javascript"
  src="http://ajax.googleapis.com/ajax/libs/angularjs/1.2.0rc1/angular-route.js">
  </script>
<script type="text/javascript"
  src="http://ajax.googleapis.com/ajax/libs/angularjs/1.2.0rc1/angular-mocks.js">
  </script>
<script type="text/javascript"
  src="../../../../../main/resources/META-INF/resources/webjars/core/graph.js">
  </script>
<script type="text/javascript" src="assert.js"></script>
</head>
<body>
    <h1 id="qunit-header">QUnit Test Suite</h1>
    <h2 id="qunit-banner"></h2>
    <div id="qunit-testrunner-toolbar"></div>
    <h2 id="qunit-userAgent"></h2>
    <ol id="qunit-tests"></ol>
</body>
</html>
```

Our *assert.js* is then free to contain the QUnit functions that define our client-side test suite:

```
module("Service OPTIONS", optionsInit)
asyncTest("can get?", 1, function() {
    this.$initGraph('GET', function(node) {
        ok(node.canGet(), "Should be able to create Resource")
    })
});
asyncTest("can remove?", 1, function() {
    this.$initGraph('DELETE', function(node) {
        ok(node.canRemove(), "Should be able to remove Resource")
    })
});
```

When we execute the GraphTestCase Java class as part of the test execution, Arquillian QUnit will create and configure Drone (*https://docs.jboss.org/author/display/ARQ/Drone*) and Graphene (*https://community.jboss.org/wiki/ArquillianGraphene2*) to represent our defined environment. It then parses the QUnit JavaScript to extract the real test names and replace the Java JUnit defined ones. That means that in our test results we'll see test names like "can remove?" and "can get?" as opposed to "testGraph."

We have configured Drone to use the PhantomJS browser (*http://phantomjs.org/*); this headless browser allows us to run on a CI server without a graphical environment. This is easily configurable via *arquillian.xml*.

With this setup we now have control over our JavaScript client code and can integrate JavaScript tests in our test pipeline.

Functional Behavior

We still have functional behavior in our application that goes beyond how the JavaScript code itself runs. Are the page elements displaying properly? Does the end user see what is expected?

One could argue that we're now moving over from integration into functional testing. Either way, we need to set up our functional tests to be maintainable, robust, and easy to read.

We use Drone to control the lifecycle of the browser and Graphene to wrap the browser and provide client-side object injection.

We rely on a pattern called PageObjects (*http://bit.ly/1noOxoo*) from Selenium to encapsulate the logic within a page in a type-safe and programmable API. With Graphene we can take the PageObject concept one step further and use PageFragments. PageFragments are reusable components that you might find within a page. We might have a Conference object displayed on multiple different pages or a Login controller repeated in all headers.

By encapsulating the references to the HTML IDs and CSS rules within PageObjects and PageFragments, we can create reusable TestObjects that represent our application.

We start out by creating a PageObject for our application in org.cedj.geekseek.test. functional.ui.page.MainPage:

```
@Location("app/")
public class MainPage {

    @FindBy(id = "action-links")
    private ActionLinks actionLinks;

    @FindBy(id = "user-action-links")
    private ActionLinks userActionLinks;

    @FindBy(id = "resource")
    private WebElement resource;

    public ActionLinks getActionLinks() {
        return actionLinks;
    }

    public ActionLinks getUserActionLinks() {
        return userActionLinks;
    }
```

```
    ...
}
```

We use Graphene's `@Location` to define the relative URL where this page can be found. By combining Graphene with Drone we can now simply inject the `MainPage` object into our `@Test` method. The injection will carry the state navigated to the correct URL and be fully powered by `WebDriver` in the background. With this arrangement, our test class will end up with the following structure:

```
@RunWith(Arquillian.class)
public class MyUITest {

    @Drone
    private WebDriver driver;

    @Test
    public void testSomething(@InitialPage MainPage page) { ...}
```

The `testSomething` method accepts a `MainPage` object with proper state intact.

When Graphene initializes the `MainPage` instance for injection, it scans the PageObject for `@FindBy` annotations to inject proxies that represent the given element. In our case we use a second layer of abstraction, `ActionLinks`, which is our PageFragment. Each page has a menu of "what can be done next?" following the flow of the underlying REST backend. These are split in two; `actionLinks` and `userActionLinks`. The differentiator: is this a general action against a `Resource` or an action against a `Resource` that involves the `User`? An example of an action is *Add Conference*, and a `User` action example would be *Add me as a Tracker to this Conference*.

We add an `ActionLinks` abstraction to simply expose a nicer API around checking if a link exists and how to retrieve it:

```
public class ActionLinks {

    @Root
    private WebElement root;

    @FindBy(tagName = "button")
    private List<WebElement> buttons;

    public WebElement getLink(String name) {
        for(WebElement elem : buttons) {
            if(elem.getText().contains(name) && elem.isDisplayed()) {
                return elem;
            }
        }
        return null;
    }

    public boolean hasLink(String name) {
```

```
            return getLink(name) != null;
        }
    }
```

The `ActionLinks` PageFragment is very similar in how the PageObject works. The main difference is the use of the `@Root` annotation. Both `Actions` and `UserActions` are modeled as the PageFragment type `ActionLinks`. They are two lists of links in different locations on the page. In the PageObject `MainPage` we have the following two injection points:

```
@FindBy(id = "action-links")
private ActionLinks actionLinks;

@FindBy(id = "user-action-links")
private ActionLinks userActionLinks;
```

The `ActionsLinks` `@Root` WebElement is injected based on the parent `@FindBy` element and represents where on the page this fragment was found. When working within a PageFragment, all of our `@FindBy` expressions are relative to the `@Root` element.

You might remember that our application is a single page, so everything happens within the same physical URL and the content is only manipulated via JavaScript. With this in mind we've modeled in a concept of a fragment being `SelfAware`. This allows us to encapsulate the logic of knowing how to find certain fragments within the fragment itself:

`org.cedj.geekseek.test.functional.ui.page.SelfAwareFragment:`

```
    public interface SelfAwareFragment {

        boolean is();
    }
```

The `MainPage` PageObject implements the discovery logic like so:

```
        public <T extends SelfAwareFragment> boolean isResource(Class<T> fragment) {
            try {
                return getResource(fragment).is();
            } catch (NoSuchElementException e) {
                return false;
            }
        }

        public <T extends SelfAwareFragment> T getResource(Class<T> fragment) {
            return PageFragmentEnricher.createPageFragment(fragment, resource);
        }
```

Within the `MainPage` we want to set up PageFragments so they can be created dynamically based on the requested type. This is to avoid having to create a `@FindBy` injection point for all possible combinations within our application. But we still want our *on-demand* PageFragments to have the same features as the injected ones, so we delegate the actual creation of the instance to Graphene's `PageFragmentEnricher`, giving it the requested type and the `@Root` element we expect it to be found within.

After discovering and executing `ActionLinks` we can now ask the `MainPage`: "Are we within a given *subpage*?" by referring just to the class itself:

```java
public static class Form implements SelfAwareFragment {
  @Root
  private WebElement root;

  @FindBy(css = ".content.conference")
  private WebElement conference;

  @FindBy(tagName = "form")
  private WebElement form;

  @FindBy(css = "#name")
  private InputComponent name;

  ...

  @FindBy(tagName = "button")
  private List<WebElement> buttons;

  @Override
  public boolean is() {
    return conference.isDisplayed() && form.isDisplayed();
  }

  public Form name(String name) {
    this.name.value(name);
    return this;
  }

  public InputComponent name() {
    return name;
  }

  ...

  public void submit() {
    for(WebElement button : buttons) {
      if(button.isDisplayed()) {
        button.click();
        break;
      }
    }
  }
}
```

As shown in this example in one of our `SelfAwareFragment` types, `Conference.Form`, we continue nesting PageFragments to encapsulate more behavior down the stack (mainly the `InputComponent`). Whereas an HTML Form `<input>` tag knows how to input data, the `InputComponent` goes a level up:

`textfield.html`:

```
<div class="col-md-8 form-group" data-ng-class="{'has-error':error}">
    <label class="control-label" for="{{id}}_field">{{name}}</label>
    <input class="form-control" type="text" id="{{id}}_field"
        data-ng-model="field"
        required placeholder="{{help}}" />
    <div class="has-error" data-ng-show="error">{{error}}</div>
</div>
```

The complete state of the input is required—not only where to put data, but also the defined name, "help" text, and, most importantly, is it in an error state after submitting?

We also have a custom extension to Drone and Arquillian: we need to ensure that "click" and "navigate" events wait for the loading of async calls before doing their time check. For this, we have the `org.cedj.geekseek.test.functional.arquillian.AngularJS DroneExtension`, which defines:

```
public static class AngularJSEventHandler
    extends AbstractWebDriverEventListener {

        @Override
        public void afterNavigateTo(String url, WebDriver driver) {
            waitForLoad(driver);
        }

        @Override
        public void afterNavigateBack(WebDriver driver) {
            waitForLoad(driver);
        }

        @Override
        public void afterNavigateForward(WebDriver driver) {
            waitForLoad(driver);
        }

        @Override
        public void afterClickOn(WebElement element, WebDriver driver) {
            waitForLoad(driver);
        }

        private void waitForLoad(WebDriver driver) {
            if(JavascriptExecutor.class.isInstance(driver)) {
                JavascriptExecutor executor = (JavascriptExecutor)driver;
                executor.executeAsyncScript(
                    "var callback = arguments[arguments.length - 1];" +
                    "var el = document.querySelector('body');" +
                    "if (window.angular) {" +
                        "angular.element(el).injector().get('$browser').
```

```
                          notifyWhenNoOutstandingRequests(callback);" +
                     "} else {callback()}");
               }
          }

     }
```

The `waitForLoad` method, triggered by all of the action handlers, contains the logic to wait on an async call to return.

With all the main abstractions in place, we are now free to start validating the application's functional behavior:

- Given the User is *Creating a new Conference*
- When the Conference has no start/end date
- Then an error should be displayed

To satisfy these test requirements we have, for example, `org.cedj.geekseek.test.func` `tional.ui.AddConferenceStory`:

```
@RunWith(Arquillian.class)
public class AddConferenceStory {

    @Drone
    private WebDriver driver;

    @Test @InSequence(1)
    public void shouldShowErrorMessageOnMissingDatesInConferenceForm(
        @InitialPage MainPage page) {

        ActionLinks links = page.getActionLinks();
        Assert.assertTrue(
            "Add Conference action should be available",
            links.hasLink("conference"));

        links.getLink("conference").click();

        Assert.assertTrue(
            "Should have been directed to Conference Form",
            page.isResource(Conference.Form.class));

        Conference.Form form = page.getResource(Conference.Form.class);
        form
            .name("Test")
            .tagLine("Tag line")
            .start("")
            .end("")
            .submit();

        Assert.assertFalse("Should not display error", form.name().hasError());
        Assert.assertFalse(
```

```
        "Should not display error", form.tagLine().hasError());
    Assert.assertTrue(
        "Should display error on null input", form.start().hasError());
    Assert.assertTrue(
        "Should display error on null input", form.end().hasError());
}
```

The `shouldShowErrorMessageOnMissingDatesInConferenceForm` test method takes the following actions:

- Go to the `MainPage` (as injected).
- Get all `ActionLinks`.
- Verify there is an `ActionLink` named *conference*.
- Click the *conference* `ActionLink`.
- Verify we're on the `Conference.Form`.
- Input given data in the form and submit it.
- Verify that name and `tagLine` input are not in error state.
- Verify that start and end input are in error state.

As we can see, Arquillian Drone, together with Selenium and QUnit, makes for an integrated solution to testing frontend code with a Java object model. Running the full suite on your own locally should be instructive.

CHAPTER 11

Assembly and Deployment

The road to success is always under construction.

— Lily Tomlin

To this point, we've focused primarily on the testable development of our modules and have taken some selective slices out for examination and testing. The time has come for us to address full integration by bringing everything together into a single deployable unit.

Additionally, we'll look at some alternative (and arguably more enterprise-ready) runtimes for our application. Ideally, we'd like to be in a position where our test environment is aligned as closely as possible to what will be run in production, and we'll further aim to automate the process of deployment. By removing human interaction as much as possible, our potential for mistakes decreases and we learn to rely instead on our test suite as a guardian of code quality.

This chapter will ultimately link a `git push` to validate new commits in a *continuous integration* server before deploying the new version of our application into the publicly accessible Web. Whether you go straight to production or first to a staging environment, these steps should outline a smooth transition from development to real application use.

Obtaining JBoss EAP

JBoss Enterprise Application Platform (EAP) is Red Hat's supportable application server distribution born from the community open source *WildFly* project (formerly known as the JBoss Application Server). A full discussion of the relationship and differences between community and supportable middleware is detailed by Red Hat (*http://red.ht/1noPPQf*), and some of the most important points are as follows:

- The community projects are built to innovate quickly and push new features at a rapid rate.
- Supportable products are intended to have a multiyear life span, and receive updates and bug fixes over this time period.
- A support contract and SLA can be purchased for supportable products.

In March of 2013, the JBoss Senior Director of Engineering announced (*https://commu nity.jboss.org/blogs/mark.little/2013/03/07/eap-binaries-available-for-all-developers*) that EAP binaries and their dependencies will be made freely available (at no monetary cost) via a *0-dollar subscription* through Red Hat. Because this runtime comes with no obligation and allows us a migration path to support if our little *GeekSeek* business were to need it, we'll opt for EAP as our target runtime.

EAP has some additional differences with WildFly, which become very apparent during our development experience. Though EAP is available for free, there is a *Terms and Conditions* prerequisite to its use, and therefore it is not currently available in the JBoss Nexus or Maven Central repositories. We'll have to perform some extra steps to set up our environments for EAP before we can enable this option in our builds.

First, let's obtain the EAP distribution and private JBoss EAP Maven repository from the JBoss Downloads page (*http://www.jboss.org/jbossas/downloads/*), as shown in Figure 11-1.

Figure 11-1. Download JBoss EAP

Once we agree to the Terms and Conditions, the links to download will begin the process. Both the EAP distribution and the EAP Maven Repository are bundled as ZIP files.

Let's install EAP by unzipping it into a location on the filesystem. Anywhere will do; for instance, in *nix-like systems we can handle this from the command line:

```
~ $> mkdir -p /home/alr/opt/jboss/eap; cd /home/alr/opt/jboss/eap
eap $> mv /home/alr/Downloads/jboss-eap-6.1.0.zip .
eap $> unzip jboss-eap-6.1.0.zip
```

Using this, we'd now have EAP installed at *home/alr/opt/jboss/eap/jboss-eap-6.1/*.

Now let's place our EAP Maven repository somewhere useful. It might be enticing to mix in these artifacts with our default Maven repository (typically located at *USER_HOME/.m2/repository*), but let's keep things separated and create a new extension repo for our product bits. This way we'll have the option of enabling this repository explicitly in our builds and won't ever have to worry about placing these artifacts alongside ones found in Maven Central. We'll choose *USER_HOME/.m2/jboss-eap-6.1.0.GA-maven-repository* (the default folder name contained inside the ZIP, under our user's Maven directory):

```
Downloads $> unzip jboss-eap-6.1.0-maven-repository.zip
Downloads $> mv jboss-eap-6.1.0-maven-repository ~/.m2/
Downloads $> rm jboss-eap-6.1.0-maven-repository.zip
```

Running Against JBoss EAP

With our EAP installation in place, we're now in a position to exercise our application against this server instead of WildFly, which we've used up to this point as a convenient default.

Using the EAP Remote Container

First we'll run EAP as a standalone process. Opening a terminal or console window, let's cd into the directory in which we unzipped the distribution. From there we can export an environment variable to set *JBOSS_HOME* to the present working directory (using the export command on *nix systems or simply set on Windows machines):

```
$> cd /home/alr/opt/jboss/eap/jboss-eap-6.1/
jboss-eap-6.1 $> export JBOSS_HOME=`pwd`
```

Now we'll launch the EAP server in standalone (nondomain) mode by using the provided scripts in the *bin* directory:

```
jboss-eap-6.1 $> cd bin
bin $> ./standalone.sh
=================================
  JBoss Bootstrap Environment
  JBOSS_HOME: /home/alr/opt/jboss/eap/jboss-eap-6.1
  JAVA: /home/alr/opt/oracle/java/jdk7/bin/java
  JAVA_OPTS:  -server -XX:+UseCompressedOops -Xms1303m
    -Xmx1303m -XX:MaxPermSize=256m -Djava.net.preferIPv4Stack=true
    -Djboss.modules.system.pkgs=org.jboss.byteman
    -Djava.awt.headless=true
=================================
...output trimmed
02:57:43,593 INFO  [org.jboss.as] (Controller Boot Thread) JBAS015874:
    JBoss EAP 6.1.0.GA
    (AS 7.2.0.Final-redhat-8) started in 2404ms -
```

```
Started 123 of 177 services (53 services
are passive or on-demand)
```

And with that, we have our server process running and ready to receive deployments or service requests. As noted in the preceding output, the startup sequence is complete on our machines in about 2.4 seconds. You can ensure that everything is working correctly or find links to the web-based management interface by pointing your browser to *http://localhost:8080*, as shown in Figure 11-2.

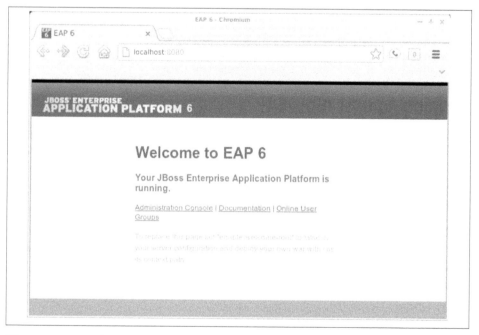

Figure 11-2. EAP home page

Let's leave this as is for the time being, and open a new console window (or tab) in the GeekSeek application's source root.

Our experience with Arquillian up to this point has been using a *managed* container configuration; this has ceded the responsibility of server startup and shutdown to Arquillian during the Before Suite and After Suite test lifecycle events. Now that we've already got a server booted, we can let Arquillian bypass these steps to use a previously bootstrapped process, which gives us some benefits:

- We save the time needed to start and/or stop a server alongside each test suite.
- A server does not have to be running locally; the server process may be housed on a separate physical machine accessible on the network.

We've provided a Maven profile, `arq-jbosseap-remote`, to run our Arquillian tests against a running EAP process on the local machine. From the GeekSeek source code root, simply pass this profile as an argument using the -P switch to the mvn command, and instead of using the default WildFly managed container (which will automatically start and stop), we'll instead use the running server that we started earlier:

```
code $> mvn clean install -Parq-jbosseap-remote
```

The build will run as we've seen before, only this time we'll be able to see some activity in the server console resulting from the deployments made and tests run. For instance:

```
03:35:30,984 INFO  [org.jboss.as.server]
  (management-handler-thread - 1) JBAS018559:
  Deployed "015c84ea-1a41-4e37-957a-f2433f201a23.war"
  (runtime-name : "015c84ea-1a41-4e37-957a-f2433f201a23.war")
```

This may be a preferable technique to employ while developing; at the start of the day you can launch the server and keep it running as an external process, and run your tests without the overhead of waiting for server start and stop, as well as the unzipping process (and resulting file I/O) to create local WildFly installation directories under `target` for testing. On our machines, this cuts the total build time from around 3:30 to 2:11, as we exercise quite a few test suites and hence remove a good number of start/stop lifecycle events by using the remote container.

Because we're done with the EAP instance we started earlier, let's end the process:

```
bin $> ^C
03:45:58,876 INFO  [org.jboss.as]
  (MSC service thread 1-5) JBAS015950:
  JBoss EAP 6.1.0.GA (AS 7.2.0.Final-redhat-8)
  stopped in 127ms
```

Using the EAP Managed Container

Of course, the GeekSeek examples also make EAP available for use in *managed* mode, as we've used before. Because EAP is not currently available as a distribution in a Maven repository, it'll take a few extra steps for us to enable this layout.

Remember that we downloaded the EAP Maven repository earlier. This is an *extension* repo; it's meant to serve as an addition to a standard repo like that offered by JBoss Nexus or Maven Central. As such, it contains EAP-specific artifacts and dependencies only.

Let's begin by unpacking this into a new repository alongside the default `~/.m2/repository` repo:

```
~ $> cd ~/.m2/
.m2 $> mv /home/alr/Downloads/jboss-eap-6.1.0-maven-repository.zip .
.m2 $> unzip jboss-eap-6.1.0-maven-repository.zip
.m2 $> rm jboss-eap-6.1.0-maven-repository.zip
```

This will leave us with the new EAP extension repository `jboss-eap-6.1.0.GA-maven-repository` under our *.m2/* directory.

Now we must let Maven know about our new repository, so we can define it in the default user-level *~/.m2/settings.xml*. Note that we're actually free to use any settings file we choose, though if we opt outside of the default settings file we'll have to manually specify our settings configuration to the `mvn` command using the `-s /path/to/settings/file` switch.

We'll add our repository definition inside a profile, so that we can enable this at will without affecting other projects. In this case we create the `jboss-eap-6.1.0` profile:

```xml
<?xml version="1.0" encoding="UTF-8"?>
<settings xmlns="http://maven.apache.org/SETTINGS/1.0.0"
          xmlns:xsi="http://www.w3.org/2001/XMLSchema-instance"
          xsi:schemaLocation="http://maven.apache.org/SETTINGS/1.0.0
              http://maven.apache.org/xsd/settings-1.0.0.xsd">
...
<profiles>
  <profile>
    <id>jboss-eap-6.1.0</id>
    <repositories>
      <repository>
        <id>jboss-eap-6.1.0-maven-repository</id>
        <name>JBoss EAP 6.1.0 Repository</name>
        <url>file://${user.home}/.m2/jboss-eap-6.1.0.GA-maven-repository</url>
        <layout>default</layout>
        <releases>
          <enabled>true</enabled>
          <updatePolicy>never</updatePolicy>
        </releases>
        <snapshots>
          <enabled>false</enabled>
          <updatePolicy>never</updatePolicy>
        </snapshots>
      </repository>
    </repositories>
  </profile>
  ...
</profiles>
...
</settings>
```

Now, we'll need to again find our EAP ZIP. Then, using the profile we've created, we'll deploy our EAP distribution ZIP as a proper Maven artifact into the repository using the Maven `deploy` plug-in. We must remember to pass in our profile using the `-P` switch:

```
mvn deploy:deploy-file -DgroupId=org.jboss.as \
  -DartifactId=jboss-as-dist \
  -Dversion=eap-6.1.0 \
  -Dpackaging=zip \
```

```
-Dfile=/home/alr/Downloads/jboss-eap-6.1.0.zip \
-DrepositoryId=jboss-eap-6.1.0-maven-repository \
-Durl=file:///home/alr/.m2/jboss-eap-6.1.0.GA-maven-repository \
-Pjboss-eap-6.1.0
```

If we've set everything up correctly, we'll see output:

```
[INFO] Scanning for projects...
...
[INFO]
[INFO] --- maven-deploy-plugin:2.7:deploy-file (default-cli) @ standalone-pom ---
Uploading: file:///home/alr/.m2/jboss-eap-6.1.0.GA-maven-repository/
org/jboss/as/jboss-as-dist/eap-6.1.0/jboss-as-dist-eap-6.1.0.zip
Uploaded: file:///home/alr/.m2/jboss-eap-6.1.0.GA-maven-repository/
org/jboss/as/jboss-as-dist/eap-6.1.0/jboss-as-dist-eap-6.1.0.zip
(112789 KB at 50828.7 KB/sec)
Uploading: file:///home/alr/.m2/jboss-eap-6.1.0.GA-maven-repository/
org/jboss/as/jboss-as-dist/eap-6.1.0/jboss-as-dist-eap-6.1.0.pom
Uploaded: file:///home/alr/.m2/jboss-eap-6.1.0.GA-maven-repository/
org/jboss/as/jboss-as-dist/eap-6.1.0/jboss-as-dist-eap-6.1.0.pom
(431 B at 420.9 KB/sec)
Downloading: file:///home/alr/.m2/jboss-eap-6.1.0.GA-maven-repository/
org/jboss/as/jboss-as-dist/maven-metadata.xml
Uploading: file:///home/alr/.m2/jboss-eap-6.1.0.GA-maven-repository/
org/jboss/as/jboss-as-dist/maven-metadata.xml
Uploaded: file:///home/alr/.m2/jboss-eap-6.1.0.GA-maven-repository/
org/jboss/as/jboss-as-dist/maven-metadata.xml (313 B at 305.7 KB/sec)
...
[INFO] BUILD SUCCESS
[INFO] Total time: 2.911s
[INFO] Finished at: Mon Jun 03 05:30:53 MST 2013
[INFO] Final Memory: 5M/102M
```

And in the ~/.m2/jboss-eap-6.1.0.GA-maven-repository/org/jboss/as/jboss-as-dist directory, we should see our EAP distribution ZIP along with some Maven-generated
metadata files:

```
$> ls -R
.:
eap-6.1.0           maven-metadata.xml.md5
maven-metadata.xml  maven-metadata.xml.sha1

./eap-6.1.0:
jboss-as-dist-eap-6.1.0.pom
jboss-as-dist-eap-6.1.0.pom.md5
jboss-as-dist-eap-6.1.0.pom.sha1
jboss-as-dist-eap-6.1.0.zip
jboss-as-dist-eap-6.1.0.zip.md5
jboss-as-dist-eap-6.1.0.zip.sha1
```

Now, assuming we enable the jboss-eap-6.1.0 profile in our builds, we'll be able to
use EAP just as we did for WildFly, because we've assigned it to a proper Maven artifact
in the coordinate space org:jboss.as:jboss-as-dist:eap-6.1.0.

To run our GeekSeek build with tests against EAP in managed mode, we apply the `jboss-eap-6.1.0` profile to enable our custom repository, and the `arq-jbosseap-managed` profile to configure Arquillian with the proper adaptors:

```
code $> mvn clean install -Parq-jbosseap-managed,jboss-eap-6.1.0
```

In this fashion, we can now automate our testing with EAP just as with WildFly.

Continuous Integration and the Authoritative Build Server

The practice of *continuous integration* involves the frequent pushing of code to a shared mainline, then executing a robust test suite against it. Ideally, each commit will be tested in this fashion, and though we should strive to run as many tests as are appropriate locally before pushing code to the source repository for all to see, the most reliable agent to verify correctness is our *authoritative build server*.

Our goal here is to set up a continuous integration environment that will serve two primary purposes:

- Run the test suite in a controlled environment when a `git push` is made to the authoritative source repository
- Trigger the deployment of the latest version of our application upon build success

In this way we chain events together in order to automate the human action of a code commit all the way through deployment to a publicly accessible application server.

Although we have our choice of build servers and cloud services backing them, we've chosen for our examples the Jenkins CI Server (*http://jenkins-ci.org/*) (the project forked off Hudson (*http://hudson-ci.org/*)) run by the CloudBees service (*http://www.cloud bees.com/*). Of course, we could install a CI server and maintain it ourselves, but the excellent folks at CloudBees have proven more than capable at keeping our infrastructure running, patched, and updated. Additionally, they offer a few extension services (which we'll soon see) that fit well with our desired use cases.

It's worth noting that the CloudBees team has kindly provided the Arquillian and ShrinkWrap communities with gratis service and support over the past several years, so we'd like to thank them for their contributions in keeping the open source ecosystem running smoothly.

Configuring the GeekSeek Build on CloudBees

Because our eventual deployment target will be EAP, we're going to configure CloudBees as our authoritative build server to execute Arquillian tests against the EAP runtime. Just as we ran a few extra steps on our local environment to equip the backing Maven repositories with an EAP distribution, we'll have to make the same artifacts available to our CloudBees Jenkins instance. Luckily, we've already done most of that work locally, so this will mainly be an issue of copying over the EAP Maven repository we already have.

First we'll log in to our CloudBees account and click Select to enter the Jenkins Dashboard from within CloudBees Central, as shown in Figure 11-3.

Figure 11-3. CloudBees Jenkins

We'll create a new job, assigning it our project name of *GeekSeek* and selecting a `Maven2/Maven3 Build` configuration template, as shown in Figure 11-4.

Figure 11-4. CloudBees new job

The next step is to configure the build parameters, as shown in Figure 11-5. First let's set the SCM section to point to our authoritative Git repository; this is where the build will pull code.

Figure 11-5. CloudBees SCM

Now we'll tell Maven how to run the build; remember, we want to enable the `arq-jbosseap-managed` profile, so we'll note that in the "Goals and options" section (see

Figure 11-6). Also, we'll enable our alternative settings file, which will expose our private repository to our build.

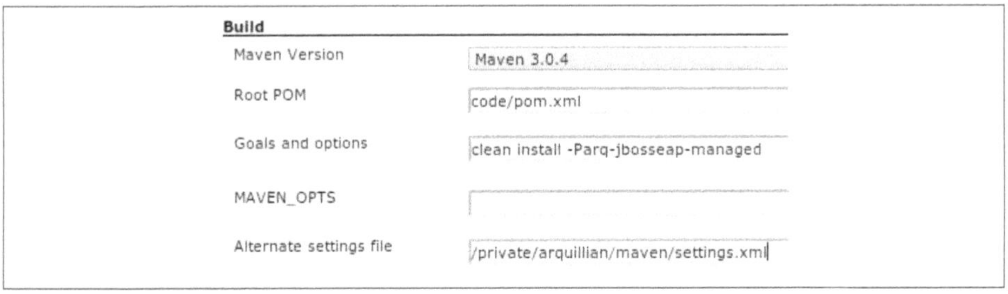

```
Build
Maven Version           Maven 3.0.4

Root POM                code/pom.xml

Goals and options       clean install -Parq-jbosseap-managed

MAVEN_OPTS

Alternate settings file  /private/arquillian/maven/settings.xml
```

Figure 11-6. CloudBees build config

Populating CloudBees Jenkins with the EAP Repository

CloudBees offers a series of Maven repositories associated with each Jenkins domain. These are documented here (*http://bit.ly/1noQ7Xh*), and of particular note is the private repository that is made available to us. We'll be able to write to it and place in artifacts demanded by our builds, yet the visibility permissions associated with the private repo will block the rest of the world from seeing or accessing these resources.

To copy our EAP Maven Repository into the CloudBees Jenkins private repo, we'll make use of the WebDAV protocol, an extension of HTTP that permits writing to WWW resources. There are a variety of system-dependent tools to mount DAV volumes, and CloudBees addresses some known working techniques in its documentation (*http://bit.ly/1noQ91B*). For illustrative purposes, we'll apply *nix-specific software in this guide, loosely based off the CloudBees Linux Documentation (*http://bit.ly/1noQaCq*).

First we need to install the davfs2 project (*http://bit.ly/1noQelN*), a set of libraries enabling the mounting of a WebDAV resource as a standard logical volume. In most Linux-based systems with a package manager, installation can be done using apt-get or yum:

```
$> sudo apt-get install davfs2
```

or:

```
$> sudo yum install davfs2
```

Next we'll ensure that our */etc/conf/davfs2/davfs2.conf* configuration file is set up appropriately; be sure to edit yours to match the following:

```
$> cat /etc/davfs2/davfs2.conf
use_locks 0
ask_auth 1
if_match_bug 1
```

The last line is unique to Ubuntu-based x64 systems (*http://bit.ly/1noQj95*).

Now we can create a directory that will act as our mounting point; we've chosen */mnt/cloudbees/arquillian/private*:

```
$> mkdir -p /mnt/cloudbees/arquillian/private
```

The `fstab` utility on *nix systems acts to automatically handle mounting to registered endpoints. It's configured in */etc/fstab*, so using your favorite text editor, add the following line (replacing your own parameters) to the configuration:

```
# Arquillian WebDAV on CloudBees
https://repository-{domainId}.forge.cloudbees.com/private/ {/mnt/location/path}
    davfs rw,user,noauto,conf=/etc/davfs2/davfs2.conf,uid=$UID 0 0
```

The `private` repository requires authentication, so we must add authentication information to */etc/davfs2/secrets*:

```
{/mnt/location/path}   {cloudbees username}   {password}
```

Note the CloudBees username here is available on the details page under "Authenticated access" (as shown in Figure 11-7), located at *https://forge.cloudbees.com/a/domainId/repositories/private*.

Figure 11-7. CloudBees Authenticated access

Now we should be ready to mount our volume (subsequent reboots to the system should do this automatically due to our `fstab` configuration):

```
$> sudo mount /mnt/cloudbees/arquillian/private/
```

With our volume mounted, any file activities we make under */mnt/cloudbees/arquillian/private/* will be reflected in our remote `private` CloudBees Maven Repository. Let's copy the contents of the JBoss EAP Maven Repository into `private`:

```
sudo cp -Rv ~/.m2/jboss-eap-6.1.0.GA-maven-repository/* \
    /mnt/cloudbees/arquillian/private/
```

This may take some time as we copy all artifacts and the directory structure over the network.

We must also enable this private repository in our build configuration. In the private repo (which we have mounted) is a file called *maven/settings.xml*. We'll edit it to add the following sections.

Under `<servers>`:

```
<server>
  <id>cloudbees-private-maven-repository</id>
  <username>{authorized_username}</username>
  <password>{authorized_password}</password>
  <filePermissions>664</filePermissions>
  <directoryPermissions>775</directoryPermissions>
</server>
```

And under `<profiles>`:

```
<profile>
  <id>cloudbees.private.maven.repository</id>
  <activation>
    <property>
      <name>!cloudbees.private.maven.repository.off</name>
    </property>
  </activation>
  <repositories>
  <repository>
    <id>cloudbees-private-maven-repository</id>
    <url>https://repository-arquillian.forge.cloudbees.com/private</url>
    <releases>
      <enabled>true</enabled>
    </releases>
    <snapshots>
      <enabled>false</enabled>
    </snapshots>
  </repository>
  </repositories>
</profile>
```

Keep in mind that some mounting systems (including `davfs2`) may cache content locally, and avoid flushing bytes to the remote CloudBees DAV repository immediately for performance reasons. To force a flush, we can unmount, then remount the volume:

```
$> sudo umount /mnt/cloudbees/arquillian/private
$> sudo mount -a
```

Note that it's not atypical for large hold times while the cache synchronizes over the network:

```
/sbin/umount.davfs: waiting while mount.davfs (pid 11125) synchronizes the cache
....
```

Now we can manually trigger a build of our project, and if all's set up correctly, we'll see our test result come out clear.

Automatic Building on Git Push Events

Let's take things one step further in terms of automation. We don't have to click the Build Now button on our CI server every time we'd like to run a build. With some extra configuration we can set up a trigger for new `git push` events on the authoritative source repository to start a new CI build.

CloudBees documents this process (*http://bit.ly/1noQQYE*), and we'll follow along these guidelines.

First we must log in to the CloudBees Jenkins home and select the GitHub plug-in for installation at the Manage Jenkins → Manage Plugins screen. Jenkins will download and install the plug-in, then reboot the instance. Then we can go to Manage Jenkins → Configure System and select "Manually manage hook URLs" under the "GitHub Web Hook" setting. Save and exit the screen.

With our Jenkins instance configured, now we should enable GitHub triggers in our build job configuration. Check the box "Build when a change is pushed to GitHub" under "Build Triggers" on the build configuration page, then save.

That will handle the CloudBees Jenkins side of the integration.

In GitHub, we can now visit our repository's home, and select Settings → Service Hooks → WebHook URLs (see Figure 11-8). Add a URL with the format `https://domainId.ci.cloudbees.com/github-webhook`. This will instruct GitHub to send an HTTP `POST` request to CloudBees containing information about the new push, and CloudBees will take it from there.

Figure 11-8. GitHub WebHook URLs

From here on out, new commits pushed to the GitHub repository will trigger a build on the CloudBees Jenkins instance. In this way we can nicely create a pipeline of build-related actions, triggered easily by our committing new work upstream.

Note that this is simply one mechanism of chaining together actions from a `git push`, and it relies on the GitHub and CloudBees services specifically. Of course, there are many other custom and third-party services available, and the choice will ultimately be yours based on your needs. This configuration is offered merely to prove the concept and provide a base implementation (and it also drives the software examples for this book).

Pushing to Staging and Production

With a working build to validate our tests and assemble the final deployable unit(s), we're now free to push our application out to a publicly accessible runtime. In most cases, we'd like to first target a staging server that can be accessed only by members of our team before going public, but the choice for that extra stage is left to the reader's discretion. For the purposes of our GeekSeek application, we'll allow commits that pass the test suite to go straight to the public WWW on OpenShift.

Setting Up the OpenShift Application

First, let's create our new application by logging in to OpenShift and selecting Add Application, as shown in Figure 11-9.

Figure 11-9. Add Application

Because EAP will be our target runtime, we'll select the "JBoss Enterprise Application Platform 6.0" cartridge, a prebuilt environment for applications targeting EAP (see Figure 11-10).

Figure 11-10. JBoss EAP cartridge

Next we'll assign our application with a name unique to our account's domain, as shown in Figure 11-11.

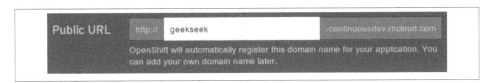

Figure 11-11. New app name

And when we've reviewed the configuration, clicking Create Application, as shown in Figure 11-12, will instruct OpenShift to provision a new namespace and backing infrastructure for our application.

Figure 11-12. Create Application

When the process is completed, a default landing page will be accessible to us (and anyone in the world) from the browser, as shown in Figure 11-13.

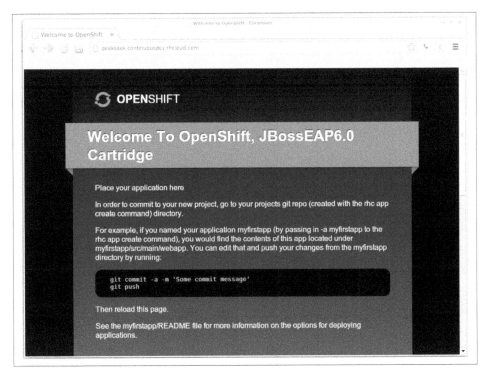

Figure 11-13. Welcome to OpenShift

The default DNS record will be in the format *http://appName-domainId.rhcloud.com*. It's likely that this isn't really the name we desire for public consumption, so let's add our own custom DNS name.

This is a two-step process:

1. Create a DNS entry with your domain registrar or DNS Management interface to point to *http://appName-domainId.rhcloud.com*. In our case, we'll opt for a subdomain, which amounts to a CNAME record. Consult your domain authority for the specifics of this step, but generally you might be presented with a screen that looks similar to Figure 11-14.

Figure 11-14. Add CNAME

2. Add an "alias" in your OpenShift application's configuration. You can do this via the web interface shown in Figure 11-15.

Figure 11-15. Add alias

Alternatively, you can acquire the OpenShift client-side command-line tools (*https:// www.openshift.com/developers/rhc-client-tools-install*). These rely on a Ruby installation of 1.8.7 or greater on your system, and are obtained by installing a Ruby gem:

```
$> sudo gem install rhc
```

Once the gem is installed, you can add the domain record to OpenShift using the command rhc alias add *appName alias* -l *username*. For instance:

```
$> $ rhc alias add geekseek geekseek.continuousdev.org -l admin@continuousdev.org
Password: *****************

Alias 'geekseek.continuousdev.org' has been added.
```

Assuming the CNAME is properly set up with your domain registrar, the record has percolated through the network's DNS tree (which may or may not take some time), and the alias is set up correctly, your application should now be available directly at the provided alias. In our case, this is http://geekseek.continuousdev.org/.

Removing the Default OpenShift Application

Now let's clear the way for our real application. First we'll clone the OpenShift application repository into our local workspace. The Git URL for your application is displayed on the application's status screen on your OpenShift account. The git clone command will look a little like this:

```
$> git clone ssh://(somehash))@geekseek-continuousdev.
rhcloud.com/~/git/geekseek.git/
Cloning into 'geekseek'...
The authenticity of host 'geekseek-continuousdev.rhcloud.com (72.44.62.62)'
can't be established.
RSA key fingerprint is cf:ee:77:cb:0e:fc:02:d7:72:7e:ae:80:c0:90:88:a7.
Are you sure you want to continue connecting (yes/no)? yes
Warning: Permanently added 'geekseek-continuousdev.rhcloud.com,72.44.62.62'
(RSA) to the list of known hosts.
remote: Counting objects: 39, done.
remote: Compressing objects: 100% (31/31), done.
remote: Total 39 (delta 1), reused 0 (delta 0)
Receiving objects: 100% (39/39), 19.98 KiB, done.
Resolving deltas: 100% (1/1), done.
```

Now we have a full copy of the OpenShift application's repository on our local disk. Because we don't need the default landing page shown in Figure 11-13, we can safely remove it. We can do this easily by cd-ing into our repository directory, removing the files in question with git rm, committing the changes, and then pushing the commit to the remote OpenShift repository:

```
$> cd geekseek
geekseek $>  git rm -rf pom.xml src/
rm 'pom.xml'
rm 'src/main/java/.gitkeep'
rm 'src/main/resources/.gitkeep'
rm 'src/main/webapp/WEB-INF/web.xml'
rm 'src/main/webapp/images/jbosscorp_logo.png'
rm 'src/main/webapp/index.html'
rm 'src/main/webapp/snoop.jsp'
geekseek $> git commit -m 'Remove OpenShift default application structure'
geekseek $> git push origin master
```

When the git push command concludes and the remote build is complete, reloading our application in the web browser should now yield us a blank page, because we've deleted the only content in the OpenShift repo. We'll replace that with fresh content from our CI builds.

Pushing from the CI Build Job to OpenShift

The final piece of the automated deployment puzzle lies in deploying artifacts built from our CI server into our runtime environment. In our case, this amounts to configuring the CloudBees Jenkins instance to perform some Git operations against our OpenShift repository.

We'll need to allow access for CloudBees Jenkins to interact with the OpenShift repository. On the Configure screen for our CI job is a section named CloudBees *DEV@Cloud* Authorization, which contains our public key (see Figure 11-16). Copy this to your OS's clipboard.

Figure 11-16. CloudBees SSH public key

Then log in to your OpenShift Management Console and select Settings (*https://open shift.redhat.com/app/console/settings*); there will be a dialog to manage the public keys allowed access to our repository (see Figure 11-17). Add the CloudBees Jenkins key by pasting it here.

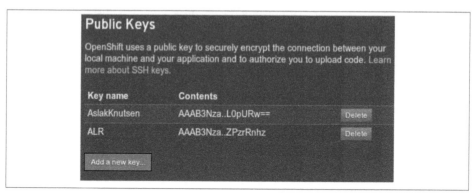

Figure 11-17. OpenShift public keys

Switching back to our Jenkins job configuration screen, toward the bottom is a section where we can add "post-build" steps (see Figure 11-18). Let's create a shell-based action that will be set to execute only upon successful build.

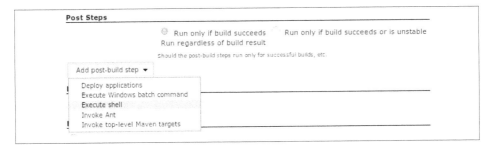

Figure 11-18. CloudBees post-build steps

The following script will handle the task for us:

```
if [ -d geekseek ]; then
  cd geekseek
  if [ -f deployments/ROOT.war ]; then
    rm -rf deployments/ROOT.war
  fi
  git pull origin master
else
  git clone ssh://51abd6c84382ec5c160002e2@geekseek-continuousdev.rhcloud.com/
  ~/git/geekseek.git/
  cd geekseek
fi

cp $WORKSPACE/code/application/application/target/*.war deployments/ROOT.war
touch deployments/ROOT.WAR.dodeploy
git add -Av
COMMIT_MESSAGE='Updated application from '
COMMIT_MESSAGE=$COMMIT_MESSAGE$BUILD_URL
git commit -m "$COMMIT_MESSAGE"
git push origin master
```

Let's see what's going on here. First we have some bash logic to either clone the remote OpenShift repository if this node hasn't already, or update the existing copy. Then we copy the final deployable web application. We'll WAR into the *deployments* directory of the repository, renaming it to *ROOT.war* so that this acts as our application servicing requests from the web root. Also, we'll add or update an empty *ROOT.war.dodeploy* file to let OpenShift know that we want this application deployed when it's discovered (full documentation on this feature is available on the OpenShift site (*http://red.ht/1nop6U6*)). Finally, we add our changes to be staged for commit, perform the commit, and then push the changes to our remote OpenShift repository.

As we've seen before, OpenShift will dutifully exercise the remote operations to redeploy our application and make it available for our use.

Using the OpenShift client command-line tools, we can tail the server logs for the application to monitor status:

```
$> rhc tail {openshift_appname} -l {openshift_username}
```

If we look closely, we'll see that the application has deployed, and is ready for use!

```
2013/06/04 05:38:52,413 INFO  [org.jboss.as.server]
   (ServerService Thread Pool -- 36) JBAS018559:
   Deployed "ROOT.war" (runtime-name : "ROOT.war")
```

CHAPTER 12

Epilogue

Now this is not the end. It is not even the beginning of the end.
But it is, perhaps, the end of the beginning.

— Winston Churchill

Enterprise Java is, as technologies go, not a highly opinionated landscape; it does not prescribe only one way of accomplishing a task. Although Java EE provides a suite of APIs, we've seen in our GeekSeek example that it may be appropriate to look outside the platform and integrate with external frameworks. This freedom carries with it a burden of choice: developers new and seasoned alike may find that bringing together a working application at all layers may carry complexity.

We've set out to show one cohesive application, but this is not a book of best practices. We've taken one approach of many, and it fit our requirements.

What we *do* intend to underscore is the importance the role of testing takes in responsible development. The applications we deploy into production are composed of much more than what we write on our own; we need to be sure that all components are working in concert. Additionally, it's helpful to isolate business logic where we can, and further ensure that everything is connected properly when integrated. The Arquillian project in particular has been a wonderful means for us to explore the bounds of how simple we can make testing of even the most complex use cases, and its community has been instrumental in pushing the limits of testability in a landscape that has historically been cumbersome to manipulate.

We hope that the techniques outlined here, on the companion source repository, and running proof in production on *http://geekseek.continuousdev.org* are beneficial to your own path in building reliable applications in Enterprise Java.

Index

We'd like to hear your suggestions for improving our indexes. Send email to index@oreilly.com.

mock objects, 7, 20
Model, View, Controller (MVC) pattern, 198
modulars, 18
MongoDB, 73, 79
multiuser access, 84
MySQL, 79, 101

N

Neo4j, 73, 79, 106
nodes, 106
normalized forms, 67
NoSQL systems, 102

O

OAuth, 192–195
   Agorva and, 182
   sessions, 184
object relational mapping, 82
objects, managed, 83
one-to-many relationships, 66
one-to-one relationships, 66
OpenJPA, 82
OpenShift application service, 38
   default application, removing, 227
   deploying applications to, 224–230
   deploying to, via JBDS, 55–62
   pushing build jobs to, 227–230
   set up, 224–226
optional dependencies, 32
Oracle, 101

P

PageFragments, 203
PageObjects, 203
performance testing, 6
persistence, 78
   unit, 83
PhantomJS browser, 202
PicketLink, 178–182
   project source, 74
Platform as a Service (PaaS), 38
POJO (Plain Old Java Object), 7
   entities, 82
   programming model, 20
POM
   files, resolving artifacts with ShrinkWrap, 34
   models, 34

post-conditions, 8
PostgreSQL, 79, 101
precondition checks, 2
primary key, 81
proactive quality policies, 2
projects, creating, 40–48
provided scopes, 32
pull models, 19
push models, 19
pushing repositories, 69

Q

query caches, 102
query results, joining, 105
QUnit, 201
   execution, 201

R

reactive error handling, 1
Red Hat, 211
regression testing, 6
relational database management systems
   (RDBMS), 79, 101, 104
   binary data and, 102
   data grids vs., 103
   graph theory vs., 105
   relationships and, 104
   relationships, handling in separate layer,
      111–119
   testing, 127–129
relational databases, 79
   binary data and, 102
   relationships, handling in separate layer,
      111–119
relational mapping, 82
relational models, 73
relationships
   between entities, 66
   cardinality of, 66
Remote Procedure Call (RPC), 74, 151
replication, 103
repository EJBs, 91–93
repostitory resources, 157–168
representation converters, 161–163
Representational State Transfer (see REST)
requirement test scenarios, 93–99
   of business logic, 140–148
   CRUD functions, 95–99

test frameworks, 8–13
   JUnit, 10–12
   TestNG, 12
test harness setup in Warp, 173
test platforms, 20–37
   Arquillian, 21
   ShrinkWrap, 22–27
test scopes, 32
testable development, 48, 93
testing, 5–8
   CRUD functions, 95–99
   frameworks for, 8–13
   functional behavior of UI, 203–209
   HTTP contracts, 174
   integration, 7
   levels of, 5
   relationships, 127–129
   requirements, 93–99
   security, 186–195
   transactional integrity, 123–127
   unit, 6
TestNG test framework, 12
tools, 15–38, 21
   (see also Arquillian)
   Apache Maven, 16
   bootstrapping, 15–18
   for building file systems, 15–18
   JBoss Forge, 17
   version control, 18
transactions
   database, 85
   integrity testing, 123–127
   invoking, 131
   managing, 8
transitive relationships, 106
Twitter, 64, 102, 182
   (see also authentication, authorization)
typesafe injection, 20

U

unit testing, 6
University of California at Irvine, 150

unreserved checkouts, 19
upstream repositories, 68
use cases, in Warp, 172
user interface, 197–209
   Drone, testing with, 203–209
   functional behavior of, 203–209
   Graphene, testing with, 203–209
   implementing, 198–200
   JavaScript and, 201
   QUnit, testing with, 201
   requirement test scenarios for, 201–209
users
   perspective of, 84
   requirements of, 83
   security and, 177

V

value DBMS, 79
value equality, 113
version control systems (VCS), 18
   Git, 19
   Subversion, 19
vertices, 106
Vogels, Werner, 101

W

Warp (Arquillian), 74, 171–175
   deploying, 172
   frameworks, 173
   test harness setup, 173
Waterfall development model, 3
Web Archives (WARs), 51
white-box testing, 6
WildFly application service, 37, 154, 211
world wide web, origins of, 149

X

XACML, 179
XP (see Extreme Programming)

About the Authors

As senior software engineer at JBoss, a division of Red Hat, **Andrew Lee Rubinger** is primarily responsible for development of the company's EJB 3.x implementation. He was an early adopter of Java EE technologies and is an active contributor in the tech community.

Aslak Knutsen, the project lead of Arquillian, is a senior software engineer at JBoss, by Red Hat. He's involved in projects such as Arquillian, ShrinkWrap, Weld, and Seam 3 and is one of the founders of the JBoss Testing initiative, as well as a speaker at major industry conferences including Devoxx, JavaOne, Jazoon, JFokus, and Geecon.

Colophon

The animal on the cover of *Continuous Enterprise Development in Java* is a Violet Turaco (*Musophaga violacea*), also known as a Plantain Eater, a large bird inhabiting West Africa in tropical savannas, wetlands, woodlands, and forests. Its plumage is a glossy violet color except for its thick orange bill, yellow forehead, and crimson crown. The main flight feathers on the wings are also crimson in color. However, despite these bright colors, the birds are often quite indistinguishable in the dense canopy of their forest home.

Like all turacos, the Violet Turaco is an important disperser of seeds. When flying in search of fruit, rounded wings and a long, widespread tail give the turaco great agility when maneuvering through the dense treetops. Its flight is characterized by irregular, flapping wing beats interspersed with gliding. To cross an open space, they fly single file.

Their diet consists of fruit, and they are quite partial to figs, but they will also eat leaves, buds, flowers, insects, snails, and slugs.

For savanna species, the widespread destruction of gallery forest and riverine woodlands is a big threat. However, because of its wide distribution and great numbers, the Violet Turaco is not in imminent peril. For the same reason, it's not in danger from trapping for the pet trade, though local people hunt them for their ostentatious red feathers.

The cover image is from Wood's Animate Creation. The cover fonts are URW Typewriter and Guardian Sans. The text font is Adobe Minion Pro; the heading font is Adobe Myriad Condensed; and the code font is Dalton Maag's Ubuntu Mono.

Get even more for your money.

Join the O'Reilly Community, and register the O'Reilly books you own. It's free, and you'll get:

- $4.99 ebook upgrade offer
- 40% upgrade offer on O'Reilly print books
- Membership discounts on books and events
- Free lifetime updates to ebooks and videos
- Multiple ebook formats, DRM FREE
- Participation in the O'Reilly community
- Newsletters
- Account management
- 100% Satisfaction Guarantee

Signing up is easy:

1. Go to: oreilly.com/go/register
2. Create an O'Reilly login.
3. Provide your address.
4. Register your books.

Note: English-language books only

To order books online:
oreilly.com/store

For questions about products or an order:
orders@oreilly.com

To sign up to get topic-specific email announcements and/or news about upcoming books, conferences, special offers, and new technologies:
elists@oreilly.com

For technical questions about book content:
booktech@oreilly.com

To submit new book proposals to our editors:
proposals@oreilly.com

O'Reilly books are available in multiple DRM-free ebook formats. For more information:
oreilly.com/ebooks

O'REILLY®

Spreading the knowledge of innovators   oreilly.com

Lightning Source UK Ltd.
Milton Keynes UK
UKHW031232070621
385078UK00006B/280